Deconstruction is/in America

Deconstruction is/in America

A New Sense of the Political

Edited by Anselm Haverkamp

NEW YORK UNIVERSITY PRESS
New York and London

NEW YORK UNIVERSITY PRESS
New York and London

"Burning Acts: Injurious Speech" (Chapter 10) also appears in *Performance and
Performativity*, Andrew Parker and Eve Kosofsky Sedgwick, eds. (Routledge,
1994).

"The Disputed Ground: Deconstruction and Literary Studies" (Chapter 4), by J.
Hillis Miller, draws upon parts of an earlier essay, "Is Deconstruction an
Aestheticism?", which was published in *Nineteenth-Century Prose*, vol. 20, no.2
(fall 1993), pp. 23–41. Permission to reprint is gratefully acknowledged.

Library of Congress Cataloging-in-Publication Data
Deconstruction is/in America : a new sense of the political / edited
by Anselm Haverkamp.
p. cm.
Chiefly based on papers presented at a conference in the fall of
1993.
Includes bibliographical references.
ISBN 0-8147-3518-5 (alk. paper). — ISBN 0-8147-3519-3 pbk. :
alk. paper)
1. Criticism—Congresses. 2. Deconstruction—Congresses.
I. Haverkamp, Anselm. II. Title: Deconstruction in America.
III. Title: Deconstruction is America.
PN98.D43D42 1995
801'.95—dc20   94-38318
                    CIP

New York University Press books are printed on acid-free paper, and their
binding materials are chosen for strength and durability.

Manufactured in the United States of America

10 9 8 7 6 5 4 3 2 1

Contents

Acknowledgments

In the fall of 1993, the Poetics Institute and the Center for French Civilization at New York University took advantage of Jacques Derrida's presence in New York for a conference on the present state of deconstruction in America—as evidenced, at least in part, by the yearly event of Derrida's seminar at the Poetics Institute on *The Politics and the Poetics of the Secret*. Special thanks are due to Thomas Bishop, the chairman of the French Department of New York University, for organizing the conference from which the contributions for this volume derive or take their departure. He, together with the Center for French Civilization and the Florence Gould Foundation, made the event possible. The French and English Departments shared the work of presenting the conference, but special recognition is due to Carol Downey for her role in managing the important details. To Peggy Kamuf goes particular gratitude for her timely translation of Derrida's contribution to this volume. Thanks also go to Anthony Reynolds for his help in completing the manuscript, and to Jane B. Malmo for her dedicated editorial work.

Contributors

Derek Attridge is the author of *Peculiar Language: Literature as Difference from the Renaissance to James Joyce* (1988) and *The Rhythms of English Poetry* (1982) and is the editor of *The Cambridge Companion to James Joyce* (1992). He is a Professor in the English Department of Rutgers University.

Michel Beaujour is Professor of French at New York University and the author of *Poetics of the Literary Self-Portrait* (1991), translated from the French *Mirroirs d'encre* (1980).

Judith Butler is Professor of Rhetoric at the University of California at Berkeley. Her books include *Gender Trouble* (1990) and *Bodies that Matter* (1993).

Cynthia Chase is Professor of English at Cornell University and the author of *Decomposing Figures* (1985) and the editor of *Romanticism* (1993).

Jonathan Culler is Class of 1916 Professor of English and Professor of Comparative Literature at Cornell University. His books include *On Deconstruction* (1982), *Flaubert: The Uses of Uncertainty* (1985), and *Framing the Sign* (1988).

Jacques Derrida is Jacques Derrida.

Peter Eisenman is the Irwin S. Chanin Distinguished Professor of Achitecture at Cooper Union and principle of Eisenman Architects of New York.

Rodolphe Gasché is Eugenio Donato Professor of Comparative Literature at the State University of New York at Buffalo and the author of *The Tain of the Mirror* (1986).

Anselm Haverkamp is Professor of English and Director of the Poetics Institute at New York University. He has recently written *Laub voll Trauer* (1991) and has edited *Gedächtniskunst* and *Memoria* (with Renate Lachmann, 1991, 1992) and *Gewalt und Gerechtigkeit: Derrida—Benjamin* (1993).

Peggy Kamuf is Professor of French and Comparative Literature at the University of Southern California. Her publications include *Fictions of Feminine Desire* (1982) and *Signature Pieces: On the Institution of Authorship* (1988). She edited the recent collection *A Derrida Reader: Between the Blinds* (1991) and has translated numerous works by Jacques Derrida, including *Specters of Marx* (1994).

Perry Meisel is Professor of English at New York University and the author of *The Myth of the Modern* (1987).

J. Hillis Miller is Distinguished Professor of English at the University of California at Irvine and the author of many books, including *The Ethics of Reading* (1987) and *Visions of Pygmalion* (1990).

Avital Ronell is Professor of Comparative Literature at the University of California at Berkeley. Her books include *Dictations: On Haunted Writing* (1986), *The Telephone Book* (1991) and *Crack Wars* (1992).

Gayatri Chakravorty Spivak is the Avalon Foundation Professor in the Humanities at Columbia University. She has translated Jacques Derrida's *Of Grammatology* (1977), edited *Selected Subaltern Studies* (1991) with Ranajit Guha, and authored *In Other Worlds* (1989) and *Outside in the Teaching Machine* (1993).

Barbara Vinken has been a Visiting Professor in the Department of French and the Department of Comparative Literature at New York University. She now teaches at the University of Hannover, Germany. She is the author of *Unentrinnbare Neugierde* (1991), *Dekonstrucktiver Feminismus* (Ed., 1992) and *Mode nach de Mode* (1993).

Elisabeth Weber is Assistant Professor of German at the University of California at Santa Barbara. Her book on Emmanuel Levinas, *Verfolgung und Trauma* (1989), is to appear in English under the title *Persecution and Trauma: On Emmanuel Levinas's Otherwise Than Being or Beyond Essence.*

Samuel Weber is Professor of English at the University of California at Los Angeles. Following the publication of *Institution and Interpretation*, (1985), his earlier books, *Rückkehr zu Freud* (1978) and *Freud-Legende* (1979) appeared in English as *Return to Freud* (1991) and *The Legend of Freud* (1987).

David Wills is Professor of French at Louisiana State University. His publications include *Writing Pynchon* (with Alec McHoul, 1982), *Screen/play: Derrida and Film Theory* (with Peter Brunette, 1989), and the forthcoming *Prothesis*.

Deconstruction is/as Neopragmatism?

Preliminary Remarks on Deconstruction in America

Anselm Haverkamp

The first part of the following is a revised version of the author's opening remarks to the conference *Deconstruction is /in America* in the fall of 1993, which appears in this volume in a rearranged and supplemented form. The second part underlines some of the political implications of the conference after the event. The sketchy character is deliberate, since the intention of the conference was not to arrive at a new narrative on the subject of deconstruction but to offer a highly selective approach to certain problems. That other problems are missing or remain underrepresented is a part of the problem to being with.

The reasons for looking back on *Deconstruction in America* are obvious enough. Looking back, certainly, is not the same as giving up, and in spite of the notorious task of facing the future in, and of, say, future deconstructions, the possibilities of such a facing ask for a review, an *account* of the future that has passed, the future left behind in the years of deconstruction in America. As the slogan "Deconstruction is America" suggests, that the fate of deconstruction in America is as hard to determine as the project of America. A conference that would reconsider the role of deconstruction in America over the last two decades would have to take into account the particular role of America for deconstruction: not only for the development of deconstruction's philosophical and critical arguments, but for its political adaptation to, and involvement with what was left in American universities after the academic dispute of the Sixties and Seventies—that came under the heading of "The Structuralist Controversy"—had run its course.[1]

Looking back on the seminal Johns Hopkins conference of that title some 25 years ago, we realize that this controversy closed an age-old debate on the limits of man and humanist principles of education rather than opening a new one—however manifest and visible the outline of the new may already have been at the time. The beginnings of deconstruction in America had to remain for a quarter of a century associated with bringing to an end an educational era whose aftermath had to be faced, while deconstruction's own—and one is tempted to add, its *substantial*—contribution was to surface much more quietly. "A new sense of the political" seems the most persuasive name for this quiet advent whose agenda has never been destruction, nor resurrection, but a pursuit of happiness. "The Politics of Friendship," about which the American Philosophical Association was recently reminded by Jacques Derrida, points in the direction of such a new sense of what politics might be, and might become, against the grain of what it has not ceased to be instead.[2] A sense to be recovered of a politics to come, to be approached.

There is, however, no happy success story to be told about deconstruction in America, and there is no salvation history to be related, as one would wish for, and fall for, in a country dedicated to success and salvation. On the contrary, one has to admit from the start that "nothing fails like success" in deconstruction, as Barbara Johnson put it when she saw the need to use history differently and decided "to use history deconstructively," in order to avoid the false success of "answers, causes, explanations, or origins."[3] In order, that is, not to lose track of the problems, questions, and impasses. Among them, though not most urgently, the issues of self-interpretation and self-implication had to be taken into account, those auto-interpretive figures of self-deconstruction that make it difficult to tell the story of deconstruction in America in the form of a metahistory of bygone possibilities, remaining resistances, or persisting side effects.

When Derrida delivered the 1985 Wellek Library Lectures at Irvine, he discarded the title of *Deconstruction in America* in favor of *Memoires for Paul de Man*, who had died in December 1983, ten years ago now, and whose memory is implied in this conference, as the topic of this conference was already contained and explained in Derrida's dedication of 1985. "Geopolitics does not suffice," said Derrida at the time, but he was ready to "risk," as he added ("with a smile"), "the following hypothesis: America *is* deconstruction—l'Amérique, mais *c'est* la deconstruction."[4] The image discarded—America as geopolitical enterprise—does not disqualify the "toponymy" of *America* for deconstruction, that is, America as deconstruction's hypothetical "residence" at a specific moment, a moment whose historicality might be most appropriately captured by calling it *in* deconstruction. Deconstruction may be America to the extent that America *is in* deconstruction.

Beside the many good reasons why one could think so, it is important to note that it could be otherwise. Deconstruction could be everywhere, and is everywhere, but the fact that America happens to be an exemplary place for deconstruction is not a coincidence, the coincidence, say, of America's nostalgia for the appeal of French thought. Deconstruction could not be turned into some generalizable humanism that would feed into America's concern for Western values. It would not exist everywhere in the same way, as McDonald's and Coca Cola do, the simulacra of America's being worldwide. On the contrary, deconstruction should be expected to exist in different places in very different ways. No, what keeps it in America rather than elsewhere, say Europe, and gives it a specific American place value is a *sense of difference* in America that is different from Europe—although one could also say that it *is* Europe's sense of difference, but in a very different way. And it is the additional difference, the differentiating *momentum* within that difference, that comes to count (as in any difference), and is to be investigated, through deconstruction.

Deconstruction in America, one could speculate, takes advantage of the difference America makes with respect to Europe; and pragmatism is the American name for this difference in the realm of philosophy, a difference which seems indifferent to what it has left behind, and keeps leaving behind, in *This New*—I quote from

Stanley Cavell's reading of Emerson—*Yet Unapproachable America.*[5] Yet the hope against lost hopes, the loss of European hopes, to be precise, cannot be theory-hope again, according to older and newer pragmatists alike. Their declared indifference to philosophy and "theory as such" is no longer to be consoled by theory-hope.[6] They remain inconsolable to the point of abandoning pragmatism itself—thus hoping to bring it back to where it began, to the vision of the new, yet still unapproachable America. Back to the old pragmatism's vision of "making our future different from our past," as Richard Rorty keeps underlining the difference in question, in the name of solidarity instead of objectivity, democracy instead of philosophy, or fairness as justice.[7]

It is here that pragmatism meets deconstruction, although for reasons other than neopragmatists seem able to see. It is not deconstruction's antiessentialist, antifoundationalist side effect, let alone a new "kind of writing" that would account for this meeting.[8] Rather, it seems to be pragmatism's insistence on the impossible difference traditional philosophy kept promising without ever being able to deliver; to go, for example, for fairness, while justice may seem as yet, and maybe forever, unapproachable. The crucial place of *A Theory of Justice* for any pragmatist attempt toward making a difference, is also deconstruction's *topos* for investigating the force of law and maintaining the difference in which legal regulations fall short with respect to the justice approached.[9] Justice may be nothing but the name for this difference between legal practice and the law's force, which both carries on this practice and, in carrying it out, transgresses what is carried out with respect to the justice to be done. Likewise fairness may be the best possible name for this imperative to transgress, rather than toward prosecution, enforcement, and execution. Justice may be, and may have to remain forever, out of reach, but nonetheless approachable—if and only insofar as fairness is, indeed, applied. How, if not pragmatically, with respect to a given situation, and given the time, can justice be assessed? No instance is better suited to exemplify the paradoxes of pragmatism than justice in America.

But more than just this remains to be said for the exemplary role of justice in the American "drama of consent."[10] After the first and, so to speak, primal difference that America had promised to accomplish with respect to the difference that Europe was unable to make—and European philosophy was unable to ensure— America had to take on, and has taken on, differences of another dimension that are completely incommensurable with the older, European one. In an America whose future is less approachable than ever the urgency seems desperate. As Cornel West expressed his frustration with Rorty's *Consequences of Pragmatism*, "no philosophical case can be made for this civilization" as long as this pragmatism's attitude is not up to coping with differences other than the European one.[11] One cannot but ask for a pragmatism newer than the one given up by Rorty and added by West to the nuisance of philosophy's old European, and now renewed American, identity. But where should it come from? Within neopragmatism's own historical account of paradigm shifts, the exhaustion of one paradigm cannot account for the succeeding shift, nor can this shift be in any way commensurable with the preceding set of assumptions—except for the problems left over, the mortgage to be transcribed to a new account.

In America's multifaced landscape of differences, the European tradition has turned into a mortgage of uncanny proportions. Quite against the grain of leaving it behind, the European difference returns as the repressed and reveals what had to remain repressed in its difference. That great design of America as a radically open space to newcomers meant more than just the erasure of these newcomers' histories; it meant the retroactive idolization of one particular difference erasing all others— including and foreclosing those others already implied and foreclosed before.[12] Thus, deconstruction in America may appear as the return of the repressed within America's indifference to Europe, an indifference yet to be exhausted with respect to the differences yet to be expected. "Might one find some ground to deconstruct before there are any philosophical foundations in place?" wonders Stanley Cavell about America's lack of metaphysical talent, its lack, as it were, of a philosophical homeground.[13] This lack, as a matter of fact, has reproduced the ground to be deconstructed far more effectively than this ground, as a homeground, would have lent itself to deconstruction. In displacing the "West-

ern Canon," American literature and philosophy not only reproduced what they attempted to rewrite, but re-deconstructed what
they found deconstructed (and, that is, already "in deconstruction").

Within the succession of paradigms of knowledge and learning,
deconstruction seems to have succeeded in opening up a new
space for transformation within which pragmatism has to be replaced, its mortgage transcribed and its hopes, not to forget them,
reiterated. In settling his account with *Limited Inc*, the linguistic
orthodoxy of ordinary language politics, Derrida had already
identified the tentative perspective of his *Grammatology* as "a sort
of pragmatics," or future "pra[gma]-grammatology (to come)"; a
grammatologically articulated pragmatism that would also have
to account for "the *possibility* of transgression [which] is always
inscribed in speech acts"—and not just for the limitations usually
associated with these speech acts' institutionalized uses.[14] Justice,
again, is the most prominent, and most urgent, domain of application here, although the sphere of the "literary" would lend itself
much more readily to a congenial linguistic analysis.

If the sphere of the "literary" (for the sake of a better term) was
an exemplary case in point, the point consisted precisely not in
opening up the aesthetic possibility of a "living in beauty," set free
from all normative expectations, or even from the strain of being
ironic all the time.[15] The rare uses that analytical philosophy
and analytically minded critics have made of deconstruction in
adapting the "literary" to the pragmatics of a democratically
open, public sphere cannot, or should not have to, contend with
shrugging off the obsolete aesthetic normativity and its hermeneu-
tic twin, semantic holism. With a payoff like this, the "nihilistic"
temptation of an advanced liberalism would have proved to be
much greater than the all-pervasive fear of deconstruction's destructive force.

Quite to the contrary, one must face frustrations like Cavell's in
Disowning Knowledge: the "failure to acknowledge" and "avoid-
ance of love" in Shakespeare, encounters not to be compensated
for in advance.[16] An "aesthetics" of undisturbed living cannot
compensate for philosophy's failure to come to terms with what
is, nor for skepticism's desperation about what is to be done.

Rather, the skeptic's acknowledgement of the possibilities of transgression asks for an ethics of reading prior to an ethics of what there is to be done or not to be done (and, finally, to be denied). However multiple the interpretations may be, and however flexible interpretors may become, there is simply no point in *Doing What Comes Naturally*, if it is only to console us with, and relieve us from, the burden of reading. To turn the tropes of persuasion into tropes of reasonable conviction asks for a responsibility beyond and, that is, before the mechanism of what comes naturally; it needs analysis in the first place. And no pathos can, in the second place, compensate for what has been missed in the first place—although one has to put up with the pathos in the first place, along with the loss of pathos in the end.[17]

It would be an extra task, and would take another time, to reconsider the reception of deconstruction in America in the light not so much of its detotalizing strategies, but of its pragmatic impact on the rethinking and rereading of crucial concepts. Not only the necessary defiguration of the old, but also the opening of new possibilities—call it refiguration. Deconstruction's sensitivity to pragmatic issues is best documented in its growing interest in the performativity of acts and their institutional setting, a perspective more crucial than the much bedeviled, or else applauded, antiessentialism, not to mention the now out-of-fashion "play of signifiers." I think, the once-feared danger of "domesticating" deconstruction's philosophical impact into a domestic brand of pragmatism—certainly a thing to be avoided—is less relevant than the opposite danger of taking the pragmatic acuity out of deconstruction and turning it back into a merely critical, even hypercritical "theory." Deconstruction is a kind of pragmatism, insofar as it is able to replace a disabled pragmatism. It may even turn out to be pragmatism's better equipped, and more pragmatic, version.

Deconstruction, however, is also more than a kind of pragmatism, if only in that it aims beyond pragmatism's anxieties of influence and desperation. The literary and philosophical issues of deconstruction have had, among many other important academic effects, a political effect and outcome, in which reading—the reading of difference—arrived at working results far from the alleged effects of mere irony and mere play. As it turns out, the terms "irony" and "play" are not what they merely seem. In literature's ways of exposing rhetorically what in philosophy was meant to persuade "naturally," authentically, difference turns up in the undisguised undecidability of figuration. Reading the literary and philosophical double bind: deciphering, more precisely, philosophy's difference inscribed within literature's indifference to this very philosophy's authority was the model, and is still a model, for reading difference beyond the quests for identity. The "irony" needed in acknowledging what has to be decided, as well as the "play" needed in dealing with the consequences, are not merely tropes of a stimulus-response-like reaction-formation; they have to be taken on as figures of response, as responsibility.

The legal debate should be mentioned first here but also, and not without legal implications, sexual politics. It was through the difference of the sexes, and not by coincidence, that this model of metaphor, or transference, was to be applied in the most rigorous way and delivered pragmatic impact.[18] *Deconstructive Feminism* has practiced this mode of reading to the extent that there is, at present, hardly any other direction of criticism that could compete with it both in analytical refinement and pragmatic pertinence. Compared to this, the encounter of deconstruction with the *Critical Legal Studies Movement* was bound to remain metapragmatic; but as I have indicated there may be an additional point of constitutional importance to the metapragmatic role of legal theory in a country where the law is the law.

Not that we can ever be too sure about the "critical function" of literature's disfigurative work. Not that we can ever be too clear about philosophy's task "as such." What is to be elaborated are the problems, if the responsibility of solutions is ever to be met. Therefore, a topology of impossibilities is needed rather than a system of the restricted possible. According to the much older pragmatism that was rhetoric (an art whose analytical potential has been on the agenda of deconstruction from the beginning), topology has to map the relevant *topoi* under consideration; a heuristics of differences to be reconsidered in their manifestations and underlying mechanizations—the gift, for example, or the crypt, or the secret. As far as inventiveness is concerned in these matters, *poietic* imagination in the precise sense, I see nobody to whom we owe as much as we owe to Jacques Derrida for his unfailing dedication to America.

Take the gift, for example. "For finally, if the gift is another name of the impossible, we still think it, we name it, we desire it. We intend it."[19] America is by now the age-old name for the thought, the desire, and the intention towards the impossible, like the gift (not a given, but to be given). Like that "other cape," Cape Europe, as Derrida has called a collection of recent writings on deconstruction in Europe, America has become a *paleonym*, the re-citation of an old name for some hope not altogether lost. Or is it lost, after all? Answering the French President François Mitter-and's hopeful remark on the future of Europe as "returning in its history and its geography like one who is returning home—chez soi," Derrida asks, "Is it possible? Desirable? Is it really this that announces itself *today?*"[20] Cavell did not hesitate to confront "the place or the topic of the place" that America is for him as it was for Emerson and Thoreau with the European predicament, the essential, nostalgic Heideggerian version of being at home: "The substantive disagreement with Heidegger," writes Cavell—as with Mitterand, wonders Derrida—is the disagreement shared by Emerson, Thoreau and Cavell himself, "that the achievement of the human requires not inhabitation and settlement but abandon-ment, leaving."[21] If the given is to be abandoned in favor of the impossible, of the gift that would have announced itself once in America and may announce itself today in Europe again, what politics does this announcement entail?

The handy reversal of terms which predicts the politics of de-construction as a deconstruction of politics is as well put as it is badly meant. Because it is the *caesura* of what is going on as politics that defines the "new sense of the political"—of politics deconstructed not in the sense of giving up the space of the politi-cal, but in the sense of keeping it deconstructible. Open to revi-sion, but in a radical sense. Thus Derrida's "The Politics of Friend-ship" cites the classical sources, through whom this *topos politic* is defined and in whose redefinition a new sense of the political is to be refound, remade and regained. This may not seem enough for

those who overlook in this review the pragmatics of the *caesura*—
a pragmatics involved in the application of rupture (as in the
classical instance of strike)—and therefore complain about a
"withdrawal from the specificity of politics and of empirical social
research."[22] But is it not the very specificity of politics that asks
for a refocusing within the frame given, "democracy," and even of
a refocusing of the frame as it is given and too easily taken for
granted? The democracy that is as yet fully to come cannot be
simply deduced, and thus be taken for coming, from a democracy
as yet insufficiently reached. Unfortunately, one cannot say that
the political critique and social research in question had come
forward with what it had hoped for, and keeps hoping for on
the premises of a critical theory that is obviously not critical
enough to avoid turning hypocritical and cutting the wrong way
now.

As Derrida has put it most pertinently in his closing remarks to
this conference (I quote from memory): "What we have to do is to
politicize the problems in a way that politics become just; not in
politicizing as such and in itself, but in politicizing differently."
This includes a work of differentiating much easier to invoke than
to carry out. A differentiation also of the politics of friendship, no
doubt, that is still suffering from Euro-American self-cen-
teredness, deeply buried in what Derrida most recently came to
investigate as the "secret of European responsibility."[23] But the
patient work of deconstructing philosophy on the grounds of its
particular European sources is not in itself Eurocentric, if it politi-
cizes differently. It demands, as Gayatri Spivak has pointed out
more than once, a decentering of deconstruction's politics from its
Euro-American homeground, the pretext of the Euro-American
difference of this conference included. Deconstruction in America
implies, and therefore will have to take care of, Americas beyond
this America, in an America yet to be given.

In the world of difference to which America is more exposed
than any other part of the world, Europe to follow, no principle of
identity has to be erected. The state of difference in America asks
for a differentiation of deconstruction's "differing" the *topos* of
difference with respect to the differences inscribed therein. "The
challenge of deconstruction," Rodolphe Gasché emphasizes, is the

paradoxical necessity of taking the other as the other, *other* than me (and not just: the other *me*); it "is how to distinguish without judging and deciding; in other words how to do justice to what requires recognition on the basis of its singularity."[24] That singularity is defined by difference and not to be mixed up with individuality in the older sense of an undivided, self-contained self, the subject of philosophical reflection. The politics of singularity, therefore, has to cope with another spacing, some "kind of asymmetrical and heteronomical curvature of the social space" according to Derrida's description. Peter Eisenman has translated this spacial peculiarity into the time-qualification of a "presentness" in architecture other than the time-effacing pomposity of the uniformly postmodern. Architecture as the pragmatic challenge to all utopias can be taken as the deconstructive chance of a nonutopian politics in many a sense, but most decidedly not in the sense of a preestablished symmetry to be imposed upon public places.

Let me risk an example, if only to do justice to the spirit of the place. Take the theatricality of a city like New York, a place in permanent destruction, in continuous decay, as it seems, but more precisely a city in permanent change, in gender trouble and racial controversy. It is here that one gets, now and then, a new sense of the political qua deconstruction. I do not refer to the corrupted state of city politics, which proves the old sense of the political to be "out of joint." What I would rather refer to is how the failure of ordinary politics to "become just" has provoked a sense of the political expressing itself differently here—in mixed identities barely controlled by means of the police force and, by the way, only badly translated into the language of the media. A movie such as *Paris is Burning*, already noteworthy for its unfailing play on the Euro-American paleonym, had to compromise itself with the pathos of accredited concerns (the human interest stories of those involved), in order to deliver its message of drag and mimetic desire, of unsettling comedy. The discarded name of Harlem, which never comes up in the picture except in reference to the river, on whose distant banks the towers of wealth rise, points to no *u-topos*.[25] On the contrary, the utopian-minded Venus from the house of Xtravaganza dies shortly after the film was completed. Likewise the quotation of Paris stands for no burning other than the urgency of the performative. Nowhere else in America (and certainly not in the literal burning of L.A.) is the destabilization of established politics, the bastardization of race, the queering of gender more effective, and thus the constructive potential of deconstruction more obvious—not just in destroying the patterns of domination, and not only in ridiculing the pretensions of identity (both already considerable achievements in their own right) but in creating modes of transition, sex untroubled by gender, the frail acceptance of the other before and beyond affirmation. Sure, there is no such thing as ungendered sexes, but the parodic decomposition of gender—and there is hardly an example more significant these days—asks for the unconditional acceptance that is necessary for "becoming just." Come, and see.

Notes

1. *The Structuralist Controversy: The Languages of Criticism and the Sciences of Man*, eds. Richard Macksey, Eugenio Donato (Baltimore: The Johns Hopkins University Press, 1970), notably Jacques Derrida's closing remarks, following his intervention on "Structure, Sign, and Play in the Discourse of the Human Sciences," pp. 270–272.
2. Jacques Derrida, "The Politics of Friendship," as read at the 85th annual meeting of the American Philosophical Association, Eastern Division, in December 1988, *Journal of Philosophy* 85 (1988), pp.632–645.
3. Barbara Johnson, *A World of Difference* (Baltimore: The Johns Hopkins University Press, 1987), p.15.
4. Jacques Derrida, *Memoires for Paul de Man* (New York: Columbia University Press, 1986), p.18.
5. Stanley Cavell, *This New Yet Unapproachable America* (Albuquerque: Living Batch Press, 1989), p.91.
6. See, most prominently, Stanley Fish, *Doing What Comes Naturally: Change, Rhetoric, and the Practice of Theory in Literary and Legal Studies* (Durham: Duke University Press, 1989), p.342.
7. Richard Rorty, "The Priority of Democracy to Philosophy," in *Objectivism, Relativism, and Truth—Philosophical Papers* I (Cambridge: Cambridge University Press, 1991), p.175.
8. Richard Rorty, "Philosophy as a Kind of Writing: An Essay on Derrida," *Consequences of Pragmatism* (Minneapolis: University of Minnesota Press, 1982), pp.90, 109.

9. See, paradigmatically, Jacques Derrida, "Force de Loi" (The Force of Law), *Cardozo Law Review* 11 (1990), pp.919–1045.

10. See, paradigmatically, Stanley Cavell, *Conditions Handsome and Unhandsome* (Chicago: The University of Chicago Press, 1990), p.102.

11. Cornel West, Afterword, *Post-Analytic Philosophy*, eds. John Rajchman, Cornel West (New York: Columbia University Press, 1985), p.267.

12. See, for instance, Philip Fisher, "Introduction," *The New American Studies* (Berkeley: University of California Press, 1991), pp.xxi–ii.

13. Stanley Cavell, "Naughty Orators," *Languages of the Unsayable*, eds. Sanford Budick, Wolfgang Iser (New York: Columbia University Press, 1989), p.365.

14. Jacques Derrida, "Toward an Ethic of Discussion," Afterword, *Limited Inc* (Evanston: Northwestern University Press, 1988), pp.133, 148 (159.16).

15. See, most recently, Richard Shusterman, *Pragmatist Aesthetics: Living Beauty, Rethinking Art* (Oxford: Blackwell, 1992), p.246.

16. Stanley Cavell, *Disowning Knowledge in Six Plays of Shakespeare* (Cambridge: Cambridge University Press, 1987), pp.39, 138.

17. See, most recently, Gary Wihl, *The Contingency of Theory: Pragmatism, Expressivism, and Deconstruction* (New Haven: Yale University Press, 1994), p.182.

18. See, paradigmatically, Shoshana Felman, "Rereading Femininity," *Yale French Studies* 62 (1981), pp.19–44.

19. Jacques Derrida, *Given Time: I. Counterfeit Money*, trans. Peggy Kamuf (Chicago: The University of Chicago Press, 1992), p.29.

20. Jacques Derrida, *The Other Heading: Reflections on Today's Europe*, trans. Pascale-Anne Brault, Michael Naas (Bloomington: University of Indiana Press, 1992), pp.8–9.

21. Stanley Cavell, *The Senses of Walden*, (Chicago: Chicago University Press, expanded edition 1992), p.138.

22. See, most pointedly, Thomas McCarthy, "The Politics of the Ineffable: Derrida's Deconstructionism," *The Philosophical Forum* 21 (1989/90), pp.160; 146–168.

23. Jacques Derrida, *Donner la mort*, trans. David Wills (Chicago: Chicago University Press, forthcoming).

24. Rodolphe Gasché, "On Critique, Hypercriticism, and Deconstruction," *Cardozo Law Review* 13 (1991), pp.1115–1132.

25. On *Paris is Burning* see Barbara Vinken, *Mode nach der Mode* (Frankfurt/M: Fischer, 1993), pp.45–47; Judith Butler, *Bodies That Matter* (New York: Routledge, 1993), pp.129–137.

The Time is Out of Joint

Jacques Derrida

"So long? . . . "
    (Hamlet)

I

Forgive me for thanking you in my language. I am very grateful to you, in the first place, for allowing the foreigner here at New York University—and this is hospitality itself, with which you are unstinting—to thank you in his language. To thank you all, and especially the two friends and colleagues who had the fortunate idea of this colloquium, Tom Bishop and Anselm Haverkamp.

I thank them in my name, of course, since they have done me the honor of confiding this perilous task to me: to address to the experts and the redoubtable readers that you are, a *key word*, a keynote, at the halfway point, right in the middle of the colloquium, at the very time when the colloquium seems to pivot on itself. Like time, like deconstruction perhaps, like a door on its hinges, our colloquium would turn in this way, and *folding* back on itself, it would also *bend to* and obey itself, without the least certainty.

As for deconstruction, it has never been at peace with its hinges—which is perhaps its way of tirelessly reminding us of disjointment itself, the possibility of any disjunction. Since I am speaking in my language, I underscore here that *"disjoncter,"* in a kind of modern slang, can also mean *"délirer,"* to become mad or deranged. Whether Hamlet played or lived his madness, whether he was able to mimic it only *in order to* think it (in view of thinking it and because already he thought of himself on the basis of madness), the one who said "The time is out of joint" knew in any case, as nearly as possible, what *"disjoncter"* means. What happens if time is mad? And what if what time gives is first of all the measurelessness of all madness?

To be *hors de ses gonds*, off one's hinges, may be translated by "out of joint." "The time is out of joint": this is the mad thinking that I will often speak about this evening.

I ought to begin by rereading a passage that you all know by heart:

> Hamlet: . . . . Swear
> Ghost [beneath]: Swear
> [They swear]
> Hamlet: Rest, rest perturbed Spirit! So Gentlemen,
> With all my love I do commend me to you;
> And what so poor a man as Hamlet is
> Do t'express his love and friending to you,
> God willing, shall not lack: Let us go in together,
> And still your fingers on your lips, I pray.
> The time is out of joint: Oh cursed spight,
> That ever I was born to set it right.
> Nay, come, let's go together. [Exeunt]

I thank you thus in my name—I insist on this point—and not at all in the name of some entity nicknamed "Deconstruction." I have never claimed to identify myself with what may be designated by this name. It has always seemed strange to me, it has always left me cold. Moreover, I have never stopped having doubts about the very identity of what is referred to by such a nickname. Finally, and especially, presuming that *it* exists and that *it* can be identified, there is no way one can give thanks in its name since deconstruction will always maintain a relation that is as enigmatic as it is disjointed to gratitude, more precisely, to commerce, to the market, and to the thankfulness of thanking. On the one hand, it is the most thankless thing in the world, a kind of ethics of ingratitude (elsewhere and at length, I have tried to justify this, if one may still say that), a practice of implacable ingratitude, without thanks, *sans merci*. Deconstruction is merciless. On the other hand, as a thinking of the gift, of a gift beyond the debt and a justice beyond the law, deconstruction should, on the contrary, be devoted to grace and gratitude, thus to a gratitude without thanks, without exchange or, if you prefer, according to an exchange that carries beyond exchange. It should be only at the moment—and on the condition—of opening itself to the possibility of the gift, as to a kind of ecstatic and boundless caress of mute gratitude. It learns only by receiving/It teaches only to receive *[Elle n'apprend qu'à recevoir]*. It cultivates the experience that consists in receiving from the other the very thing that it can never be a question of restituting and inscribing in the commerce of thanks or the market of commodities.

Enough on the thanks and the thanksgiving of deconstruction.

Now, after the merciless gift, the request for forgiveness. Yes, forgive me if I severely limit my remarks this evening to the risky interpretation of a single word.

A very little word, the minuscule coupling of *two letters*, a copula or copule, a *minuscopule*.

I am, therefore, speaking my language, as if I had already, on the eve of my coming departure, left to return to France. And yet the two chosen letters will be those of an English word, of a verb in truth. Politeness requires, as does hospitality, that English be the chosen language of this verb.

Such a password might pass unnoticed because it is so common. It belongs to the most common language and it is common to two little phrases that seem to turn on it as on a hinge. What is this word? It is "is." Here it is:

"The time **is** out of joint"

says Hamlet and, to cite the title of our colloquium,

"Deconstruction **is**/in America."

How is one to understand this copula? Does the "is" have the same meaning? Does it perform the same function, or rather the same dysfunctioning, in both propositions? Why should we cross these two quotations—because they are both quotations—at the disjointed juncture, at the crossroads or the crossing of this little "is"? Should we also inscribe it under some erasure in the form of a cross?

These are, we were saying, two quotations. Two quotations in English. And doubtless there were those who were surprised to see me announce with an English title a lecture concerning which it was made clear, at my request, that it would be given in my language, French. This was not done to be intriguing; nor was it done out of playfulness, nor out of courtesy. Why then?

First of all, in order to signal that if there is a problem around "Deconstruction in America," or "Deconstruction being America, *as* America, or *in* America," it is an adventure of translation, at the very least it is a history from which one cannot efface the singular experience of translation and transference. Let us understand these words in all their senses and all their dimensions, which are not only linguistic. At stake is presence and event: of what comes to pass or what takes place.

(I have often had occasion to define deconstruction as that which is—far from a theory, a school, a method, even a discourse, still less a technique that can be appropriated—at bottom *what happens or comes to pass* [ce qui arrive]. It remains then to situate, localize, determine what happens with what happens, *when* it happens. To date it. Has deconstruction happened? Has it arrived? Of course it has, if you like, but then, if it has, so many questions arise: How? Where? When? On what date exactly? Was it so long ago, already? Or perhaps not yet? Supposing that deconstruction has a *shibboleth*, I remind you that the question of the date is inseparable from it and that the link between *shibboleth* and *date* is an insistent theme of what is called deconstructive readings, one of the most apparent themes *of* deconstruction.)

Now, Hamlet is mad about dates. His phrase ("The time is out of joint") does not betray only the symptomatic anxiety of someone whose memory is suffering. His memory is suffering in fact from a death, and a death is never natural. His memory is suffering from the death of a king, a father, and a homonym, but it is suffering first of all and by that very token, *as memory*, from amnesia, from an amnesia that is not natural either. It is suffering because it cannot remember, thus because it cannot think the event of this so unnatural death, because it is not a memory that is sure of being able to situate, date, determine, objectify the event that the son must account for and to which he must render accounts in rendering justice, in making justice of a crime, through the vengeance and punishment to which he has committed himself with an oath. That the event has taken place and that he remembers it, that it concerns the violent death of his father, that there seems to be unimpeachable testimony in this regard, all of this does not rule out madness. This structuring event may still belong to what Freud called "psychic reality," as opposed to "material reality"; it may still testify to the phantasmatic dimension of a repetition *en abîme,* of the theater within the theater that is reflected in the heart of the play.

The proof? The proof that "the time is out of joint"? One proof at least? Well, no one can agree about the time, about the date of the King's death, and about the time that separates present speech from this event which, in spite of or because of all that destines it to repetition, plays an inaugural, founding, or instituting role in the story. No one can agree about the time of mourning, which is finally the true subject of the play. It is just now, upon rereading the play recently, that I have noticed this, so late, too late, as if by *countretemps.* Hamlet in fact haunts the book I have just written, *Specters of Marx.* The phrase "The time is out of joint" is cited, recited, analyzed, and also loved there like an obsession. And yet, after the fact, I read it today differently. Here then is a contretemps, one more contretemps in contretemps itself. Until today, I had not noticed what, lying inhumed in "The time is out of joint", in the subterranean strata of the text, could also resonate secretly with that essential pathology of mourning. I have become aware of it too late; it is too late, for *Specters of Marx,* where mourning, the dis- or anachrony of mourning is in some way the very subject. This tragedy of dating has become apparent to me today, too late. But this contretemps is a contretemps within the contretemps because it is a question of a contretemps on the subject of an utterance that says the contretemps. Repetition, the law of iterability, is still the law of differance here. This is not the first time I have given myself over to the Shakespearian contretemps. A few years ago, after an unforgettable trip to Verona, I wrote an essay on *Romeo and Juliet,* "Aphorism Countertime." Like *Specters of*

Marx, it crossed the themes of anachrony, mourning, haunting, oath, survival, and the name—which in the that instance as well is the name of the father (*Juliet:*—" 'Tis but thy name that is my enemy . . . O! be some other name./What's in a name? . . . Deny thy father, and refuse thy name . . . Romeo, doff thy name"). To analyze "the fatedness of a date and a rendezvous" and the "traps in contretemps," I then tried to demonstrate in what way "dates, timetables, property registers, place-names, all the codes that we cast like nets over time and space—in order to reduce or master differences, to arrest them, determine them—these are also contretemps-traps." And so as to clarify this question of time, of the being of time, of what then *is,* in its impossible present, time itself, I continued: "Intended to avoid contretemps, to be in harmony with our rhythms by bending them to objective measurement, they produce misunderstanding, they accumulate the opportunities for false steps or wrong moves, revealing and simultaneously increasing this anachrony of desires: *in the same time.* What is this time?"[1]

A delirium of the date thus confers on the incredible sentence "The time is out of joint" more than one supplementary meaning, to be sure, but *at the same time,* just as many more madnesses. *At the same time. At once* [Sur l'heure]. As if there were a dead time in the hour itself.

Everything in fact begins, in *Hamlet,* with the dead time of this "dead hour," at the moment when, in an already repetitive fashion, the specter arrives by returning. At the first hour of the play, the first time already marks a second time (Act I, sc.i, *Marcellus:* "Thus twice before, and jump at this dead hour,/ With martial stalk hath he gone by our watch"). The vigilance of the watching guard, the very watch of consciousness, is also a maddened watch or timepiece that, turning on itself, does not know how to guard or regard the hour of this "dead hour." It is delivered over to another time for which the timeclock and the calendar no longer are the law. They no longer are the law or they are not yet the law. Dates have come unhinged.

Then there's Claudius who wants to have done with mourning, without delay, so he begins by encouraging himself to cut short this time of mourning and to take advantage of time: "Though yet of Hamlet our dear brother's death/ The memory be green, and that it us befitted/ To bear our hearts in grief, and our whole kingdom/ To be contracted in one brow of woe,/ Yet so far hath discretion fought with nature/ That we with wisest sorrow think on him/ Together with remembrance of ourselves." Soon, in the same speech he uses words that announce Hamlet's sentence, "The time is out of joint." He speaks at this point of the State, such as it appears in the dreamy eyes or the wild imagination of the son of Fortinbras, the one who will, let us not forget, end up on the throne. The King pretends to thank his guests: "For all, our thanks,/ Now follows that you know young Fortinbras,/ Holding a weak supposal of our worth,/ Or thinking by our late dear brother's death/ Our state to be *disjoint* and out of frame,/ Col-leaguèd with this dream of his advantage,/ He hath not failed to pester us with message . . ." (Act I, sc.ii; emphasis added).

A little later, the King, once again, encourages Laertes to take his time, to appropriate it ("time be thine"), to use the seal of his father, Polonius, and with the authorization thus obtained, to go away (the time it takes, his time—in fact in the logic and the chronology of the play, all the time it will take for his father to die in his turn by Hamlet's hand, and so forth): "Take thy fair hour, Laertes. Time be thine,/ And thy best graces spend it at thy will./ But now, my cousin Hamlet, and my son . . ." (ibid.).

After which, turning to the one who refuses the name of son, he exhorts Hamlet to count the days, to cut short the time of mourn-ing, to measure it in a measured fashion, "for some term," to put a *term* to it; a term, that is, at once the engagement, the terms of a mourning contract, so to speak, and the limit, the boundary, the endpoint, or the moderation that is appropriate. One must, he tells him in effect, know how to put an end to mourning. This presumes (but this is one of the enigmas of the play, as it is of mourning) that mourning depends on us, in us, and not on the other in us. It presumes above all a knowledge, the knowledge of the date. One must indeed know *when: at what instant* mourning began. One must indeed know *at what moment* death took place, really took place, and this is always the moment of a murder. But Hamlet, and everyone in *Hamlet*, seems to be wandering around in confusion on this subject. Now, *when* and *if* one does not know *when* an event took place, one has to wonder *if* it indeed took place, or in any case if it took place in "material reality" as Freud might have said, and not only in the fabric of some "psychic reality," in phantasm or delirium. A date, which is to say, the objectivity of a presumed reference, stands precisely at the joining of the "material" and the "psychic."

To carry mourning beyond its "normal" term is no longer the gesture of a son, says the King to Hamlet; and it is even "unmanly," thus perhaps inhuman, he suggests, not realizing that he has just said very well that the question of mourning, which is the very heart of any deconstruction, carries beyond the human (or the viril) the only possibility of interrogating the human (or the viril) as such:

> *King:* 'Tis sweet and commendable in your nature, Hamlet,
> To give these mourning duties to your father,
> But you must know your father lost a father,
> That father lost, lost his, and the survivor bound
> In filial obligation for some term
> To do obsequious sorrow. But to persever
> In obstinate condolement is a course
> Of impious stubbornness. 'Tis unmanly grief. . . .
> . . . 'tis a fault to heaven,
> A fault against the dead, a fault to nature,
> To reason most absurd, whose common theme
> Is death of fathers, and who still hath cried,
> From the first corse till he that died today,
> "This must be so." We pray you throw to earth
> This unprevailing woe, and think of us
> As of a father . . .
>
> (Act I, sc. ii)

Exhorting him to put a *term* to his grief, to *comprehend* his mourning, to comprehend it between two dates, the beginning and the end, the King proposes to Hamlet, with the same gesture, to replace his father. He confirms thereby that if, according to the common prejudice and one which Freud (the Freud of *The Rat Man*) did not escape, a mother is, by universal testimony, naturally irreplaceable, the father, on the other hand, remains that "legal fiction" that Stephen talks about in *Ulysses*, not far from a

meditation on Hamlet. A legal fiction, yes, especially when a father is the father in the figure of the king. For one of the king's
"two bodies" can always, by definition, be replaced.

It seems then all the easier to put a term to mourning: everything happens as if the father were not dead, as if the murder had
not taken place, as if it were impossible to testify to it and to
assign it a date. Since, Claudius says, the "death of fathers" is a
"common theme" of reason, a father who always dies never dies,
he is replaced on the very date on which he dies. If this death is
always a murder, there is always someone—and occasionally it is
the murderer—to offer his paternity to the orphan. *A priori*, always and without delay, on the very date of a death concerning
which one immediately wonders if it took place, someone comes
to say to the orphan: "I am your true father, be my son."

Now, you will have noticed, in the same scene, what cannot be a
chronological coincidence: Remaining alone on stage after having
heard his uncle-King, which is to say from now on his stepfather,
or as one says in French his *beau-père*, his legal father, his father
according to the law (or his father-in-law), Hamlet seems no
longer to know *when* his father died. On what date? Since when?
The confusion seems to cause his memory to go astray. Since
when is he in mourning? Two months or one month? "That it
should come to this:/ But two months dead, nay, not so much, not
two . . . " And less than ten lines later he says "and yet within a
month—/Let me not think on't; frailty, thy name is woman— . . .
O god, a beast that wants discourse of reason/ Would have
mourned longer—married with my uncle,/ My father's brother,
but no more like my father/ Than I to Hercules. Within a
month . . ."

When he accuses his mother of not respecting the terms, the
dates, and the time of mourning, he returns the accusation of
inhumanity. The King his stepfather had said to him: to maintain
mourning beyond the normal time, beyond the term appropriate
to human mourning, is inhuman, it is a crime against the dead
and against reason. Hamlet, for his part, accuses the woman, the
mother, he accuses feminine-maternal frailty of giving itself up to
the replaceability of a surrogate mother, there where the father is
irreplaceable, and of conducting itself like a beast, that is, in an

inhuman fashion. Mourning is human, only beasts do not wear mourning and know nothing of dates. And the rationalism of the reasonable, the invocation of reason, of the "discourse of reason," is also on the side of this inhuman bestiality; it is a strategy of rationalization destined to serve and to hide the interests of a crime.

Time passes. As time passes, time passes. Instead of taking place, it disappears, it ceases to take place. It mourns itself. Instead of stretching out, instead of growing larger, it shrinks, it recalls mourning to the chronological paradox of its economy. The two months, then the month, the less than a month of the "within a month," and then without delay they will become hours, less than two hours—"within two hours"—or else "twice two months" depending on the place mourning assigns to one or to the other, Hamlet or Ophelia. We say that this happens "without delay"; we could say the opposite: it will "delay," but without delay, because the more it delays, the less time is long, thus the less it delays. It is a matter of thinking what "delay" means and of putting this delay in relation to the time of mourning (is there a time that is not a time of mourning?) and to the time of mourning as messianic time of imminence. Here the term of mourning gives the measure. But it is the impossible measure of time. And thus the impossibility of an objective and stable reference to the violence of the founding event—which always has something to do with a phantasm. To have said "two months," then twice "within a month," in a play whose chronology is so difficult to follow and whose calendar so difficult to reconstitute (the play's action stretches over several months), will not in fact prevent Hamlet from reducing, much later (Act III, sc. ii) the months into hours. But one does not know then, no more than ever, if for the time being he is speaking figuratively, if he is truly raving or if he is playing at madness in order to outmaneuver his partners, fool everybody, and put the event back on stage, by organizing the theatrical repetition in which it already consists, with the sole aim of ensnaring the criminal, trapping him, catching him with his symptom ("The play's the thing/ Wherein I'll catch the conscience of the king . . ."). To Ophelia, after having pretended to want to put Hamlet's head between her legs, as if to mimic penetration or birth—which would have made of his beloved his surrogate mother, his replacement mother, his virgin mother—to Ophelia who says to him "You are merry, my lord," Hamlet responds as if he were looking at his watch. And naming survival ("outlive"), he counts the hours: "What should a man do but be merry? For look you how cheerfully my mother looks, and my father died within's two hours. *Ophelia:* Nay, 'tis twice two months, my lord. *Hamlet:* So long? Nay, then, let the devil wear black, for I'll have a suit of sables. O heavens! Die two months ago, and not forgotten yet? Then there's hope a great man's memory may outlive his life half a year. But, by'r Lady, he must build churches then . . ."

II

If I chose this title, "The time is out of joint," would it be merely so as to recall these supplementary disturbances of an abyssal mourning or just to attempt in vain to make up for my own lateness? No, it is also out of fidelity, out of a taste for memory and repetition. In this case I wanted to thematize what may be a traditional gesture of deconstruction, at least the deconstruction that interests me. This gesture would consist in interrogating, so as to put them back into play, titles in general: the title of the title, the justification and authority of the title. And to do so by marking a multi-referentiality, which is to say (forgive me this suitcase word) a *differeferentialty* [différéférentialité] of the title that is thus suspended. The reference of the title, that to which it refers, the thing in play becomes at once multiple, different, and deferred. Thus for example "The time is out of joint" does not announce only the dislocations, disjunctions, disjoinings, disarticulations, anachronies, contretemps, all the untimeliness that I will be speaking about this evening. In other words, this title does not anounce only the *subject* or the *content*, the *stakes* of this discourse (and this subject is already a certain difference within time, a temporal and temporalizing differance). "Out of joint" also describes in advance what will be the time of these remarks. Disorganization, disarticulation: these are *both the thematic stakes and the form* of these out-of-joint remarks, the dis-junction at the heart of the "is" that is so poorly defined, and with so much difficulty, by the third person singular present indicative of the verb *to be*.

Two quotations therefore. Two reported sentences neither of which (because I am quoting them) is, as one says, by me, signed or countersigned by me:

1. "The time **is** out of joint."
2. "Deconstruction **is**/in America."

I signed neither the one nor the other, that is true, but I have loved both of them. Moreover, one can never love anything other than that: what one cannot sign, he or she in the place of whom one neither can nor wants to sign.

I loved them for a time, and it is about them, which I loved for a time, and which therefore I still love inasmuch as they are not mine, that I would like to talk a little.

What do they have in common, these two beloved sentences? First of all, I have loved them, which at least for me is priceless. This love renders them desirably ineffaceable within me. Next, these two sentences pretend to say what is, what is "is," only in order to end up also by forcing me to relinquish the "is," by dis-locating, discrediting, and suspending the very authority of the "is."

And perhaps deconstruction would consist, if at least it did consist, in precisely that: deconstructing, dislocating, displacing, disarticulating, disjoining, putting "out of joint" the authority of the "is." Or yet again, rather than doing that, sooner, even before doing that, and doing it methodically, it would be a matter for deconstruction of measuring itself against the *historical* experience—and this is history itself—against the experience of that which in the "is," in time or in the present time of the "is," remains precisely "out of joint."

I will come back to this later while insisting on what Hamlet says to me today in America when he pronounces in English "The time is out of joint." And I will say why I cannot separate this extraordinary sentence from the one that, modestly, is murmuring, far from the stage and the theater: "Deconstruction is/in America."

Concerning this latter sentence, one of the two quotations therefore, forgive me if I recall, still in a preliminary fashion, that I in fact pronounced it but without assuming it, without subscribing to it, without ever believing it. It was in 1984; in America, at the University of California, Irvine, where I had not yet begun to teach regularly. At that time, and for some time yet to come, I remained more of an East-coast American since I was teaching every year for several weeks at Yale after having done the same thing at Johns Hopkins. In 1984, then, I had been invited to give the Wellek Lectures at Irvine. David Carroll and Suzanne Gearhart had suggested that I speak—this was ten years ago—on what already for some time had been called "Deconstruction in America." This was also the title of a book published in 1983 at University of Minnesota Press, *The Yale Critics: Deconstruction in America.* I had explained the reasons—there were four of them—for which I thought I had to renounce, as I must also do this evening, talking about "Deconstruction in America." I will not recall these reasons because all this has since been published in *Mémoires for Paul de Man.* But permit me to say, in the most neutral fashion possible, that these reasons seem to me still to withstand all the considerable transformations that have occurred in the last ten years and, however presumptuous this may sound, I would not change a word of what I said then on the subject.

Having arrived at the fourth of these reasons, I risked putting forth an hypothesis according to which, if it is impossible to talk about deconstruction in America, this is because "America *is* deconstruction [l'Amérique, mais *c'est* la déconstruction]."

I had tried, then, to explain why it was impossible and illegitimate to speak about "Deconstruction in America," but also and above all that, in marking one of the reasons not to speak about "Deconstruction in America," the sentence "Deconstruction is America" formulated merely an hypothesis. Better yet, it formulated an hypothesis that I finally relinquished and to which, however seductive it may remain, I would not in any case subscribe.

This abandoned hypothesis was not merely what I called then a "fiction of truth." We must recognize in the two open sets, in the "allegorico-metonymical figure" that they describe, the power to dislocate and destabilize the "is" as well as the "in."

This is what puts into deconstruction the very thing that confers its title on the present conference. The history of deconstruction or the deconstruction of history perhaps roams around the disjointed pivot of this copula "is," this clause of inclusion "in," or this conjunction "and" by which one seeks at the same time to couple, enclose, or conjoin a subject and a predicate. For example here," Deconstruction and (in, is, as) America."[2]

Instead of prolonging these preliminary precautions that could go on infinitely, I am not going to delay jumping to the second quotation, "The time is out of joint." It will help me to say something about what is happening today, ten years later, for me, *for me at least*, with deconstruction in America.

Before making the jump, however, allow me a few steps by way of take-off. *Four little steps* the last of which will lead me to speak in English.

1. *First step*. The first step passes by way of the passage, namely translation. It is not merely for the sake of facility that I decided to speak several languages this evening, yours and mine, and then to announce in Shakespeare's English that I was going to speak French. I do it for at least three reasons:

a) Deconstruction, as we know it, will have been first of all a translation or a transference between French and American (which is to say also, as Freud has reminded us about transference, a love story, which never excludes hatred, as we know).

b) In the passage from *Mémoires for Paul de Man* that turns around Deconstruction in America, is the only definition that I have ever in my life dared to give of deconstruction: "more than one language" (p. 15). But I insisted then on an obvious point that had to be taken into account: "more than one language" does not constitute a sentence, it is not a proposition of the kind S is P. In the sense in which Austin understands meaning, therefore, this phrase does not have a meaning. It was then necessary for me to underscore that, contrary to what is often thought, deconstruction is not exported from Europe to America. It has in this country several original configurations that in their turn produce singular effects. I said that this American radiation or hegemony must be interrogated, which sometimes means contested, in all its dimensions (political, technical, economic, linguistic, academic, editorial). Deconstruction is often perceived in Europe as an American brand of theorems, a discourse, or a school.

Is there an irreplaceable place and a proper history for this thing, deconstruction? Is there anything else in it but transference in all the senses this word assumes in more than one language, and first of all in the sense of transference among languages? Allow me once again this quotation: "If I had to risk a single definition of deconstruction, one as brief, elliptical, and economical as a password, I would say simply and without overstatement: *plus d'une langue*—both more than one language and no more of just one language. In fact it is neither a statement nor a sentence. It is sententious, it makes no sense if, at least as Austin would have it, words in isolation have no meaning. What makes sense is the sentence. How many sentences can be made with 'deconstruction'?" (*ibid;* trans. modified).

2. *Second step.* This translativity of deconstruction destines it to erring and voyage, which is to say, to a destination and destinerrance. Now, when I discovered with some surprise the title of this colloquium, the title such as is it was chosen not by me but by Tom Bishop and Anselm Haverkamp, I let myself dream about all the readings one could give of it. I read it suddenly as if in a newspaper, a travel diary, or a press release: Hey, deconstruction, on this date, finds itself here these days, it is in America, it landed yesterday at JFK and is just passing through, more or less incognito and for a little while. Today, deconstruction is, happens to be; it turns out that it is in America. Where was it yesterday? Where will it be tomorrow? etc. With that slash in the middle (is/ in America) which interrupts the reverie and gives us a start by marking clearly with an implacable injunction that we have to choose: either *is* or else *in*.

Here then again the difference of a single letter, *n* or *s*. It marks for us very well, *in the first place*, that if deconstruction *is in America*, "in" can indicate inclusion as well as provisional passage, the being-in-transit of the visitor (Deconstruction is just visiting—and from visitation one passes quickly to the visor, to the visor and haunting effect in Hamlet—return to Hamlet's father.) If, then, *Deconstruction is in America,* that means also, *in the second place,* that it is not America. If D is in A, it is not A; if D is A, it is not in, etc. The slash indeed inscribes or incises a disjunction in the copula "is," in the coupling of the present that interests me here. How can the *is* itself be disjoined from itself, out of joint?

When Hamlet says "The time is out of joint," he says, to be sure, many things (we will come back to that); but he says at least and first of all this, by folding the proposition back on itself in advance: that time itself, the present indicative of the verb to be in the third person singular, the "is" that says what time is, this tense of time is out of joint, itself and by itself out of joint. And the shock waves of such a disjoining doubtless affect the heart of the question "to be or not to be." The essence of Being is often determined, in a non-fortuitous fashion, as Heidegger often insists, on the basis of the third person singular of the present indicative, so that what happens to "is" happens to the bar that separates to be and/or not to be. There would no longer even be a question without this disjoinng of the "is."

Perhaps deconstruction has never done anything but *interpret* this extraordinary phrase of Hamlet's; to interpret it in the sense in which the hermeneut interprets, interpret it in the sense in which the actor interprets, interpret it in the sense of the play or the performancc, interpret it in the sense in which one must still, beyond reading and theater, interpret interpretation.

And if this interpretation is neither America nor in America, not only America nor in America, then what is America today? What is deconstruction doing at this very moment in America? Before outlining a partial and preliminary response to that question, here is a third step.

3. *Third step.* If the slash between "is" and "in" says in silence something about what "The time is out of joint" may mean, if that is the very affirmation of deconstruction, then the good and the wicked fairies that for more than thirty years have been following

its destiny, proliferating teleological verdicts, eschatological prognoses, or organicist diagnoses concerning the birth, growth,
health, sickness, and death of deconstruction, all these voluble
fairies begin by not knowing what they are talking about. This
does not mean that no historian or sociologist of deconstruction
ever says anything pertinent. Nor that one has to reduce all their
plotted curves to so much silliness—which they are sometimes. It
remains necessary, no doubt, to attempt to analyze the becoming,
the genesis, and the decline of what is thus reduced to a fashion, a
school of thought, an academic current, a theory, or a method. But
even there where they do not fall into unfortunate stereotypes,
even there where they are more rigorous and more lucid, these
historico-sociological analyses encounter several limits: a) They
miss the most acute aspect of deconstruction, that which exceeds,
in their very deconstructibility, the themes, objects, methods, and
especially the axiomatics of this historical or sociological knowledge; b) they already incorporate and import from deconstruction
what they attempt to objectify; c) they most often resemble performatives disguised as constatives: they would like to make happen what they claim to describe in all neutrality. For more than
twenty-five years, in fact, we have been told that deconstruction is
dying or that it is "on the wane." And in a certain way this is true!
Since it has been true from the beginning, and that's where the
question is, since deconstruction begins by being in poor shape
(being out of joint) and even by dying, since that is all anyone
talks about, one must stop believing that the dead are just the
departed and that the departed do nothing. One must stop pretending to know what is meant by "to die" and especially by
"dying." One has, then, to talk about spectrality. You know very
well who pronounces the sentence "The time is out of joint":
Hamlet, the heir of a specter concerning which no one knows
any longer *at what moment* and therefore *if* death has happened
to him.

The diagnoses and the prognoses are here at once more true
and (as many signs also attest) less true than ever. This implies
that the teleological schema (birth, growth, old age, sickness, end
or death) can be applied to everything, and to everything about
deconstruction, except, in all certitude and in the mode of a deter-

minant knowledge, to that which in it begins by questioning, displacing, and dislocating the machine of this teleology, and thus this opposition between health and sickness, normality and anomaly, life and death.

With that I undertake my *fourth step*, to say a few words about what is going on in America today. Not about what deconstruction may represent there, here, now, today, but what, far more modestly, I am doing there, myself, or believe I am doing there in this very moment.

To take a shortcut and get very quickly to the point, I will distinguish two times in my work, two recent upheavals. The one and the other had their place, their landscape, as well as their language, in this country, in the East and then in the West, in New York and in California. Such as I first felt them in myself, these upheavals will not have failed to be announced, like all phenomena of this type, by long-range waves whose traces can be found in my work for the last thirty years. But this does not mean that they were any less irruptive and sudden.

The first, about which I will say only a word, was on the occasion of a colloquium organized by Drucilla Cornell at the Cardozo Law School around the theme "Deconstruction and the Possibilities of Justice." In "Force of Law," I tried to demonstrate that justice, in the most unheard-of sense of this word, was the undeconstructible itself, thus another name of deconstruction (deconstruction? deconstruction *is* justice). This supposed a decisive distinction and one of incalculable scope between law and justice. Such a distinction of principle, joined to a certain thinking of the gift (a thinking which had also begun long ago and in a more visible fashion in recent publications) will have allowed me to knot or unknot, in a more political book on Marx which I have just finished, a great number of threads that were already crossing throughout all the earlier texts, for example on the gift beyond debt and duty, on the aporias of the work of mourning, spectrality, iterability, and so forth.

And last Spring, once again in the United States, on the other side, on the other coast, on the occasion of a keynote address that I was generously invited to deliver at a large colloquium, "Whither Marxism" at the University of California, Riverside, I was finally able to hazard a discourse that would have liked to be something other than a Marxist discourse, something other than a discourse *on* Marx or a reading *of* Marx, in the conventional, academic, or exegetical sense of this word. What I try to make understood there corresponds first to a political position-taking: it was uttered first of all *in* America, but surely also *on the subject of* America, and doubtless, to an extent that remains to be determined, *against* a certain America in the new world order that is attempting to impose itself today.[3]

III

An epilogue for today, a word for the end on all the possible ends of the Nation-State and of that which in the Nation-State will have always been, no doubt, "out of joint." For Hamlet's phrase must also describe and interpret that State which was the rotten state of Denmark.

This word for the end brings me back again to the United States. It reawakens in me, moreover, the living and, in many regards, happy memory I retain of that moment in October 1966 when I was so generously invited to speak there for the first time. I am referring to the conference at Johns Hopkins University on Critical Languages and the Sciences of Man. I will recall merely that my remarks on that occasion concerned the concept of interpretation. They opened with a quotation from Montaigne ("We need to interpret interpretations more than to interpret things") and they closed with the distinction between two interpretations of interpretation, more precisely, with a "second interpretation of interpretation, to which Nietzsche pointed the way," although I then added that, between these two interpretations, it is not a question for us today of "choosing."

Returning in conclusion to Nietzsche, to Nietzsche's testimony concerning Hamlet's phrase, I would like to weave together the eschatological motifs of interpretation, the last word, testimony, and the work.

Bearing witness for itself, but no less for all the *shoahs* of history, "Aschenglorie," the poem by Celan (who was a great translator of Shakespeare), declares the enigma itself:

Niemand
zeugt für den
Zeugen.

No one
bears witness for
the witness.

In the seminar on testimony I have been conducting for several years, we are trying to interpret all the possible interpretations of these three lines. They say to us, among so many other things, both the eschatology of a witness who is always a last survivor, or even a last man, and the absolute immanence, that of a testimony without outside other than the infinite, irreducible, and spectral alterity of another witness, of the witness of the witness as other. There is no witness for the witness, but there are only witnesses for the witness.

Now, in *Hamlet*, the dramatization deploys a spectacular and supernaturally miraculous *mise en abîme* of testimonies. Each witness is always *alone in bearing witness* in general (this is of the essence of testimony) and thus of testifying to the impossible possibility of testimony, thereby "testifying for the absence of attestation" as Blanchot puts it.[1] Hamlet is alone in being able to bear witness in this way to the testimony. The play named *Hamlet* thus becomes, like "Aschenglorie," a testimony on the essence of testimony, which also becomes the absence of testimony.

For this final word today, I would thus like to return once more to Hamlet. To Hamlet as read by Nietzsche. Not to what I may have said about being "out of joint" in *Specters of Marx*, but to what I added a moment ago when, concerning the disorder or the inadequation that marked the dating, the calendar, or the timetable, namely, the impossibility of assigning a real date, thus an external, objective reality, to the death of Hamlet's father, we considered the impossibility of measuring time and thus of measuring the measure of all things.

Measurelessness thus becomes the law. The law of the law is what measurelessness will always have been. For justice and for injustice, justly and unjustly. This inadequation is a dismembering, an essential disjoining, and first of all of time, of the present that is also out of joint. Among all the consequences and the interpretations that may thus be authorized, let us limit ourselves to one, whose trail I have just picked up thanks to a recent rereading of *The Birth of Tragedy*. Hamlet makes a strange apparition there. The latter apparition seems to disturb all the great interpretations, notably the psychoanalytic readings (Freud, Jones) of Hamlet and of Oedipus.

Nietzsche wants to see in this apparition of Hamlet a Dionysiac figure, which is already odd in itself. But he also sees there someone who renounces action (this time it is the classic vision of a paralyzed Hamlet, unable to decide, the neurotic Hamlet who no longer knows what to do and becomes a witness, merely a powerless witness, a profoundly indifferent observer beneath all his apparent passions). In the withdrawal that immobilizes him, this witness is now but a spectator of the play: passive and apathetic, pathetically patient and apathetic, pathologically apathetic in his very passion. It is in these terms that, most often, the witness is determined, the witness-witness, the one who attends [assiste] but does not intervene, the one who no longer even bears witness to what he has been a witness to. It is always supposed that the "good" witness, the one who attends, finds himself in this situation of the spectator who is neutral or neutralized, that is, paralyzed, turned to stone, stupefied, stunned, struck by lightning, thunderstruck by the flash of lucidity.

When we speak of testimony as active or performative, we are talking about bearing witness, the declaration, the oath, and so forth. But the witness-witness, the one who sees, is in principle passive, as passive as the camera that he can never be.

Now what does Nietzsche say? How does he *see* Hamlet? Because the latter was able to see what he saw, because he saw as a witness, and because he saw absolute disorder, the world out of joint, measurelessness, monstrosity (the ghost, his murdered father, his mother as merry widow, the political disorder that accompanies all this and perverts all the reasons of family and state, etc.), but also because he perhaps saw, through all of this, something that he cannot even say or admit to himself, Hamlet *glimpsed* [entrevu] such a terrifying thing, the Thing itself, that he decides to make no further move: he will remain but a discouraged witness, paralyzed, silent, made desperate by the being "out of joint" of time, by the disjoining, the discord, the terrible dismembering of the world in its present: originary Dionysianism, the Dionysiac itself.

But this witness will have been the witness of a witness, and the oath of secrecy binding all these testimonies. If Hamlet resolves not to decide, if he resigns himself to remaining the mute witness of the naked and monstrous truth that, in the blink of an eye, has been given to him in a blinding, thundering, traumatizing intuition, it is because he was first of all the witness of that witness that was his ghost of a father, of the violent death and the betrayal of which the latter claims he has been the victim, in the course of a supernatural and spectral attestation (which, in this regard, is like every attestation). Having known this, having *believed* it, having put faith in it, but having perhaps glimpsed something still worse behind it, the worst which the play would thus have actively silenced, Hamlet can no longer act. A more than lucid knowledge has killed off the action in him. He is from then on a pure witness, he is alone, alone and inconsolable; he ceases to act there where he is alone in having seen, known, alone in being able to bear witness.

He is alone in bearing witness.

Like every witness—and he bears witness also for every witness. He says no more than that, while keeping it secret: I am alone in being able to bear witness to it. A witness is always alone in being able to bear witness. Like a prophet who gives up speaking and acting or causing to act, precisely because he has seen too much. This "too much," that which goes beyond measure, is the "out of joint" (*aus den Fugen* in German, which is the common expression for "out of joint," something I noticed in Heidegger's text on the *Dikē* in *Der Spruch des Anaximander*).

In the long passage that I will now read, I am not sure whether the Nietzschean interpretation of Hamlet and of the experience of being "out of joint" could not be dissociated from the theory of art, of salvation through art, of the sublime and the comic that Nietzsche nevertheless manifestly attempts to attach to it. I will thus leave that question provisionally supended.

In this sense the Dionysian man resembles Hamlet: both have once looked truly into the essence of things, they have *gained knowledge,* and nausea inhibits action; for their action could not change anything in the eternal nature of things; they feel it to be ridiculous or humiliating that they should be asked to set right a world that is out of joint. Knowlegde kills action; action requires the veils of illusion: that is the doctrine of Hamlet, not that cheap wisdom of Jack the Dreamer who reflects too much, and, as it were, from an excess of possibilities does not get around to action. Not reflection, no—true knowledge, an insight into the horrible truth, outweights any motive for action, both in Hamlet and in the Dionysian man.

Now no comfort avails any more; longing transcends a world after death, even the gods; existence is negated along with its glittering reflection in the gods or in an immortal beyond. Conscious of the truth he has once seen, man now sees everywhere only the horror or absurdity of existence; now he understands what is symbolic in Ophelia's fate; now he understands the wisdom of the sylvan god, Silenus: he is nauseated.

Here, when the danger to his will is greatest, *art* approaches as a saving sorceress, expert at healing. She alone knows how to turn these nauseous thoughts about the horror or absurdity of existence into notions with which one can live: these are the *sublime* as the artistic taming of the horrible, and the *comic* as the artistic discharge of the nausea of absurdity. The satyr chorus of the dithyramb is the saving deed of Greek art; faced with the intermediary world of these Dionysian companions, the feelings described here exhausted themselves.[4]

In sum, Hamlet, surviving witness, is also the one who has seen death. He has seen the impossible and he cannot survive what he has survived. After having seen the worst, after having been the witness of the worst disorder, of absolute injustice, he has the experience of surviving—which is the condition of witnessing— but in order to survive what one does not survive. Because one *should not* survive. And that is what Hamlet *says,* and that is what *Hamlet,* the work, *does.* The work alone, but alone with us, in us, as us.

This is what one has to know: It is against the background of this disaster, it is only in the gaping and chaotic, howling and famished opening, it is out of the bottomless bottom of this open mouth, from the cry of this *khaein* that the call of justice resonates.

Here then is its chance and its ruin. Its beginning and its end. It will always be given thus as the common lot *[en partage]*, it will always have to be at once threatened and made possible in all languages by the *being out of joint: aus den Fugen.*

—Translated by Peggy Kamuf

Notes

1. Trans. Nicholas Royle, in Jacques Derrida, *Acts of Literature*, ed. Derek Attridge (New York: Routledge, 1992), p. 419.
2. "The fourth reason is that of a singular circle, one which is 'logical' or 'vicious' in appearance only. In order to speak of 'deconstruction in America,' one would have to claim to know what one is talking about, and first of all what is meant or defined by the word 'America.' Just what is America in this context? Were I not so frequently associated with this adventure of deconstruction, I would risk, with a smile, the following hypothesis: America *is* deconstruction [*l'Amerique, mais c'est la deconstruction*]. In this hypothesis, America would be the proper name of deconstruction in progress, its family name, its toponymy, its language and its place, its principal residence. And how could we define the United States *today* without integrating the following into the description: It is that historical space which today, in all its dimensions and through all its power plays, reveals itself as being undeniably the most sensitive, receptive, or responsive space of all to the themes and effects of deconstructon. Since such a space represents and stages, in this respect, the greatest concentration *in the world*, one could not define it without at least including this symptom (if we can even speak of symptoms) in its definition. In the war that rages over the subject of deconstruction, there is no front; ther are no fronts. But if there were, they would all pass through the United States. They would define the lot, and, in truth, the partition of America. But we have learned from 'Deconstruction' to suspend these always hasty attributions of proper names. My *hypothesis* must thus be abandoned. No, 'deconstruction' is not a proper name, nor is America the proper name of deconstruction. Let us say instead: deconstruction and America are two open sets which intersect partially according to an allegorico-metonymic figure. In this fiction of truth, 'America' woud be the title of a new novel on the history of deconstruction and the deconstruction of history" (*Memoires for Paul de Man*, rev. ed. [New York: Columbia University Press, 1989), pp. 17–18.

3. Since then, this *reading* has become a book. It will appear this year in France and next year in the United States. Once again Peggy Kamuf did me the favor of translating it, a favor I will never be able to match with my gratitude.
4. *Le pas au-delà* (Paris: Gallimard, 1973), p.107.
5. Friedrich Nietzsche, *The Birth of Tragedy*, trans. Walter Kaufmann (New York: Random House, 1967), p.60.

I

The Time of Analysis

1

Deconstruction and the Lyric

Jonathan Culler

It seems thoroughly appropriate for a conference on Deconstruction in America to begin with literature, since literature—the study thereof—is where deconstruction in America itself began to take root. But one might also suspect that, if we lead off with literature, it is in order to get it out of the way and to get down to the important stuff—philosophy and politics. Crucial in a sense, yet perhaps inconsequental, there to be passed beyond—is that of the condition or the fate, shall we say, of literature today?

My subject is that combination of importance and inconsequentiality known as the lyric—which for me at least is the most economical if not quintessential instantiation of literature.

Jacques Derrida has always written about authors deemed literary but recently he has dealt more frequently with the idea of literature itself. For example, he speaks of literature as

[an] historical institution with its conventions, rules, etc., but also this institution of fiction which gives *in principle* the power to say everything, to break free of the rules, to displace them, and thereby to Institute, to invent and even to suspect the traditional difference between nature and institution ... The institution of literature in the West, in its relatively modern form, is linked to an authorization to say everything and doubtless too to the coming about of the modern idea of democracy. Not that it depends on a democracy in place, but it seems inseparable to me from what calls forth a democracy, in the most open (and doubtless itself to come) sense of democracy.[1]

Here is another passage from the same text; an interview with Derek Attridge in *Acts of Literature* (1992):

This experience of writing is "subject" to an imperative: to give space for singular events, to invent something new in the form of acts of writing which no longer consist in a theoretical knowledge, in new constative statements, to give oneself to a poetico-literary performativity at least analogous to that of promises, orders, or acts of constitution or legislation which do not only change language, or which, in changing more than language, change more than language. . . . In order for this singular performativity to be effective, for something new to be produced, historical competence is not indispensable in a certain form (that of a certain academic kind of knowledge, for example, on the subject of literary history), but it increases the chances.[2]

Or again, Derrida remarks that deconstruction, in this historical moment, is crucially conditioned by "l'événement de la littérature depuis trois siècles, en tant que système de possibilités performatives. Elles ont accompagnées la forme moderne de la démocratie. Les constitutions politiques ont un régime discursif identique à la constitution des structures littéraires" ["the event of literature for the past three centuries, as a system of performative possibilities. They have accompanied the modern form of democracy. Political constitutions have a discursive regime identical to that of the constitution of literary structures."][3]

Finally, here is a passage from "Passions: 'An Oblique Offering,' " which recapitulates with a difference:

Literature is a modern invention, inscribed in conventions and institutions which, to hold on to just this trait, secures in principle its *right to say everything*. Literature thus ties its destiny to a certain non-censure, to the space of democratic freedom. No democracy without literature; no literature without democracy. It is always possible to want neither one nor the other, and there is no shortage of doing without them under all regimes, . . . But in no case can one dissociate one from the other. No analysis would be equal to it. . . . The possibility of literature, the legitimation that a society gives it, the allaying of suspicion or terror with regard to it, all that goes together—politically—with the unlimited right to ask any question, to suspect all dogmatism, to analyze every presupposition, even those of the ethics or the politics of responsibility.[4]

Thinking about literature thus seems directed to work eventually to elucidate a certain relation between literature and democracy: is it a metonymical relationship (where literature is linked to what gives rise to democracy), or a metaphorical relation (where literature's performativity is at least analogous to that of acts of constitution), or a relation of identity of discursive regimes, or a relation of mutual entailment (you can't have one without the other)?

The relationship as sketched here seems based on two interrelated factors—two factors which bring together the modern ideas or institutions of literature and democracy: first, a freedom which involves a special kind of responsibility, a hyper-responsibility, which includes a right to absolute nonresponse. The writer, like the citizen, must, Derrida writes, "sometimes demand a certain irresponsibility, at least as regards ideological powers . . . This duty of irresponsibility, of refusing to reply for one's thought or writing to constituted powers, is perhaps the highest form of responsibility."[5] There are important questions to be pursued in this domain, apropos both literature and democracy and the freedom and responsibility they involve; but the wager is that these questions will more likely be elucidated if, as they are pursued, the cases of literature and democracy are kept in view together.

The second connecting factor in these passages is the performativity of literature and of the discursive regimes of politics, both of whose discourses work to bring into being the situations they purport to describe. Since appeal to the notion of performativity has become very widespread of late, as the success of Judith Butler's brilliant *Gender Trouble* has led people in gender studies and queer theory to take up the notion, it is important to stress that performativity is the name of a problem rather than a solution, that it draws attention to the difficulty of determining what can be said to happen, under what conditions, and to the fact that the event is not something that is simply given. Once again, it is the conjunction of literature and politics through the notion of performativity that gives the complexity of the problem a chance of being elucidated.

But the idea of literature that emerges from such deconstructive reflections on the relation of literature and democracy is not itself my subject, though I hope we may have the opportunity to pursue it. In discussions of the sort I have been quoting, Derrida distinguishes between literature—this modern institution, with its possibility of *tout dire*—and something else: poetry (or sometimes *belles lettres*). And so it is in this context, where literature is linked with democracy and described in terms of a certain hyper-responsibility and a performativity of the word, that I want to ask about poetry, particularly the lyric. To put the problem most simply, if we can maintain "no democracy without literature," it seems considerably harder to imagine claiming, "no democracy without poetry," or vice versa. What, then, can we say of lyric? What is its relation to the freedom and the performativity that are crucial to the modern idea of literature?

Northrop Frye defines the lyric as utterance overheard, a notion Paul de Man partly takes up in calling it "the instance of represented voice."[6] In an essay on Théodore de Banville, Baudelaire writes of the lyric, "Constatons que l'hyperbole et l'apostrophe sont des formes du language qui lui sont non seulement des plus agréables mais aussi des plus nécessaires . . . " [Note that hyperbole and apostrophe are the forms of language which are not only the most agreeable but also the most necessary to it].[7] And it is in this tradition that de Man, Barbara Johnson, and I have argued that the fundamental tropes of lyric are apostrophe (the address to something that is not an empirical listener) and prosopopoeia (the giving of face and voice to and thus the animation of what would not otherwise be a living interlocutor).[8] Both apostrophe and prosopopoeia work to create *I-you* relations and structures of specularity, which seem characteristic of the dramas projected by lyric. Whether we think of the address to apparently inanimate objects—"O Rose thou art Sick!" "O wild West Wind!" "Sois sage, o ma douleur!"—or the address to the beloved, apostrophes are not only endemic in lyric, they are the moments chosen for satirizing poetic discourse, as in, for example,

> O Huncamunca, Huncamunca, O!
> Thy pouting breasts, like kettledrums of brass,
> Beat everlasting loud alarms of joy, . . .
> For what's too high for love, or what's too low?
> O Huncamunca, Huncamunca, O! "[9]

Now apostrophes, whatever they are invoking, seem to end up posing, explicitly or implicitly, questions about the performative efficacy of poetic rhetoric itself. So as Baudelaire's "Ciel Brouillé" concludes,

O femme dangereuse, O séduisants climats!
Adorerai-je aussi ta neige et vos frimas,
Et saurai-je tirer de l'implacable hiver
Des plaisirs plus aigus que la glace et le fer?

[O dangerous woman, o seductive climates!
Will I also adore your snow and ice,
And will I be able to draw from implacable winter
Pleasures that are sharper than ice and steel?][10]

This is a question about the performativity of lyrical discourse: will it work? will it bring about the conditions it describes? To take a more familiar example, Shelley's "Ode to the West Wind" insistently invokes and conjures the wind in the apparent hope that it will, in the end, be what the speaker demands:

Be thou, spirit fierce,
My spirit! Be thou me, impetuous one![11]

In concluding, the speaker urges the wind to "Be through my lips to unawakened earth/The trumpet of a prophecy"—a prophecy which consists of the incantation of these verses asking the wind to bear, sustain, repeat, proliferate a poetic enunciation or performance whose content is this performance itself; namely, the articulation of the hope that the natural cycle of the seasons ("If winter comes, can spring be far behind!") will, through the agency of the wind, animate the speaker's voice. That is, the speaker urges the wind to "be through my lips the trumpet of a prophecy," but there is here no other prophecy than this hopeful calling on the wind to advance the poetic voice.

When lyrics thematically pose the question of the performative power of lyric rhetoric, it is often in this form: will you be as I describe you when I invoke you? will you be what I say you are? And when they do appear to answer the question, it is often by finding some way of formulating the request so that it is by definition fulfilled if we hear it. If one takes such cases as exemplary of the performativity of lyric, then one would see lyric, in principle and often in practice as well, as a poetic naming that performatively creates what it names. So poems that invoke the heart—"O mon coeur, entend le chant des matelots" or "Be still, my heart"— create what we have come to call "the heart."

This locating of lyric value in performativity is, perhaps, the contemporary deconstructive version of Heidegger's poetic *aletheia*, poetry as the happening of truth at work. But there are lots of lyric examples which make one uncomfortable with such a claim, where the operations of apostrophe and prosopopoeia create not the heart but speaking birds, animated sofas, or daggers full of charm: "Charmant poignard, jaillis de ton étui." Indeed, Heidegger emphatically moves to separate his true *dichtung* from frivolous play of the imagination—the sort of play that seems most at work in apostrophic lyrics, which animate all kinds of things in ways that frequently seem embarrassing.[12] If one focuses on the performative functioning of a lyric conceived as fundamentally apostrophic and prosopopoeic, then it seems overweening to link these figures, which so often foreground a conspicuously bizarre or arbitrary figurality, to the happening of truth.

What happens through the performativity of lyric is exceedingly difficult to say, but whether or not lyric is the happening of truth it does seem to happen as singular concatenations of words—"Shivelights and shadowtackle in long lashes lace, lance, and pair"[13]—combinations difficult to reduce to theme or to infer from particular empirical situations. The happening of lyrics is linked to a strangeness or alterity which, if it works, may lodge itself in memory. If the lyric happens, it does so as a form of radical singularity whose value is linked to a certain memorable otherness. So, if the "Ode to the West Wind" has in any sense made the wind be come the spirit of the speaker—"Be thou me, impetuous one"—it is because this verbal connection has been inscribed in memories here and there, has proliferated in its iterability.

Educational tradition, from Plato to the present, has distinguished good memory from bad—the memory of understanding or assimilation (which is to be encouraged and which is what tests should test), from the memory of rote repetition or mere memorization. On the one hand there is what you have made your own and can recall, reformulate, and produce as knowledge because you have understood it; on the other, there is what you repeat without necessarily understanding, what remains lodged within mechanical memory *(Gedächtnis)* as a piece of otherness. Now if the novel is writing you assimilate—that is, when you remember novels you recall, in your own words, as we say, what happens, what they are about—lyrics, on the contrary, retain an irreducible otherness: to remember them at all is to remember at least some of their words; they ask as Derrida puts it in "Che cos'è la poesia? " to be learned by heart. "Le poétique, disons-le, serait ce que tu désires apprendre, mais de l'autre, grâce à l'autre et sous sa dictée, par coeur: *imparare a memoria*." ["The poetic, let us say it, would be that which you desire to learn, but from the other, thanks to the other, and at his or her dictation, by heart: to learn by heart."][14] This brief text of Derrida's takes as the figure for the lyric not the phoenix nor the eagle but the modest, prickly yet pathetic hedgehog, *l'hérisson*. Neither *héritier* nor *nourisson*, *l'hérisson* is a creature which, as in Giraudoux's *Electre*, "se fait écraser"—indeed, whose nature is to "se faire écraser sur les routes."[15] The poem is addressed to you—a generalized, fictional you which it posits, which it tries to create—but it can always miss its mark, can be ignored, even ridiculed. It exposes itself to being dismissed. So, while at one level, lyrics thematize the problem of whether they will make things happen and sometimes find ways of insuring that what they want to have happen does happen through the form of articulation of the desire, their performativity consists also in their success in creating the listeners/readers they attempt to address and in making themselves remembered.

On the question of the freedom and performativity of literature, Derrida writes:

it is an institution which consists in transgressing and transforming, thus in producing its constitutional law; or, to put it better, in producing discursive forms, "works," and "events" in which the very possibility of a fundamental constitution is at least "fictionally" contested, threatened, deconstructed, presented in its very precariousness. Hence, while literature shares a certain power and a certain destiny with "jurisdiction," with the juridico-political production of institutional foundations, the constitutions of states, fundamental legislation, and even the theological-juridical performatives which occur at the beginning of law, at a certain point it can only exceed them, interrogate them, "fictionalize" them: with nothing, or almost nothing, in view, of course, and by producing events whose "reality" or duration is never assured, but which by that very fact are more thought-provoking, if that still means something.[16]

Though we might not wish to claim for lyric the juridico-political productive power that literature is here said to share, lyric does partake in that excess of fictionalized foundational performatives, as it posits conditions in poetic events whose reality or duration is never assured and which may indeed seem to have "almost nothing" in view. Formal structures that pose a certain resistance to understanding, they may or may not succeed in inscribing themselves on the memory, with what de Man calls "the senseless power of positional language."[17]

There would seem then to be two interpretations of the performativity of lyric. One sees poems as creating what they name or describe, in a work of truth—*dichtung*—and would stress in particular the crucial role of metaphor in poetic naming. It would be less comfortable when the tropes of lyric are apostrophe and prosopopoeia and might be sorely tempted to distinguish a true lyric performativity from the facile play of rhetoric. In 1977, in an article entitled "Apostrophe," I tried to resist that temptation, while pursuing this option, by identifying apostrophe with the fundamental structure of lyric but at the same time with everything that is potentially most pretentious, mystificatory, and embarrassing in the lyric; and I sought to work out how these tropes could be said to make things happen—for example by thrusting their animate presuppositions on the reader or listener with the force of an event.[18] Lamartine's "Objects inanimés, avez vous donc une âme?,"[19] like the question "Have you stopped beating your wife?," creates a structure from which a reader has trouble disengaging, except by ignoring the poem altogether. The problem, for me, was to find cases where one might argue convincingly that a poem made something happen. The "Ode to the West Wind" would be a case in point, because of the special self-reflexive character of its formulations. And I concluded with the example of Keats's "This Living Hand," which, I argued, dares readers to resist it but compels their acceptance of a presence the poem performatively produces.[20]

Against this account of poetic performativity, the second account of performativity would insist, rather, on the unverifiable and problematic nature of such events and link performativity rather to a performative iterability whose best instance is the lodging of singular formulations in memory. This second account might stress, as Derrida does in "Che cos'è la poesia?," that the poem, vulnerable like the hedgehog rolled into a ball, makes you want to protect it, learn it by heart, in a "passion de la marque singulière." Here the oddity of the poem, its vulnerability to dismissal, is what calls to us, and one might speculate that criticism's inclination to demonstrate the necessity, the inevitability of poetic combinations—why the poem needs just these words and no other—comes from the knowledge that it is the contingency, the accidents, the otherness of poetic phrases that creates their appeal.

Now it may be that there can be no question of choosing between these accounts—between performativity as the happening of truth or the poem's creation of what it describes, and the performativity of, shall we say, what manages to repeat, happens to lodge itself in mechanical memory as iterable inscription. There may be no question of choosing because the lyric might be precisely the name of the hope that iterable inscription will be the happening of truth—or, on the contrary, the name of the concealment of inscription and the play of the letter by a thematics of specularity and self-creation, or perhaps—one other possibility—the name of the oscillation between these perspectives.

These possibilities, it seems to me, help to make sense of part of Paul de Man's complicated and discontinuous account of lyric. De Man speaks of lyric (and other names for genres) as a defensive motion of understanding. This passage, from "Anthropomorphism and Trope in the Lyric," needs to be quoted at length:

What we call the lyric, the instance of represented voice, conveniently spells out the rhetorical and thematic characteristics that make it the paradigm of a complementary relationship between grammar, trope, and theme. The set of characteristics includes the various structures and moments we encountered along the way [i.e., in the interpretation of Baudelaire's "Obsession," which de Man sees as translating the sonnet "Correspondances" into lyric intelligibility]: specular symmetry along an axis of assertion and negation (to which correspond the generic mirror images of the ode, as celebration, and the elegy, as mourning), the grammatical transformation of the declarative into the vocative modes of question, exclamation, address, hypothesis, etc., the tropological transformation of analogy into apostrophe, or the equivalent, more general transformation . . . of trope into anthropomorphism. The lyric is not a genre, but one name among several to designate a defensive motion of understanding, the possibility of a future hermeneutics. From this point of view there is no significant difference between one generic term and another: all have the same apparently intentional and temporal function.[21]

Here the suggestion is that lyric, like other genres, is a "term of resistance and nostalgia," the name we have for a particular way of convincing ourselves not only that language is meaningful and that it will give rise to an intuition or understanding, but that this will be an understanding of the world—an understanding to come.[22] But in de Man's essay there is something else that stands against the lyric thus conceived. Of Baudelaire's "Correspondances," he writes, "All we know is that it is, emphatically, *not* a lyric. Yet it, and it alone, contains, implies, produces, generates, permits (or whatever aberrant verbal metaphor one wishes to choose), the entire possibility of the lyric."[23] De Man's phrase "it alone" warns us against distinguishing between two kinds of poetry, one of which is lyric and the other of which—like "Correspondances"—remains unnamed. "Correspondances" seems rather to be a textual singularity—he speaks of its "stutter"—that gets translated into lyric, into lyric intelligibility. "Correspondances" permits him to infer a materiality of language which cannot be isolated as such, as a "moment" or an origin, but which, by standing, as it were, "beneath" lyric (or whatever aberrant formulation one wishes to choose), enables us to identify the figurative structures and operations constitutive of the lyric.

Today, as critical accounts appeal to a performativity which is increasingly seen as both the accomplishment and the justification of literature—the source of claims we might wish to make for it—it seems to me especially important that we consider, in particular cases, what performativity involves and what kinds of distinctions we need to make to talk about such forms as the lyric, which I think merit more sustained attention than they have so far received from or in deconstruction in America.

Notes

1. Jacques Derrida, "This Strange Institution Called Literature," interview with Derek Attridge, in Derrida, *Acts of Literature*, ed. Attridge (New York: Routledge, 1992), p.37

2. Ibid. p.55.
3. Jacques Derrida, seminar on "Future Deconstructions," University of California Jumanities Research Institue, Irvine, CA, May 1992.
4. Jacques Derrida, "Passions: 'An Oblique Offering,'" *Derrida: A Critical Reader*, ed. David Wood (Oxford: Blackwell, 1992), p.23.
5. Derrida, "This Strange Institution. . . ," p.38.
6. Northrop Frye, *Anatomy of Criticism* (Princeton: Princeton University Press, 1957), pp. 249–250; Paul de Man, *The Rhetoric of Romanticism* (New York: Columbia University Press, 1984), p.261.
7. Charles Baudelaire, *Oeuvres complètes* (Paris: Gallimard, 1976) II. 164.
8. Paul de Man, "Hypogram and Inscription," in *The Resistance to Theory* (Minneapolis: University of Minnesota Press, 1986), and *The Rhetoric of Romanticism*, particularly "Anthropomorphism and Trope in the Lyric," but also "Wordsworth and the Victorians." Barbara Johnson, "Apostrophe, Animation, and Abortion" in *A World of Difference* (Baltimore: Johns Hopkins University Press, 1986). Jonathan Culler, "Apostrophe," in *The Pursuit of Signs* (Ithaca: Cornell University Press, 1981); and "Reading Lyric," *Yale French Studies* 69 (1985), pp. 98–108.
9. Henry Fielding, "The Tragedy of Tragedy, or The Life and Death of Tom Thumb the Great," *Works* (London, 1821), vol. 1, p.472.
10. Baudelaire, *Oeuvres*, I, 49.
11. Percy Bysshe Shelley, *Complete Poetical Works* (London: Oxford University Press, 1943), p.577
12. Martin Heidegger, "The Origin of the Work of Art," *Poetry Language, Thought* (New York: Harper, 1971), p.72. For apostrophe and embarrassment, see Culler, "Apostrophe."
13. Gerard Manley Hopkins, "That Nature is a Heraclitean Fire and of the Comfort of the Resurrection," *Poems* (Oxford: Oxford University Press, 1970), p.105.
14. Jacques Derrida, "Che cos' è la poesia?" *Points de suspension* (Paris: Galilee, 1992), p.304.
15. Jean Giraudoux, *Electre* (Paris: Grasset, 1937), pp. 33–37.
16. Derrida, "This Strange Institution. . . ," p.72.
17. Paul de Man, "Shelley Disfigured," *The Rhetoric of Romanticism*, p.117.
18. Culler, "Apostrophe, " *The Pursuit of Signs*, first published in *Diacritics* 7:4 (Winter 1977)
19. Alphonse de Lamartine, *Oeuvres poétiques* (Paris: Gallimard, 1963), p.392.
20. Culler, "Apostrophe," pp.153–154.
21. de Man, *The Rhetoric of Romanticism*, p.261.
22. Ibid., p.261.
23. Ibid., pp.261–262.

2

Reading Epitaphs

Cynthia Chase

You haven't really read something until you've read it as an epitaph, said a friend of a friend of mine to whom I told this title. Tell them that.

To read something as an epitaph. Not yet having begun to think, what would that mean? one recognizes the prescription, and one's head fills up with words. Wordsworth's. I want to talk about the "Essay upon Epitaphs" (the first one), which is one of the datable moments at which *literature* and *epitaph* define one another, partly in certain familiar post-Romantic terms: what more obviously than an epitaph should be universal, "permanent," and sincere? Taking the epitaph as a paradigm for writing is one of the great power plays in humanism's history, whatever else one has to say about it. By the same token, Wordsworth's "Essay upon Epitaphs" could be titled "Epitaph on Literature."

De Man's "Autobiography as De-facement" notes that the Wordsworth text states a preference for epitaphs written "in the third person," from the position of the survivor, over those in the "first person," those that "personate the deceased." I quote the reading that is for many a familiar:

Yet at several points throughout the three essays, Wordsworth cautions consistently against the use of prosopopoeia, against the convention of having the "Sta Viator" adressed to the traveler on the road of life by the voice of the departed person. Such chiasmic figures, crossing the conditions of death and of life with the attributes of speech and of silence are, says Wordsworth, "too poignant and too transitory"—a curiously phrased criticism, since the very movement of consolation is that of the transitory and since it is the poignancy of the weeping "silent marble," as in Gray's epitaph on Mrs. Clark, for which the essays strive.[1]

Citing the lines that Wordsworth's text leaves out from its quotation of Milton's sonnet-epitaph "On Shakespeare": "... thou ... Dost make *us* marble ...," "Autobiography as De-facement" remarks,

"Doth make us marble", in the *Essays upon Epitaphs*, cannot fail to evoke the latent threat that inhabits prosopopoeia, namely that by making the death speak, the symmetrical structure of the trope implies, by the same token, that the living are struck dumb. . . .The surmise of the "Pause, Traveller!" [conventional to epitaphs] thus acquires a sinister connotation that is not only the prefiguration of one's own mortality but our actual entry into the frozen world of the dead.[2]

To read great literature, Milton's "On Shakespeare" says, is to be turned to stone, and because Wordsworth's essay-epitaph perceives and performs that threat, it erases those lines of Milton that pronounce it.

In teaching a reading such as this, de Man conveyed the experience of *reading in the original*. That one might read Wordsworth in the original, not in translation. Into, say, German or Flemish or French. No one of de Man's *formation* would do such a thing, of course, but that English wasn't one's first language means something: the slight effort and unobviousness that that phrase "to read something in the original" conveys. "Death" for "dead" (and vice versa), "doth" for "dost," "debt" ("deat'") for "death"—now all those slips are finds, just because they may or may not have meaning; shells, *coquilles*. To read in the original means not to "know," right off, what counts as a mere idiom, an assonance, a cliché, and so to have to reconstruct, painstakingly, a sense, of which the stresses may be altogether different than the emphases of the spoken and "understood" text. To this day I listen with dismay and cringing to how *The Prelude* sounds as "read" by English-born actors. I mean to praise here, though, not an alternative authenticity, another "original," but a chance. "Slow reading," Barbara Johnson calls it in a recent paper on some of these same texts. It gives the chance of unwinding the words from the meanings they (in phrases, in sentences, in verses) have over and over had. Reading in the original a text in a language not your own: this is the experience promised by *literature* (not only "*Comparative Literature*"), and a tolerable metaphor, perhaps a tolerable instance, of the "experience" of history, alternately that of intelligibility and of unintelligibility in a rhythm one may or may not pick up. But I bring up the matter of language learning also because it offers a real "correlate" to the "actual entry into the frozen world of the dead" that de Man's text speaks of. Not knowing what elements of a text to "read" and what to silently read past or through: it's that banal and ghastly predicament of the language student that is the condition of "really reading something." To borrow again my opening words, and (for the longest time, if not "permanently") for all that you can say about it, that epitaph might as well be yours.

What does it mean to take as one's model for language (or even just for writing) *epitaphs*, as Wordsworth's "Essay" does? (That move compares with the stories in Rousseau's *Second Discourse* and *Essai sur l'origine des langues*, which alternately award priority to passion and to need.) Surely it means an attempt to realize, to phenomenalize, the ontology we too readily "think" (or receive the idea) is *implicit* i.e., present, in language or in writing, which to "be" language has to be able to mean something when you or I are no longer "there."

Regenerating a description of this possibility or "predicament" that would not have the illusory ease and familiarity of that description takes more care than I could manage; one goes back to *Limited Inc.* (1988) and "Sign and Symbol." So just say that there is no one time at which anything "takes place." Wordsworth's move could be seen as an attempt to translate this possibility— this "predicament"—into aesthetic and generic terms and thereby naturalize and undo or alleviate it. An apologia for language, modulating into a threat—that's how the *Essays on Epitaphs*, at a certain pace, read. Wordsworth's *Essay* would give a face to the enigma of how the meaning gets to the words. And no answers are excluded, including "from things." To say "from things" doesn't necessarily put you in empiricism or positivism, especially, in "our" traditions, if the things in question are trees, rocks, or can be called "she" or "elle" (or "T").

"It is to be remembered," the "Essay" reads, "that to raise a monument is a sober and a reflective act; that the inscription which it bears is intended to be permanent, and for universal perusal." And also:

an epitaph is not a proud writing shut up for the studious: it is exposed to all—to the wise and the most ignorant; . . . it is concerning all, and for all . . . for this reason, the thoughts and feelings expressed should be permanent also—liberated from that weakness and anguish of sorrow which is in nature transitory, and which with instinctive decency retires from notice. . . . The very form and substance of the monument which has received the inscription, and the appearance of the letters, testifying with what a slow and laborious hand they must have been engraven, might seem to reproach the author who had given way upon this occasion to transports of mind, or to quick turns of conflicting passion; though the same might constitute the life and beauty of a funeral oration or an elegiac poem.[3]

In a proper epitaph—and the epitaph is the model for literature and for history, for Wordsworth's text—the medium dictates to the message-sender, and "turns" of thought and feeling come into being only because of the materialization, the immobilization, that fixes them to a grave.

What peculiar power the text ascribes to writing with the qualities that—sometime before and after this text—were identified with literature, *great* literature: universality, universal readability, permanence. And at the same time, what a soft sell! "Have feelings that are universal and permanent," says the house of language, "—because gravestones are." The evidence suggests that Wordsworth was alarmed by and not skilled in the making of advertisements, and in this text too perhaps that shows. What peculiar power this passage in Wordsworth's "Essay" ascribes to a *kind of writing*: the power to determine what sort of feelings the writer should have: hegemonic power. And not from Gramsci's jail did "hegemony" appear more insidious or more important. But is such power, *read*—Is such power, when designated, explained, as it is in Wordsworth's text—or even when exercised (say this passage is "merely an exercise"); is such power, through such a text, being established, or being unraveled? There isn't *an* answer, but outcomes that change as one listens for them by silently deciding and redeciding how to segment the text's semantic and syntactic structures. " *'In'* Wordsworth's text," we have to concede, then, is a no-place; in what *time* we read those words, what *time* we see those words, is crucial. How much time do you have; *what time* do you take it to *be*. This seems to me a way to describe the practical difficulty of trying to practice ideology critiques *and or* deconstructions.

It's something Jacques Derrida said, I think. It could also be under his aegis that one would move from a rhetorical analysis of the Wordsworth passage to a meditation upon politics and grief, starting off from the text's oracular and circular definition of "liberation," of being "liberated from that weakness and anguish of sorrow which is in nature transitory, and which with instinctive decency retires from notice." The circular or suspended judgment implied by the restrictive clause—"*which is in nature transitory*"—empties out and mitigates the brutality as well as the rigor that could inhere in that next phrase, "instinctive decency." (And nevertheless, whether or not they can spot restrictive clauses, and whether or not it's "there" "in the original," writing students tend to get the message: "the thoughts and feelings expressed should not be those that anyone with any decency instinctively suppresses." The sheer laboriousness of language that signifies through its syntax—not just the reading teacher—inhibits, stills.) In "other" cultures, including Greek (modern *and* ancient), anguish of sorrow does *not* "with instinctive decency retire from notice" but makes itself heard in laments—women's laments in particular.[4] They are en route, no doubt, to silence, or to writing. Or at least Wordsworth's language could have the effect, the power, of making us believe that the kind of mourning and the kind of day and the kind of literature his lines evoke has all the prestige, power, and inevitability of death.

Wordsworth's lines have the signal virtue, I'd argue, of *noting* that connection; of noting that a certain kind of writing, the kind

we value, the "permanent" kind, takes its authority from a certain—very particular and peculiar—way of handling death: handling it via the word "grave" and the idea of monuments and of
inscriptions. And in this the Wordsworth passage marks a line
of thought recently taken up in Derrida's reflections on death,
particularly at the point at which they move between *Being and
Time* and its countering in texts of Levinas that suggest that *not*
one's ownmost, my own death, but *the other's* death, has priority
among our conditions of existence. Where is mourning addressed,
how is grief redressed, in *Sein und Zeit*, was more than a passing
question, in Derrida's *conférence* for the second Derrida sympo-
sium at Cérisy. How might one go between Wordsworth, Derrida,
and de Man on mourning, and Heidegger on "mood?" I'm not
competent to pursue or really even pose these questions, so I
will return to the connection of death and literature again in
another way.

I want to go on with an important idea in the "Autobiography
as De-facement" passage, that an epitaph, that literature, does not
"leave us in quiet" (to quote Wordsworth again) but repositions
text and reader and pushes you to the ground. (Albeit "marble."
Keats, in "The Fall," anyway ("life to Milton would be death to
me"), knew that even on a marble stair one could moulder away.)
De Man's reading of Walter Benjamin's essay on "translation"
generates another lurid figure of writing or reading. It is some
sentences that come back at me like the inscribed letters of a
badly written epitaph, a permanent reproach—first because these
lines have already been written about repeatedly, and second because they reproach one for the failure and the *wish* to understand
the reproach they make and the threat they bespeak. The reproach
and the threat *are* understood, I should say, in Neil Hertz's essay
"Lurid Figures." But here they are again. The lines are of Paul de
Man, from the 1983 Messenger Lecture at Cornell University entitled "'Conclusions': Walter Benjamin's 'The Task of the Translator'," and the antecedent of the "they" that is the subject of these
lines is "translations." A previous sentence links translation with
other "activities" that are "intralinguistic," namely "critical philosophy, literary theory, history." "They are all intralinguistic,"

writes de Man, "they relate to what in the original belongs to language, and not to meaning as an extralinguistic correlate susceptible of paraphrase and imitation." Then this:

They disarticulate, they undo the original, they reveal that the original was always already disarticulated. They reveal that their failure, which seems to be due to the fact that they are secondary in relation to the original [as the engraving in stone of the epitaph is secondary in relation to its writing, its composition], reveals an essential failure, an essential disarticulation which was already there in the original.

In the original feelings—"Felt," as we say, only if they were suitable for a stone. Here now is the sentence I come back to: *They kill the original, by discovering that the original was already dead.*

We are so used to violent imagery and "negativity" that it's easy to pass by on the other side (the meaning side) of these words even after, or all the more after, they were seen and read by Neil Hertz as a remarkable instance of the lurid figures in de Man's writing, and interpreted in terms of the *"pathos of uncertain agency"* that their oxymoron or equivocation—"kill," "discover dead"—summons up. So I want to broach again the question of what it could mean to *"find already dead"* a text, a work, a figure.

Instinctive knowledge that I'll be saved by our time limits leaving me only a few more minutes alone enables me to take up this text. For I don't want to think about its figures. I want only to spell out not a certain set of alternatives, but a sort of equivocal outcome that the figures may mean. "That two-handed engine at the door," says "Lycidas." Translation is such an engine, which, perhaps, "stands ready to smite once and smite no more," but, so I'd translate, never *once* smites, because *two* things, always, at least, happen. I come back to the version of this operation in de Man's lecture on Benjamin. Two pages or a couple of minutes earlier, in the same lecture, de Man said,

Both criticism and translation are caught in the gesture which Benjamin calls ironic, a gesture which undoes the stability of the original by giving it a definitive, canonical form in the translation or in the theorization. In a curious way, translation canonizes *its own* version more than the original was canonical. Once you have translation you cannot translate it any more. You can translate only an original. The translation canonizes, freezes, an original and shows in the original a mobility, an instability, which at first one did not notice.[5]

A translation *translates* the text, and so *translates* it. It betrays it to that heaven of meanings finally received up above without their original words. Translation, on the outher hand, saves the text, for it moves it, to bury it. The translated text is destabilized, deconstructed, it tips over, it bobs up and down. For the scene of this encounter is not alone a historical location (say the Place de la Concorde or the Place Vendôme); it is that stream or lake in which the figure that Shelley named "the fair shape" faded; the watery grounds, the grief, where writing and literature find the conditions of their survival. So we kill the original by finding it already dead. Does a text's work depend so much on being "living"? As when we say, "a living masterpiece, a *living* work of art"?

No. Measure the syntax differently. To find the original, if we find it, *is* to find it already dead, for finding, in this version of translation of *this* original text, means making out the shape or contour, an outline that's bound to be doubled and blurred. For a text is not a picture, shut up for the studious. It is for reading. It is "*Wort* and *Satz*,"says de Man, elsewhere in the same lecture, saying Walter Benjamin's words; it is figure and syntax, grammar and lexicon, "*Spange und Krug.*"[6]

Notes

1. Paul de Man, *The Rhetoric of Romanticism* (New York: Columbia University Press, 1984), p.76.
2. *Ibid.*, p.78.
3. W.J.B. Owen and Jane Worthington Smyser, eds., *The Prose Works of William Wordsworth* (Oxford: Oxford University Press, 1974), pp.59–60. Futher page references to this text will be given in brackets in the text, using the abbreviation *PWWW*.
4. Gail Holst-Warhaft, *Dangerous Voices: Women's Laments and Greek Literature.* (London and New York: Routledge, 1992), p.11
5. Paul de Man, *The Resistance to Theory* (Minneapolis: University of Minnesota Press, 1986), p.84.
6. Rainer Maria Rilke, *Die Sonette an Orpheus*, I. vi (Frankfurt am Main: Insel Taschenbuch, 1980), p.54.

3

Upping the Ante: Deconstruction as Parodic Practice

Samuel Weber

As the Introduction of *Du Droit à la philosophie* draws to a close, Jacques Derrida touches on the place of *knowledge* in deconstruction:

> What is involved, of course, is knowledge, still, but above all the knowledge of how, *without renouncing the classical norms of objectivity and responsibility, without menacing the critical ideal of science and of philosophy and thus without renouncing knowledge,* the obligation of responsibility can be extended. How far? Without limit, no doubt [. . .][1]

To know how to extend the demands of responsibility to the very limits of knowledge, "without renouncing knowledge"—this is the aporetical challenge to which Derrida's writing seeks to *respond*. If this task is "without limit," it is never entirely lacking in direction, as the passage I just cited—and interrupted—goes on to make clear:

> How far? There is no limit, to be sure, for consciousness of a *limited responsibility* is *"good conscience"*; but above all to the point where these classical norms and the authority of this ideal are questioned. This in turn amounts to exercising one's right to a sort of "right of response," at least in the guise of turning the question back upon its original form by asking what ties responsibility to response. Then, going even further to ask what founds or rather *engages* the value of critical questioning so as

60

to make it inseparable [from responsibility?]. And to know how to think about the provenance of such knowledge about what one can and should do with such responsibility. (p. 108)

Respond to responsibility by raising the question of what ties it "to response"; then, question its relation to "the value of critical questioning"; and finally, "know how to think the provenance of this knowledge" and what one can and should "do with it"—this constitutes a program that, it would seem, could hardly hope to avoid the most vicious and hence most debilitating circularity except, perhaps, under one condition: by *upping the ante of knowledge.*

This formulation is to be understood in several senses. First of all, it suggests that the stakes involved in knowledge may be augmented so as to increase the value of knowing itself. At the same time, to speak of "stakes" in regard to knowledge is to question the disinterested aspect often attributed to it as a condition of its validity. Where there are "stakes," there is a game, a gamble, and a relation of forces —and of chances. To up the "ante" of knowing is, in part at least, to call the neutrality often attributed to it into question. This in turn brings to the fore yet another connotation suggested by the phrase: to up the *ante* is to foreground the *before*—the *ante*—the "provenance" of the process of knowledge. From where does knowledge come? Where is it going? Can such questions, which ask about knowledge itself, be asked in a manner that avoids the most vicious circularity? In view of this supplementary question, it is not surprising to find Derrida recurring, in the text we are reading, to a certain *docta ignorantia* (p. 100) as being both the distinctive "privilege" and *privation* of the philosopher:

An essential and declared *(revendiquée)* incompetence, a structural non-knowledge constructs the concept of philosophy as metaphysics or as science of science . . . The content of historical and positive knowledge . . . remains exterior to the philosophical act as such. This exteriority . . . potentializes, heightens *(potentialise)* the philosopher's power *as well as* his powerlessness, in his posture armed with a *quid juris*—the powerless power of that essentially philosophical site, the modern university, with its vital force and its deconstructible precariousness, its continuous, in-terminable, terminable death. (p. 101)

Hardly astonishing that a university used to legitimating itself towards society and towards itself as an institution of *higher learning* and of *knowledge*—hardly astonishing that such an institution would be surprised to hear that its "site" is "essentially philosophical" and that, in consequence, its distinctive mission does not consist in the production or transmission of knowledge but rather in posing and pursuing of a formal question: *quid juris?*—"*with what right?*"—a question that *by rights* lies beyond the pale of all "positive historical knowledge."

But deconstruction does not simply reproduce this essential philosophical privilege. In discerning and delimiting it, it simultaneously calls it "in question" ("*en cause,*" pp. 101–102, note). By this calling-into-question, deconstruction does not simply *oppose itself* to knowledge, nor even to its distinctively modern modification: *criticism.* Rather, with this questioning of cognition it responds to an appeal of an utterly different character:

> *Deconstruction is an institutional practice for which the concept of institution remains a problem,* but since it is no longer a "critique" . . . it does not destroy criticism and its institutions any more than it discredits them; its transformative gesture is different, its responsibility consists in pursuing, as consistently and cogently as possible, what we have (elsewhere) called *a graphics of iterability.* This is why the same responsibility presides both over philosophy and over deconstruction in its most vigilant exercise. (p. 88, my emphasis—S.W.)

With philosophy deconstruction thus shares a certain "essential incompetence," a "structural non-knowing." Nevertheless, in remarking how this "graphics of iterability" "fractures each element" while "constituting it" at the same time—in retracing the "breaks" that constitute articulation—Derrida's writing itself becomes the exemplary site of this "graphics." The question, of course, that can hardly be avoided here, relates to this very *exemplarity:* In what way can a graphics of iterability be *exemplified?* Every exemplarity involves some sort of *iterability.* If there were no iterability, there could be no exemplification. To exemplify is to repeat in a particularly distinctive manner. But is iterability *as such repeatable?*

Much has been written, by Derrida and others, on the curious logic of exemplarity, in the light of Kant and Hegel in particular.

Without being able to dwell on these extremely complex discussions here, it may be sufficient to point out that the tension inherent in this concept is already tangible, legible, in the etymology of the word. What is *ex-emplary* is *taken out* of its initial context, and this in a double sense. It is taken to an *extreme* and yet, at the same time in so being transported, it appears to be *more itself* than ever before. Thus, if Derrida's texts can be said to exemplify the graphics of iterability, it is because they *respond* to the possibilities of repetition—repeatability—with singular intensity.

Ever since its origins in the dialogues of Plato, Western philosophy has construed itself as responding to such possibilities. But it is only with Kierkegaard that this response takes on a distinctively modern tone:

As I had long been concerned, periodically at least, with the following problem: "Is a repetition possible? What is its significance? Does a thing gain or lose by being repeated?" what suddenly occurred to me was this: "You ought to go to Berlin, where you already were once; you can then verify whether or not a repetition is possible and what it can signify." Back home, I had been virtually stopped in my tracks by this problem. One may say what one likes, this problem will end up playing a very important role in modern philosophy, for *repetition* is the decisive term for expressing what the Greeks used to mean by "*reminiscence*" (or remembrance). They taught that all knowledge is remembrance. Similarly, the new philosophy will teach that life in its entirety is a repetition . . . Repetition and remembrance are one and the same movement, but in opposed directions; for that which is remembered has been: it is repetition in reverse; whereas repetition in the proper sense is remembering ahead.[2]

If repetition and memory imply each other, and if each returns to the other its mirror-image, their difference remains appreciable. For what is remembered is thought as something that has *already taken place*, which is to say, as a *past* which can be *rendered present in its pastness*, which can be represented by and as remembrance. Repetition—which in turn implies a certain memory just as memory for its part entails a movement of repetition—is still not simply the more or less symmetrical inversion of memory. For "remembering ahead," as Kierkegaard writes, involves something far more paradoxical than merely recalling the past. As potentiality and possibility of the future, remembering "ahead" opens the way to the return of what has never been present as such and which therefore, in a certain sense, remains ever yet to come. It should be noted that the French word, *répétition*,[3] maintains this simultaneous reference to the past and to the future—as does the English word, *rehearsal*. To *rehearse* a play, for instance, entails more than the mere reproduction in the present of something that is past, once and for all. It is also in the direction of theatrical representation that the *Gjentagelsen* of Kierkegaard should be read.

In "a short annex" to *Repetition*, the signatory of the text, one Constantin Constantius, comments on the passage just cited:

> The young man's problem is: *is repetition possible?* Well, I parodied it in advance by taking a trip to Berlin to see if it is possible. The confusion resides in the fact that the profound problem of the possibility of repetition is expressed in an external manner, as though repetition, were it possible, would be situated outside of the individual, whereas in truth it must be found in the individual. (p. 304)

Constantin Constantius confesses that he has confused the issue, by treating the "possibility of repetition" as though it were a banal empirical fact, "situated outside of the individual" instead of within it. But he does not tell us, his readers, just *why* he did this. Instead, Constantin Constantius merely describes himself as having "parodied it in advance" by himself "taking a trip to Berlin to see if it [that is, repetition] is possible." One such name for this mistreatment of the intrinsic, then, appears here to be, *parody*. What does parody mistreat? It mistreats *problems* by *externalizing* them. The young man has a problem. Parody seems to offer him the possibility of a solution. But it is a confusing solution at best, and moreover not one that he devises of his own free will, as it were. Rather, the thought of returning to Berlin—the thought that Constantin Constantius calls a *parody*—comes to the young man from outside, as it were, suddenly, abruptly, as a command that he cannot resist: "You ought to go to Berlin," it tells him. And so he goes. But, it should be remembered, such a trip is anything but self-evident. For the young man's concern with repetition had left him dead "in his tracks." The problem had thus paralyzed him: he could move neither forward nor back. In this situation of total blockage, he describes how the idea to go back to Berlin "came to my mind suddenly."

In short, only by virtue of this sudden, unexpected and abrupt intrusion of a voice telling the young man that he should go somewhere else, even and especially if he had been there before— only then does he *respond* and begin to move. However confusing and misleading it may be, playing games with what is essential and internal, parody provides the point of departure; but it must also itself be left behind, if repetition ever hopes to deploy itself in its essence.

Is the situation any different when we consider the relation of parody to iterability and to deconstruction? To be sure, parody and the parodic—suspending for the moment the question of their possible differences—entail an element of memory repeated "in advance," a repetition that lives through its difference to that which it reinscribes. But already this description is couched in terms that suggest why the question of parody is so little in evidence, explicitly at least, in the writings of Derrida. One of the relatively rare—and therefore precious—occasions where parody is discussed is in another decade at Cérisy,[4] some twenty years ago. I am referring to the Colloquium devoted to Nietzsche. In the discussion that followed the lecture of Pierre Klossowski, Derrida asked the following question, which also begins to sound like a warning:

You have suggested that parody could become political, that it was ultimately disconcerting. . . . But does it make no difference how one parodies? Must not a distinction be drawn between two parodies, of which the one, under the pretext of disconcerting, plays the game of the established political order (which loves a certain type of parody and finds itself confirmed through it) and, on the other hand, a paradox that can effectively deconstruct the established political order? Is there one sort of parody that effectively marks the body politic, in contrast to a parody that would be a parody of parody, which would play at the surface of the political order and which would consist in railing at it instead of destroying it?[5]

Despite his reserve with regard to a certain reading of Nietzsche, which tended to see in parody *as such* a necessarily subversive force, Derrida here does not deny that parody *can* "effectively deconstruct." But he insists that this notion presupposes that such parody "effectively mark the body politic" and that it successfully avoid becoming a "parody of a parody." The latter phrase is curious, for it seems to suggest that if parody, which in and of itself already entails a movement of repetition, seeks to truly disconcert or deconstruct, it must not cede too readily or too much to this self-same repetition, which otherwise will render it the "parody of a parody." Would such a parody— *parody of a parody*—itself be more or less parodic than parody *itself*? The latter, it seems, can hope "to effectively mark the body politic" while the former, on the other hand, would only reinforce that body, repeating it in an identical manner. In any case, the question of parody in relation to repetition has been raised.

Twelve years after the Nietzsche Decade at Cérisy, this question returns. This time, however, the context is quite different: the point of departure, and perhaps also of arrival, is the repetition of the "yes" in Joyce's *Ulysses*. Joyce, Derrida emphasizes, is a writer who has haunted his own writing ever since its inception: "Yes, each time that I write . . . and even within the academic domain, a ghost of Joyce is always on board."[6] It is not entirely fortuitous if one of the initial instances of this "boarding" concerns the relation between history and language.[7] But let us now turn to the "return" of parody in this text on Joyce. Once again, parody seems to impose itself inexorably by virtue of its tie to a certain essential repetition of language:

The repetition of the *yes* can assume mechanical, servile forms, bending the woman to her master. But this is not by accident, even if every response to another as to a singular other should, it seems, escape such a fate. The *yes* of affirmation, of assent or of consent, of alliance, engagement, signature or of the gift should bear repetition in itself in order to merit its meaning *(pour valoir ce qu'il vaut)*. It should immediately confirm its promise and promise its confirmation. This essential repetition allows itself to be haunted by the intrinsic threat, the interior telephone of the parasite, as its mimetic-mechanical double, as its incessant parody. (p. 89)

Here, in commenting on Joyce's text, the general problematic of the iterability of every mark singularizes itself in an ambivalent manner: if all affirmation, every affirmative response should repeat itself, or at least be capable of repetition, this iterability, which is indispensable to the valorization of every element—here, the affirmation of the *yes*—bears in itself at the same time the irreducible possibility of being denatured, of becoming mechanical, even of becoming subordinated, like the woman who, in Joyce's text, makes way for her master. This possibility of being parasited in a "mimeto-mechanical" manner by a *yes* that cannot constitute or valorize itself *except* through its repetition—such a possibility, which at the same is both essential and deformative, is designated here "as its incessant parody."

Parody—or rather, a certain parody—shows itself here to be tied in a most intimate, even intrinsic manner to repetition and to language, to affirmation and even—paradoxically enough—to *singularity*. What curiously seems unheard-of in this singularity is that it remains originally and intrinsically open to the possibility of *incessant parody*. But would not a parody that is incessant run the risk of becoming *the parody of a parody*? How can the relation of parody to the general tendency of reduplication be understood? Let us for a moment follow the movement of the text that we are in the process of rereading:

We shall return to this fatality. But already we hear this grammaphonics recording the subtext under the most living voice. It reproduces it *a priori*, in the absence of every intentional presence of the affirming man or woman. Such grammaphonics respond, to be sure, to the dream of a reproduction that *keeps*, as its truth, the living *yes*, archived in its most vivacious voice. But precisely in so doing, it opens the possibility of a parody, of a technique of the *yes* that persecutes the most spontaneous desire and the most generous *yes*.

"The possibility of a parody," as "technique of the *yes*," reveals itself here as the ineluctable consequence of the iterability of this *yes*, even when it is emitted by "the most living voice." Once the voice is constituted through the emission of *marks*—which is to say, of sounds that are both accentuated and articulate, and which must be *heard*—it is inhabited, but also haunted, by the necessary and essential possibility of being *recorded*, inscribed, grammaphonically. Like writing in general, this possibility is duplicitous. On the one hand, it seeks to preserve the fleeting vitality of the voice by inscribing it in the archive. On the other hand, this very same movement of recording confirms, qua repetition, and hence separation, the "fatality" that it seeks to ward off. As is well known, the motif of writing draws its force in the texts of Derrida from the distinctively singular demonstration that these two "hands" or sides of repetition are neither entirely separable nor simply opposable, but rather ambivalently intertwined, each hand caressing and contaminating the other in a parasitic embrace.

What now emerges is that this embrace is not just parasitic, but also—*parodic*. The possibility of parody becomes inescapable once the *yes*, which marks the involvement of the other in the same, is seized by repetition and recording. Which is to say, from the very beginning. In lending itself necessarily and *a priori* to the possibility of repetition, the *yes* opens its "most spontaneous desire and greatest generosity" not just to parody but to its *persecution*, which *follows* inexorably, like a fatality. In pretending and promising to answer the appeal of the other, the *yes* affirms itself, but parodically. But as a parody of *what*? First, of a certain *desire*, which presents itself as "spontaneous" and "generous." Second, of an *affirmation* that presents itself as *self*-affirmation. And third, as a technique tied to repetition, parody also aims at *memory*, which can no longer be considered as the simple other of forgetfulness. Memory becomes parodic, perhaps, from the moment on where it can no longer demarcate itself clearly from forgetting. From this "moment" on, or rather from this confusion on, the machine is off and running:

The desire of memory and the mourning of me gets the anamnesiacal machine going. Not to mention its hyperamnesiac going-wild (*emballement*). The machine reproduces the quick, doubling it with its automaton. (p. 90)

Thus set into motion, the "machine" pursues its trajectory throughout the pages of *Ulysses gramophone* and curiously, parody seems once again to be forgotten. Its name, at least, returns only once throughout this text. But if, here as elsewhere in the writings of Derrida, the *word* is rare, that does not necessarily prove that something like a *parodic practice* is entirely foreign to them. Like the *yes* to which it seems inextricably bound, the parodic can mark a text all the more effectively for not being named in it or mentioned explicitly. Like the *yes:* "I say the *yes* and not the word yes? for there can be *yes* without a word" (p. 122).

But before arriving at this third and last fleeting apparition of the word "parody," we must first dwell a bit on the difference between "parody" and what I have just called "parodic practice." Why *parodic* and not *parody*? Here, as elsewhere, what is at stake are two distinct manners of thinking "border crossings." Such a "crossing" is not necessarily a *traversing*, in the sense of going *over* and *beyond*. In this passage, for instance, it is possible that it is the borders themselves that *pass:* the one passing over into, or beyond, the other—and vice-versa. Thus, the border that separates the repetition from the original, or that which distinguishes parody from its object—these borders become permeable and unstable. From the moment when parody is construed as the effect of an irreducible iterability, each "original," each "work," each subject and each object becomes already in and of itself a potential *self-parody*. That amounts to saying that parody can no longer be thought as a repetition that is essentially exterior and ulterior with respect to its model. The iterability of every original opens it to the possibility of self-parody.

But how is such self-parody to be understood? Should it be construed as a *form*—perhaps the last—of that reflexivity which characterizes modern thought since Descartes? Ever since Romanticism, and despite a certain ambivalence towards the exteriority and empiricity of parody, parody has been almost always understood within a horizon of reflexivity, self-consciousness and intentionality. Parody is thus conceived of as a repetition, to be sure, but one that is mimetically oriented toward a model. Thought in this fashion, parody has tended to elicit a certain reserve, as expressed by Kierkegaard, but also already by Friedrich Schlegel, who considered it more "empirical" and less "transcendental" than irony.[8]

From an esthetical perspective, parody has always been considered to be a marginal, secondary, subordinate genre, and this for two sets of reasons. Too dependent upon its model, it was also felt to be too subservient to the *effect* that it was expected to produce: which is to say, *laughter*. In repeating the work that served as its object, parody removed it not only from its origin, but from its finality qua work. Parodied, the work found itself abandoned, or sacrificed, to laughter. Because of this subordination to its result, parody has often been considered more as a rhetorical technique than a major genre.[9]

But it is precisely its lack of substance, its deficiency qua work, its dynamic, open and other-directed character that allows, and indeed compels, one to distinguish between *parody* on the one hand, as a minor genre, and *the parodic* on the other, as a repetitive practice that elicits laughter. The disappearance of the word *parody* might therefore make way for a *parodic practice* (practice of the parodic and parody of practice) that would abandon the work—and itself—to laughter. Would this then suggest that laughter remains as the horizon of parody—and perhaps of iterability "itself"?

Something like this question seems to mark the final return of the word *parody* in *Ulysses gramophone:*

Why laugh? Surely everything has already been said about laughter in Joyce, about parody, satire, mockery, humor, irony, joking. And about his Homeric or Rabelaisian laughter. All that remains, perhaps, is to think laughter as remaining, precisely. What would it mean, laughter? What would it mean to laugh?[10] (pp. 115–116)

For the word *parody*, at least, the show is now over, and this time for good. For everything has already been said, without a doubt, concerning the list that begins with "parody," whose position at the head of the procession is probably not entirely insignificant. Above all, if we take seriously the reminder, a few lines earlier, that "we are going, for essential reasons, to treat things here in terms of contiguity" (p. 115), parody thus leads the procession of forms and modes of the laughable, which must be worked through in order to get at what is left: at laughter in and of itself. Except— except that laughter in and of itself *is* nothing but what is left-over. Concerning this left-over, divested of all its codified manifestations and its regulated epiphenomena, and far from all parody, the question remains: just what does this left-over *mean?* Why does this meaning want to laugh? *Qu'est-ce que ça veut dire?*

Qu'est-ce que ça veut rire? Ça—what is left when everything has been said—is precisely, the *oui-rire*, the *yes-laughing*,

which over-marks not only the totality of writing but all the qualities, modalities, genres of laughter, whose differences could be classified in some sort of typology. (p. 116)

That over-marks *everything*, then, including *all* the "modalities," the "genres" of laughter which—like parody, for instance, and perhaps as the primary *instance*—can "be classified in some sort of typology." Parody is thus put back in its place in this ever-possible taxonomy, but which is over- and outclassed by the *oui-rire*, that *yes-laughing* whose "consonantal difference" in French hides "the sole consonants of my name." *Oui-rire:* a sort of parodic signature, perhaps?

In any case, however, the introduction of this strange mark—*oui-rire*—ups the ante. Not only because it oversees "the totality of writing" as well as "all" the taxonomic forms of laughter. Something else is involved here, something one would be tempted to designate as "temporal," were it not, in essence, *anachronistic.* In deploying a *yes* that would be the "condition of every signature and every performative," *Ulysses gramophone* ups the ante: first of all, by foregrounding the *anteriority* of the *yes* with respect to every determinate act. Second, by showing that this anteriority reaches beyond the *yes* itself since in a certain manner it constitutes it as a response and a demand:

Yes, condition of every signature and every performative, is addressed to the other that it does not constitute and of which it can only begin by *asking (par demander),* in response to an ever-prior demand—*by asking that other* to say *yes.* Time only appears after this singular anachronism. (p. 127)

The *yes* responds to the "ever-prior demand" of another "that it does not constitute" and that therefore should be situated *before* it, if this other could be said to have a site or a situation. But this other does not exist as such and above all not in a temporal dimension, in an anteriority, since "time only appears *after* this singular anachronism." This anachronism is singular because it is an event that must be thought as an event out of which time itself ensues, and thus, paradoxically enough, as happening prior to anteriority as such. The other *gives* time as the "minimal and primary" *yes* (p. 127) which responds by asking the other to respond. But this response asked of the other cannot manifest itself other than as a certain *repetition:* "It begins with the *yes*, with the second *yes*, with the other *yes* . . ."(p. 128).

Here—but where exactly?—the upping of the ante reaches a high-point. If everything must begin "with the *other yes*," then *anteriority itself becomes rigorously other:* everything begins with an *afterwards*, a *repetition* that would be, so to speak, the other in action, *the other at work*. With this repetition of a response that affirms itself by demanding another response, *the before* returns to itself as an aftershock, *un réplique*. Like the rumble of "the *oui-rire, saying-yes before and after everything*" (p. 116). Upping the ante, the *yes* responds with the *réplique*—aftershock—of laughter.

Seized by repetition, the *yes* thus replies to and with laughter. Or rather, with *laughters*. For laughter, like parody, is never simple nor solitary. "One never laughs alone" (p. 142) just as one never parodies in isolation. And if in a certain sense laughter constitutes the end of parody, it will not be entirely surprising to find a parodic binarity breaking up the description of laughter. This binarism suddenly recalls, and echoes, the Cérisy decade on Nietzsche. On the one side, "a *oui-rire*, a yes-laughing" that is "reactive, even negative" which "delights (*jouit*) in hyperamnesiac mastery." This is the laughter that *knows*—"triumphant and jubilant, to be sure" but whose jubilation "always betrays a trace of mourning" (p. 117). The "eschatological tonality of this yes-laughing" is thus

haunted, joyously ventriloquized by a very different music, by the vowels of another song. I hear it, too, very close to the other, like the yes-laughing of a gift without debt, the light-hearted, almost amnesiac affirmation of a gift or of an event that has been abandoned. (p. 120)

This other yes-laughing, the laughter of a yes that is other, which is less to be taken than to be left—this *other song* strangely recalls what parody—the *word*, "parody," *parôdia*, always meant to say: a song *beside itself*, slightly *off*, pealing away and turning into laughter. Into that other yes-laughing, which only displays or names the cycle of reappropriation and domestication ... in order to delimit the fantasy; and in so doing, manages the break-in (*ménage l'effraction*) required for the arrival of the other ... that unpredictable other for whom a place should always be kept ... (p. 120)

To be sure, such a parody has never existed in this "purity," no more than such a *yes-laughing*, and this for essential reasons. For how can an "*effraction*"—a *break-in, or break-out*—be *managed:* which is to say, both *spared (ménagée)* and yet domesticated, made safe for the *ménage*, the household? How can room be left for "that unpredictable other" without its *otherness* being made predictable and thus being taken *care of*—*i.e.* done away with?

In a word, it is the problem of *managed care*. It is a problem without a solution if solution is meant as resolution. Which is why even the second yes-laughing does not laugh simply last, or rather: its laugh does not last. For it too is haunted by the triumphant, if melancholic, first laughter:

The two laughing-yes's, although different in quality, call for one another and imply each other irresistibly ... the one doubling the other: not as a countable presence but as a specter. The *yes* of memory, with its recapitulative mastery, its reactive repetition, immediately doubles the *dancing and lightfooted yes* of affirmation. Reciprocally, two replies or two responsibilities relate to each other without having any relationship among them. (p. 141)

We began with a Conference on Nietzsche and we now see how little we have moved away from that beginning. Or rather, it has moved with us, following, or anticipating, our every step. Where, then, have those steps led us?

In the scenario of *Ulysses gramophone*, the scene is one of an invitation. A celebrated and controversial thinker is invited to hold the keynote speech at a conference, this time of Joyce scholars. Having entered the *aula* in which this "family" is gathered, the invited guest assumes an attitude that is at once both humble and provocative. Declaring himself at the outset to be entirely incompetent—"incompetence ... is the deepest truth of my relation to this work" (p. 95)—the invited guest declares that "it is high time for the swindle to end." And then, to the astonishment of his hosts, the invited guest declares that he is by no means the sole incompetent in the room. Everyone else is equally involved in the "swindle"—and above all, those who consider themselves to be specialists in Joyce. In view of the machine set into motion by the writings of Joyce, the invited guest announces to the illustrious gathering of scholars that "fundamentally, there can be no competence" where Joyce is concerned (p. 98). And he concludes:

At bottom, you do not exist, and your existence as foundation is unfounded—this is what Joyce's signature makes legible to you. And you appeal to strangers to come and tell you [that] you exist . . . (p. 104)

This scene, perhaps, tells us how far we have come! You extend a courteous invitation to someone to come spend a quiet evening in your company, in your house, and as thanks what do you get? Bottoms up! What you "get" is nothing other than the assurance that you do not exist, and that if you did, you would be incompetent to say much about it.

And why, after all, should such a "foundation" of academic scholars be "unfounded"? Because, at least as far as Joyce is concerned, "the machine of production and of reproduction" of academic scholarship is already inscribed, programmed, anticipated and recounted in the texts it seeks to interpret, to canonize, to control.

The scholarly foundation, then, has nothing further to do or to add if it is not of the order of a repetition in which, the invited guest reminds his hosts, "we are caught" (p. 97). Who, we? Hosts as well as guests, initiates no less than strangers, specialists no less than incompetents. All that allows us to tell the two groups apart, perhaps, is how well each manages to keep open a space for the parodic and the unpredictable.

Notes

1. Jacques Derrida, *Du droit à la philosophie*, Paris: Flammarion, 1990, p. 107. (My translation — S.W.)
2. S. Kierkegaard, *Repetition*, trans. Howard V. Hong and Edna H. Hong. Princeton, N.J.: Princeton University Press, 1983, p. 131 (translation modified). Future page reference will be given in brackets in the text.
3. It should simultaneously be noted that this text was initially written in French; hence, the reflection on *répétition*.

4. This paper was originally written for and presented at a Colloquium on the work of Derrida held in July of 1993, under the title: "Passage des frontières," roughly: "Border crossings." The acts of this 10-day meeting have been published in France in a copious volume edited by Marie-Louis Mallet: *Passage des frontières*, editions galilée, Paris 1994.

5. *Nietzsche aujourd'hui, 1: Intensités*, Paris, Christian Bourgeois (coll. *10/18*), pp. 111–112.

6. Jacques Derrida, *Ulysse gramophone. Deux mots pour Joyce*, p. 27.

7. "Twenty years ago, the *Introduction* to *The Origin of Geometry* compared, at the very center of the book, the strategies of Husserl and Joyce: two great models, two paradigms with regard to thought, but also with regard to a certain 'operation': the putting-to-work (*mise en oeuvre*) of the relationship between language and history" (*Ulysse gramophone*, p. 27).

8. Thus, for Friedrich Schlegel parodic poetry is "negative in both tendency and form" (p. 151), or even "absolutely antinomical" (p. 131). Parody lacks the "transcendental": "Parody is empirical poetical negation; the transcendental is no longer parodic, but rather polemical." (p. 145). E. Behler, J.-J. Anstett, H. Eicher, *Friedrich Schlegel: Kritische Ausgabe seiner Werke*, vol. 16, Paderborn/Munich/Vienna, 1981.

9. In this respect see the extremely instructive discussion of parody by Genette in his *Palimpsestes, la littérature au second degré*, Paris, Le Seuile, 1982, p. 23 ff. In the course of this work, Genette finds himself constrained to abandon the notion of parody, which he finds too confused to be able to contribute effectively to the study of texts.

10. Derrida's French here is difficult, if not impossible, to render in English: "*Qu'est-ce que ça veut dire, le rire? Qu'est-ce que ça veut rire?*"

II

The Point of Teaching

4

The Disputed Ground: Deconstruction and Literary Studies

J. Hillis Miller

An ideological story is making the rounds. Of course it does not have currency with you and me. We know better. But the traces of this story's force are widely visible. A recent book by Jonathan Loesberg, *Aestheticism and Deconstruction: Pater, Derrida, de Man* (1991)[1] defends Derrida and de Man from the claim that they are ahistorical by arguing that neither of them is really interested in reading works of literature. Of Derrida he says: "Because Derrida embeds his analysis of literary language within his analysis of foundational philosophy, it has as little relevance to the interpretation of actual literary works as his philosophical discussion has to the status of particular propositions" (106). Later he asserts categorically that "de Man's theory of literary language will no more produce practical criticism than does Derrida's" (116). Pater, Derrida, and de Man are for Loesberg essentially philosophers investigating in their own ways contradictions in the foundational moment in philosophy. Art or literature sometimes helps them in this philosophical enterprise, but is of little further interest to them.

This is said in order to be able to claim that Derrida and de Man have nothing much to teach anyone who is interested in literary studies. This point is asserted repeatedly in the invidious form of claiming that Derrida and de Man do not provide a "method" for reading works of literature. "Method" is not at all the same thing as "exemplary acts of reading," which is what I would claim they *do* provide. You can learn quite a bit, to speak in litotes, about how to read by reading Derrida and de Man. Of course no one, certainly not I, could claim to match them in rigor and insight. But that does not relieve me (or anyone else) from the responsibility to try. I am obliged to try to read as well as they do. This does not mean reading as they do, for I must read for myself, as they do. No example or presupposed theory can help me with that.

Where in the world did the strange and quite false idea that these writers are not interested in reading literature or interpreting works of art come from? What is the point of asserting this? I say "strange and quite false" because it is evident that all three of Loesberg's authors have written many essays and books of literary or art criticism. These writings on literature and art are essential to their work, not peripheral to it, though of course all three wrote or are writing on other topics and authors too—on philosophers, theologians, literary critics, political topics, literary theory, and so on. As everyone knows, these days it is impossible, and undesirable in any case, to erect uncrossable border walls between these disciplines even though each one is elaborately institutionalized with its own separate procedures, protocols, and traditions. But Pater wrote essays on Wordsworth, Coleridge, Lamb, Sir Thomas Browne, Shakespeare, D. G. Rossetti, and Du Bellay, not to speak of Botticelli, Da Vinci, and Raphael. De man wrote essays on Rilke, Proust, Wordsworth, Hölderlin, Kleist, Yeats, Hugo, Keats, Mallarmé, and of course on Rousseau as a novelist. Derrida has written books or essays on Mallarmé, Artaud, Ponge, Shakespeare, Joyce, Celan, Baudelaire, Blanchot (as a writer of fiction), Adami, Van Gogh, and others. Derrida's seminars at the University of California at Irvine in the spring of 1993 included extended readings of the Narcissus episode in Ovid's *Metamorphoses* and of two poems by Celan. Nor will it do to say these are not really "readings," but something else, for example, philosophy or aesthetic theory in disguise, or an investigation of the ideology of literary criticism. The essays and books in question, at least in the cases of Derrrida and de Man, are detailed accounts of passages from these writers or of artworks by the artists. And Pater's essays, though in a different mode, clearly intend to be interpretations of the poets and artists in question. It would not be too much to say that the readings by Derrida and de Man are "explications," though no doubt of a special kind that would need to be carefully identified. They are explications in the sense that they carefully unfold meanings in the texts in question. One of Derrida's most recent books, *Donner le temps: 1. La fausse monnaie* (1992), is an extended reading of a prose poem by Baudelaire, *"La fausse monnaie."* In "Punctuations: The Time of the Thesis" (1980), Derrida recalls that around 1957 he had " 'deposited,' as they say," a thesis subject entitled *L'idéalité de l'objet littéraire (The Ideality of the Literary Object).* A little later he indicates something of what that thesis might have contained. The title, he says, is to be understood in the context of Husserl's thought, much in the air in the fifties:

It was a question, then, for me, to deploy, more or less violently, the techniques of transcendental phenomenology in the elaboration of a new theory of literature, of this very particular type of ideal object that is the literary object, an ideality "concatenated (enchaînée)" Husserl would have said, concatenated with so-called natural language, a non-mathematic or non-mathematizable object, but nevertheless different from music or works of plastic art, that is to say, from all the examples privileged by Husserl in his analyses of ideal objectivity. For I must recall a little massively and simply, my most constant interest, I would say even before the philosophical interest, if that is possible, went toward literature, toward the writing called literary.

What is literature? And first of all, what is writing? How does writing come to upset even the question "what is? *(qu'est-ce que?)"* and even "what does that mean? *(que'est-ce que ça veut dire?)."* Put otherwise—and this is the putting otherwise that is important for me—when and how does inscription become literature and what happens then? To what and to whom does that return? *(À quoi et à qui cela revient-il?)* What happens between *(Qu'est-ce qui se passe entre)* philosophy and literature, science and literature, politics and literature, theology and literature, psychoanalysis and literature, there in the abstraction of its label is the most insistant question.[2]

So what is the motivation for saying that Derrida and the others are not really interested in literature or art when there is such massive evidence to the contrary? A superficial answer would be to say that Loesberg is deeply influenced, as he acknowledges, by

Rodolphe Gasché's distinguished and important *The Tain of the Mirror* (1986) and by other well-known essays on Derrida by Gasché. Gasché was the first to argue in detail that Derrida is really a technical philosopher in the wake of Husserlian phenomenology and that de Man, myself, and other American "deconstructionists" have falsified his work by using it in literary criticism. We have made it, so the story goes, into nothing more than a new New Criticism. But that would still leave open the question of why Gasché's argument so much appeals these days to Loesberg and others, for example to Jeffrey T. Nealon and to Mas'ud Zavarzadeh.[3] The more serious answer is that a crude form of Gasché's expert identification of an important strand in Derrida's work and intellectual heritage is part of an ideological narrative that plays an essential role these days in the reinstatement of thematic and mimetic readings of literature, in the return to "history," and in the reinstatement of traditional ideas about personal identity, agency, and responsibility. As Thomas Cohen has recognized in incisive diagnoses,[4] what has happened is the following: In order to justify certain ways of turning or returning to history, to thematic and mimetic interpretations of literature, to the social, to multiculturalism, to the widening of the canon, to cultural studies, and to "identity politics," deconstruction or poststructuralism, some scholars have mistakenly thought, had to be denigrated ("abjected" is Cohen's word). This has by no means happened universally. Many scholars in cultural or gender studies, Judith Butler for example, have acknowledged their debt to deconstruction. But for some others, deconstruction had to be falsely identified as nihilistic, as concerned only with an enclosed realm of language cut off from the real world, as destroying ethical responsibility by undoing faith in personal identity and agency, as ahistorical, quietistic, as fundamentally elitist and conservative. The Yale "deconstructors" could then be dismissed as made over New Critics (and we know what the politics of the Southern agrarians were!), while the discovery of de Man's wartime writings doubly justified writing him off. He came to be seen as both a new New Critic *and* someone with a tainted past, however the early writings were read in relation to the later.

That left Derrida. To argue, as Loesberg does, that Derrida is really a philosopher, with little or no relevance to literary studies, is to recuperate him from the "abjection" of American deconstruction. It is hard to make Derrida either a fascist or a New Critic, though his abiding interest in Heidegger puts him under suspicion of the former, while his evident interest in reading works of literature puts him in danger of being seen as a strange continental crypto-New Critic. Calling him a phenomenological philosopher in the tradition of Husserl avoids both bad names. But this recuperation is performed at the cost of neutralizing Derrida. It puts him out of literature departments and back in the philosophy department. So everyone in literature, everyone doing cultural studies, feminist studies, studies of popular culture, "new historicism," or multicultural studies can breathe a sigh of relief, and say, "Thank God. I don't have to take Derrida seriously any more. He is just a philosopher after all." Given what interests most members of American philosophy departments these days, the last thing they would be likely to take seriously is Derrida's theories about the contradictory founding moments of philosophical thinking, which is what Loesberg says is his chief focus.

This narrative, like all such ideologemes, like ideology in general, is extremely resistant to being put in question or refuted. It takes many forms and is used in aid of many different arguments, including those by people who consider themselves friendly to Derrida, such as Loesberg or Nealon. However cogently this story is shown to be a linguistic construct based on a whole set of radical misreadings, it is still likely to be unconsciously assumed, taken as a natural truth. It fits Althusser's definition of ideology as a set of unconscious assumptions that obscure one's real material conditions of existence or de Man's definition of ideology as "the confusion of linguistic with natural reality, of reference with phenomenalism."[5]

The result of this handy bit of ideological storytelling is to underwrite that return to mimetic, thematic, and biographical readings of literature so widespread today. One unfortunate result of this return is that wherever it is acccepted it disables the crucially necessary political and intellectual work being attempted today in the name of a better democracy by cultural studies, women's studies, ethnic studies, studies in "minority discourse," and so on. The disabling might be defined by saying that the left, whenever it (perhaps unconsciously) reassumes the old traditionalist ideological presuppositions of the right about mimesis, about the acting and responsible self, about thematic ways to read literature and other cultural forms, is cooperating in that return to a neo-conservative and nationalist atmosphere that is widely visible now and that the left means to be trying to forestall and contest. Another way to put this is to say that the reaffirmation of these assumptions is unable to contest the power of what Marx called "bourgeois ideology" and what is today called "the hegemony of the dominant discourse" because it is, in its essence, bourgeois ideology all over again. It leaves the dominant discourse as dominant as ever because it is another form of it. It is vulnerable to the same critique Marx made of Feuerbach or of "German Ideology" generally, that it is no more than a theoretical or mental rearrangement of the same terms it challenges and has therefore no means of touching the material world. It is incapable of producing historical events. Only a materialist inscription can do that.

Why this is so and what is at stake will be indicated in a brief concluding discussion of what Loesberg leaves out of his treatment of Derrida and de Man. He has practically nothing to say about their concepts of the performative dimensions of literature, philosophy, and criticism. This too is a complex matter, calling for lengthy development and careful discriminations. Only an all-too-rapid indication of essentials can be given here. In one way or another both Derrida and de Man hold that the performative aspect of literature, philosophy, and criticism, of language and other signs generally, makes history. What does that mean? The distinction between cognitive statements and performative speech acts is well known, as is the recognition that the separation can never be made absolute. There is always a cognitive side to performatives, and vice versa. Nevertheless the performative side of language is not something that can be known. That is what Derrida means in recent seminars when he says "the gift, if there is such a thing," "the secret, if there is such a thing," "witnessing, if there is such a thing." Since the gift, the secret, and witnessing are kinds of performatives, they are not the objects of a possible certain cognition. They must remain a matter of "if."

De Man's way of putting this was to say that the performative force of language, its power to make something happen in history and society, is linked to its materiality, that is, to a nonreferential noncognitive side of language. In the lecture on "Kant and Schiller," speaking of the passage in Kant's *Third Critique* from a "cognitive discourse as trope" to "the materiality of the inscribed signifier," de Man argues that it is only the latter that is historical, that can be a historical event. The regressive misreading of Kant initiated by Schiller is not historical, not a series of historical events. There is in Kant, said de Man, "a movement from cognition, from acts of knowledge, from states of cognition, to something which is no longer a cognition but which is to some extent an occurrence, which has the materiality of something that actually happens, that actually occurs . . . that does something to the world as such. . . . There is history from the moment that words such as 'power' and 'battle' and so on emerge on the scene; at that moment things happen, there is occurrence, there is event. History [has to do with] the emergence of a language of power out of the language of cognition." This conception of the materiality of inscription is worked out in "Shelley Disfigured," in "Aesthetic Formalization: Kleist's *Über das Marionettentheater*," and in "Hypogram and Inscription," as well as in the essays on Kant and Hegel.

The stakes are high in recognizing or not recognizing the fundamental role in Derrida's and de Man's thinking of the relation between a performative or materialist mode of language, on the one hand, and history, on the other. A major contribution that so-called "deconstruction," for example Derrida's current writing and seminars, has to make to today's frontier work in cultural studies, women's studies, historicism, and minority discourse is just in this area. What is needed is as clear as possible a recognition of a potential performative, history-making power in language, including the language of literature, philosophy, and, yes, even "practical criticism." This potential power may or may not be actualized or effective in a given case. It would be a foolhardy person who would claim that what he or she writes is a historical event. It is in any case not of the order of cognition. Nevertheless, a purely mimetic, cognitive, referential view of cultural artifacts will reaffirm precisely that same conservative ideology which cultural studies, women's studies, and the rest want to contest. To put this in de Manian terms, the "linguistics of literariness" includes the performative dimension of literary language. Understanding it will help account for the occurrence of ideological aberrations, but knowing those aberrations will not change them. Only the performative, material, "word-thing" side of language will do that.

Appropriating, transforming, and, most of all, using performatively this insight of deconstruction is a chief task of the humanities today. That would be another example of the way the act of reading, registered in the most responsible critical terms, can actively reappropriate or performatively liberate a past text for present uses. Walter Benjamin describes in consonant terms in the seventeenth of the "Theses on the Philosophy of History" the way a "historical materialist" sees "a revolutionary chance in the fight for the oppressed past" when he finds a way to "blast *(herauszusprengen)* a specific era out of the homogeneous course of history—blasting a specific life out of the era or a specific work out of the lifework."[6]

Notes

1. Princeton: Princeton University Press, 1991. My essay is drawn in modified form from a review of Loesberg's book published in *Nineteenth-Century Prose*, 20:2 (Fall 1993), pp. 23–41.
2. Jacques Derrida, *"Ponctuations: le temps de la thèse," Du droit à la philosophie* (Paris: Galilée, 1990), p.443.
3. See Jeffrey Nealon, "The Discipline of Deconstruction," PMLA (October 1992), pp. 1266–1279; Mas'ud Zavarzadeh, "Pun(k)deconstruction and the Postmodern Political Imaginary," *Cultural Critique* (Fall 1992), pp. 5–47.
4. In the introduction to his book now out from Cambridge University Press, *Anti-Mimesis*, and in "Diary of a Deconstructor Manqué; Reflections on Post 'Post-Mortem de Man,'" forthcoming in *The Minnesota Review*.
5. Paul de Man, "The Resistance to Theory," *The Resistance to Theory* (Minneapolis: University of Minnesota Press, 1986), p.11.
6. Walter Benjamin, *Illuminations*, trans. Harry Zohn (New York: Schocken, 1969); Walter Benjamin, *Illuminationen* (Frankfurt a. M.: Suhrkamp, 1955), p.278.

5

Une drôle de classe de philo

Michel Beaujour

The education of French literary scholars has traditionally been, and remains, quite different from that of their American counterparts. Two differences strike me as especially significant. First, young French students who are committed to the study of literature are wont to do a great deal of extracurricular and anticurricular reading. Second, philosophy plays an important part in their undergraduate curriculum. Thus, they are likely to keep on reading a good deal of philosophy in their free time. Conversely, American students of literature, who mostly read books that are assigned or recommended by their teachers, are neither required nor expected to receive any philosophical training. It follows that any encounter with "philosophical ideas" will take place for them on an *ad hoc* and "need-to-know" basis. When the need does arise, the graduates of our better colleges may draw on vague memories of having been—as we say—*exposed* to some philosophical ideas in the rush of a freshman survey of Western thought. It is, I believe, such a condition of philosophical innocence and, in the case of a few curious and exigent minds, of philosophical deprivation, that proved to be—at least initially—a fertile soil for the growth of so-called "deconstruction" in a few departments of French and comparative literature. In these privileged places—privileged with respect to the quality of their students, at any rate—there occurred encounters of the third kind between a couple of extraordinarily persuasive teachers steeped in Continental philosophy and a few philosophy-starved students of literature. The meetings mainly took place in the sixties, a very auspicious time for intellectual innovation. At least in the field of the humanities, everything was seemingly thrown into question, and especially the disciplinary boundaries upon which much of the established intellectual order had rested. Moreover, in the course of its precipitate expansion, the American academy as a whole came to obliterate the still more fundamental boundary that had separated an academic inside, peopled with teachers and scholars who made no great claims to being intellectuals or writers, from the outside world where (more or less) independent intellectuals and writers fought ideological battles, wrote literature and assessed cultural productions in independent reviews and in books published by non-academic presses. During the sixties and seventies, the American universities and their affluent presses, in cooperation with the foundations and the art museums, came to absorb most of the cultural activities that had not been pre-empted by the profit-making media, the art market and the capitalist trade publishers. When the sort of critical and oppositional thinking that had previously been undertaken at the writer's own risk, and mostly in precarious circumstances, was annexed by the Universities and supported by Foundation grants, it also started counting for academic tenure and preferment. In short, it became academic. These, I believe, are the general conditions under which American deconstruction came into being and thrived for a while, along with other critical discourses that would eventually shove deconstructionism aside, largely because these militant critical theories could ride on the aspirations, and fit the abilities, of expanded student bodies. Besides, they were better attuned to American traditions of pragmatism and moral righteousness than was deconstruction.

In retrospect, one wonders whether the historical and sociological situation that allowed for the academic institutionalization of dissident European theories had ever been genuinely favorable to philosophical deconstruction, to *Abbau* in the Heideggerian mode, as such. Rather, one might have anticipated that this context would entail for deconstruction a risk of rapid and massive trivial-ization. Such a paradoxical, such a counterintuitive approach to philosophical and poetic issues as is deconstruction could not help but be undermined by the need to make it accessible to philosophically untrained students, to students who never had an overwhelming commitment to literature. The democratic tenets of American education—which rule even in the most selective and transcendent reaches of the humanities—are inimical to a deconstruction which is, nonetheless, trapped within the academic Leviathan that has no outside.

Given their previous education, I doubt that most American graduate students of literature ever had a very spontaneous urge to protest the philosophical aridity of their training. In the old days, few indeed were inclined to reject the mixture of philology, unsystematic formalism and Christian ethics that dominated academic criticism before the turn to theory. How many current students do we find challenging the mix of political high dudgeon, moral inquisition and gendered self-indulgence that has taken its place? However that may be, we do know that, before theory, literary studies were generally acknowledged to be conceptually soft and comfy, which made up for the long reading lists, and fairly demanding criteria of scholarly precision.

Yet, paradoxically enough, the initial appeal of the philosophical criticism that turned into "deconstruction" resided precisely in its *difficulty*, its specific *philosophical* difficulty. A few bright and increasingly disaffected students hoped that this kind of difficulty would redeem the mediocrity they had been expected to emulate. However, these students—whose interest in literature was presumably more intellectual than aesthetic—also were American enough to expect satisfaction from the academic institution itself, rather than from the outside world, which was then receding quickly in the direction of Europe. The faith of some of those students was rewarded when they eventually encountered a providential instructor bearing the gift of Continental philosophy to the literature seminar.

Allow me now to draw on the personal memories of some colleagues, Peter Brooks for instance who, as a Harvard undergraduate in the late fifties, was about to give up the study of literature for that of history when he walked by chance into some comparative literature class. Once there, he was soon "given to understand that what was at stake in the study of literature was as difficult and demanding as philosophy or any other kind of discourse" (YFS 69, 5). The bearer of these tidings was, of course, Paul de Man. Ellen Burt, a more recent disciple, recalls that if de Man "said in an aside one day that we ought to read Hegel's *Aesthetics,* we read them, in order to understand why we must read them" (YFS 69, 11). I trust that these two examples, though they refer only to de Man's classroom teaching, are adequate illustrations of the initial response to this sort of philosophical criticism, a reaction which, I must emphasize, was induced by the immediacy of speech, by the *ethos* of such extraordinary teachers as de Man and Derrida.

"As difficult and demanding as philosophy" says Peter Brooks. Paul de Man himself was often said to be demanding, genially and legitimately so, since he pressed his demands only in the name of literature and of philosophy, of which he was the living *prosopopoeia* for his disciples. I guess that much the same could be said of Derrida and of his teaching: both de Man and Derrida played, in favor of their older but philosophically deprived students, much the same role as does a good *prof de philo* in a French lycée. He or she is the demanding magician who reveals to adolescents the difficult pleasures of thinking about the philosophical issues encapsulated in such (deconstructible) binomials as: reality and appearance, the rational and the sensible, theory and practice, being and time, etc. This teacher also is the one who explains difficult texts where the philosophers have formulated philosophical solutions—rather than empirical, poetic or sophistic ones—to these perennial dilemmas. And, of course, those French students who will eventually become serious literary critics pursue these philosophical studies for several years, closely reading the main texts of Western philosophy and writing about them. It follows that, in this respect, de Man's and Derrida's more mature American students had a lot of catching up to do. They inevitably did so in a hasty, haphazard and *ad hoc* fashion, given many other demands on their time, and an absence of follow-through which is characteristic of American humanistic studies. The philosophical texts they read, as well as the literary texts about which philosophical issues were raised, had to be mainly the ones which de Man or Derrida discussed in their courses, notwithstanding the serendipitous suggestions these teachers might also make, perhaps only in an imperative aside: "We read them in order to understand why we must read them," writes Ellen Burt very revealingly: we really didn't have a clue beforehand, because we had no background in philosophy. Paul de Man's discourse was in effect, for his students, the sole locus of philosophy, and of its demands. Not to mention the difficulty of reading on one's own Hegel's *Aesthetics* philosophically, under those circumstances. Whereas Derrida and de Man were steeped in the texts and topics of continental philosophy, their American disciples only got fragmentary and decontextualized insights. In order to obtain a solid philosophical education they would have had to embark on a course of studies that was unfortunately unavailable from most American universities. So that American deconstructionist criticism sometimes jolts the reader with the philosophical counterparts of Jean-Paul Sartre's disarming query: "Ne doit-on pas, Monsieur, éviter soigneusement les alexandrins dans la prose?" Or something like its opposite: "Are we not expected to mix the *genres?*"

This autodidactic quandary goes a long way toward explaining a rapid decline in the philosophical sophistication of American deconstructionism as it turned to quasi-rhetorical issues and became a *sui generis* critical theory that substituted discontinuities and aporias for the ironies of an older school of Anglo-Saxon criticism. The initial desire for the difficulty of philosophy—a hardness that raised the self-esteem of young critics trapped in unprestigious literary studies—was reoriented by younger scholars toward other self-valorizing gambits. Instead of rising above literature and philosophy by dint of reading literature as an allegory of philosophy, and philosophy as prone to the weaknesses of literature, the new theorists looked upon both literature and philosophy as transparent conceits for power politics and oppression. The tense elitism of deconstruction was forced to pull down its vanity and to refit itself in the democratic shirtsleeves of textbooks and easy undergraduate courses, as it attempted to hold on to an audience in the academic marketplace of diversity and

multiculturalism. And since there wasn't any extra-academic audience left for either philosophical *Abbau* or for rhetorical deconstructionism, their practitioners ended up squabbling in the back
pages of *PMLA* and the like, while the word deconstruction itself
along with a few shreds of the vulgate, after taking a quick spin
through the art-critical babble, eventually turned into nonsense
as it trickled down to the daily press.

Nevertheless, thanks to the hegemonic growth of the universities, some early American deconstructionists have enjoyed academic careers and audiences that contrast stupendously with Derrida's own, back in France. There, since a clear division still
subsists between an intellectual milieu that makes public reputa-
tions and the institutional academic world, the university can and
still does enforce its rejection of Derrida—who insists on mixing
the genres—by depriving him of an appointment commensurate
with his merit and international fame. In France—although he
has been one of those *profs de philo* who transmute generations of
students—Derrida is seen, like Maurice Blanchot and a few of
France's most interesting thinkers, as a *writer*, an independent
essayist who publishes with small presses, a writer who mainly
writes self-reflexive literature.

This brings us back to the relationship between literature and
philosophy which we envisaged in its American context—from
the vantage point of the peculiar philosophy classes taught by de
Man and Derrida to a few students of literature. My approach
manifestly left aside the specific relationship that obtains between
literature and philosophy in their respective works, although in a
sense, it is all that matters to me; but others are better qualified
than I am to deal with it.

To conclude, then, I should like to circle around the issue once
more by way of a reference to Derrida's *Passions*, a recent reply to
an American editor who had asked him to comment on essays by
various American deconstructionist hands, and also to disclose, in
a concluding piece, if only *obliquely*, his own position. Derrida (of
course) declined to do so, and gave his reasons at some length.
But, near the end of his demurral, Derrida goes on record with at
least the following:

And finally, a disclosure. Perhaps I did simply intend to disclose or confirm my liking (probably an unconditional one) for literature, more precisely for literary writing. Not that I care for literature in general, nor that I prefer it to anything else, say, for instance—as are wont to think those who are incapable of discerning either one or the other—philosophy. Not that I want to reduce everything to it, especially not philosophy. I can do very easily without literature. But without loving literature in general and for itself, I love something in it that is not reducible to some aesthetic quality, to some source of formal enjoyment, something indeed that might take the place of secrecy. In the stead of an absolute secret. There would the passion reside. (my translation)[1]

Evidently, I cannot say whether Paul de Man would have countersigned either these lines or the distinction Derrida draws thereafter between, on the one hand, poetry and belles-lettres and, on the other, literature. Derrida claims literature, as he understands it, to be inseparable from democratic freedom: the freedom to say all, but also the freedom not to answer questions, the freedom to preserve the secrecy inherent in literature as such, even though there may not be any secret hiding behind the surface of the text, for the presumption of a secret to be sought is what makes the reader passionate—a passionate reader. This presumption, I believe, raises the issues of critical deconstruction to a higher plane, a hieratic plane where a degree of tact is more advisable than are those intrusive operations that are merely intent on uncovering—no matter how cleverly and gracefully—discontinuities, contradictions, plays of the signifier and what not. For the lesson taught by de Man and Derrida in their peculiar philosophy classes—and in their idiosyncratic writings—is also one of discretion, and of passion, the one preserving and sustaining the other. However strong the temptation to reduce literature to philosophy—especially in the hope of raising literature above the triviality which those who do not like it fear to find in it; however insidious the desire to reduce whatever philosophy one may know to a bunch of unwitting tropes, these indeed are not the passions that can ignite and nurture our love—our often ironic and suspicious love—for either of them. That is why we must preserve the freedom to be tactful and silent about our passions. A democratic and totalitarian university may not be the best place to do so.

Acknowledgments

I am grateful to Philip Lewis for challenging the accuracy of this potted narrative. It is manifestly biased in its exclusive emphasis on Paul de Man and Jacques Derrida's part in the early development of deconstruction in America. Above all, I am guilty of having ignored here the important role played by Jacques Ehrmann, Philip Lewis' teacher at Yale, and my friend (see *Yale French Studies*, No. 58, 1979, "In Memory of Jacques Ehrmann").

Notes

1. Jacques Derrida, *Passions* (Paris: Éditions Galilée, 1993), 63–64.

6

Going Public: The University in Deconstruction

Peggy Kamuf

As Jacques Derrida illustrated, the title "Deconstruction is/in America" may set one to dreaming about some rather nonacademic uses for that phrase. He indulged this fancy for a moment by describing what might have been a newspaper headline or a brief story on local television: "I read it all of a sudden as if in a newspaper, a travel diary, or a press release: Hey, deconstruction, on this date, finds itself here these days, it is in America, it landed yesterday at JFK and is just passing through, more or less incognito and for a little while." One effect of this little "reverie," which was also just passing through, was to superimpose two scenes of address: the address Derrida was then delivering to a large audience at New York University and another kind of public address, that of the newspaper headline, the press release, the TV story. There may have been others then present who, like me, felt invited to consider this kind of double address as a condition of deconstruction: in America, in its universities, but at the same time not in but passing through, always crossing the borders, without permanent address.

Responding to that invitation, I want to propose some questions about the university and its borders, the university and publicity. In what sense is the university and the intellectual work that is supposed to go on there public? Who or what is the public addressed by the work of the university? Is there or can there be a sense in which that work is not addressed to any public that can be identified? On a first level, one could say that the research and teaching activity of the university is public because it is evidenced by publication. This apparent tautology merely points to the fact that the work of the university, unlike that of some other institutions one might think of, includes the generation, support, gathering, storage, evaluation, study, preservation, and publishing of all sorts of publications. In this sense, the university is perhaps the most public of all public institutions. But of course, in another sense, very little of this activity can be expected to find its way to a mass public, the undifferentiated audience sought by a commercial mass medium like television or even daily newspapers. By comparison with the publicity of these institutions, the university might as well be a secret society shrouded in obscurity. One thing the Great PC Debate will have made clear, however, is that this appearance of obscurity is itself to a considerable extent maintained and promulgated by the institutions of the mass media themselves. The media, in other words, have made it their job to inform their public that it is not addressed by the work of the university, that that work is too obscure, too technical, or too specialized for it. (When it is a matter of scientific research, these are terms of respect, but in the case of the humanities, they are marks of disdain.) This kind of reporting, with which we have now become so familiar, determines public interest in the limited sense of common sense, immediate self-evidence, and so forth—the interest, in other words, of the largely ignorant and intellectually unadventurous. Imagining that they address themselves to this public, while in fact fashioning it by means of their address, the mass media seek in effect to avoid the question: What other kinds of address might there be?

But let us bring out another sense of publicity as it pertains to the work of the university. In his "Answer to the Question: 'What is Enlightenment?'" Kant distinguishes between the public and the private use of reason. "By the public use of one's own reason I mean that use which anyone may make of it *as a man of learning* addressing the entire *reading public*. What I term the private use of reason is that which a person may make of it in a particular *civil* post or office with which he is entrusted."[1] The public use of reason must never be restricted, whereas the private use of reason can "quite often be very narrowly restricted without undue hindrance to the progress of enlightenment."[2] Kant gives several examples: a military officer must not argue with an order even if, privately, he believes it to be ill-advised. But the same officer, speaking as a man of learning, may quite justifiably criticize military policy publicly. Likewise, a clergyman may disagree privately with points of doctrine that he nevertheless must teach to his congregation as prescribed by the Church. "Conversely," Kant adds, "as a scholar addressing the real public (i.e., the world at large) through his writings, the clergyman making *public use* of his reason enjoys unlimited freedom to use his own reason and to speak in his own person" (57). It should be noted that Kant does not speak here either of that other civil servant who is the university professor or of the civil institution that is the university. Instead, all his examples assume that the "man of learning" or the "scholar" is simply the name given any educated citizen who exercises his public reason. The "man of learning," the "scholar" is the public man, who reasons with no limiting obligation to any particular institution. Now, perhaps Kant does not mention the university because that civil institution would impose no such obligation. In other words, unlike the military officer or the cleric, professional men or (*pace* Kant) women of learning, that is, members of a university faculty, would be under no constraint to suppress even in a limited manner the exercise of their private reason in order to carry out conscientiously the duties of their office. Indeed, the professional scholar as scholar would, in theory, have no such thing as private reason, or perhaps one should say that his or her private reason is indistinguishable from public reason, from reason in the service of the "real public (i.e., the world at large)." Thus, whereas every other civil institution installs a division within the faculty of reason of those appointed to uphold it, in the institution of the university; reason in principle would be upheld only to the extent that no gap between public and private reason is allowed to occur.

If that is the case, then the institution of the university would be the institution of publicness itself, which means an institution in which internal (private or intra-institutional) interest cannot or should not be disjoined from external (public or extra-institutional) interest. Rather, the two are or should be the same, which is to say that there should be no difference between the institution of the university and all that is not that institution: the public. The university would thus be an institution without division between its inside and its outside even as it divides itself off from or within the society. The instituted division ought not to exist, although it does; and it certainly ought not to enclose or define an interest that is separate from any larger public interest. Rather, the mark of instituted difference should be a kind of empty or effaced mark, a redundant trait of public reason without reason.

The short essay, "What is Enlightenment?" was published in 1784. When, more than ten years later in *The Conflict of the Faculties*, Kant returned to the subject of public-ness and publicity as regards the activity of the scholar, circumstances had changed for the philosopher of public reason. First, in the interval Kant had experienced the strictures of a state censorship put in place in Prussia in 1788, which had refused to grant permission for the publication of *Religion Within the Limits of Reason Alone*. For this reason, perhaps, he had become considerably more wary in his formulations concerning the possibility of an entirely free exercise of reason. In addition, the "public reason" that Kant had figured in the earlier essay as that of the "man of learning," the "scholar," is presented in the later text as that of the professor, appointed by the State to the faculties of its university. What has thus intervened from one text to the other is the institution of censorship and the institution of the university. These are made to coincide when Kant holds up the image of the State "whose only wish is to rule."[3] This wish, however, encounters a "stumbling-block" in the freedom of the "*freie Rechtslehrer*," "the free professors of right," that is, adds Kant, the philosophers; the latter are not, he insists, "officials appointed by the state." Now, it may at first appear unclear how one is supposed to read this latter distinction. By "freie Rechtslehrer" who are not officially appointed by the State, one may understand independent men of learning "unaffiliated," as we say today, with the university, on the model of the French *philosophes*. The fact that Kant remarks that these free professors are "given the appellation of 'enlighteners' *[Aufklärer]*, and decried as a menace to the state" would tend to support this reading. But that reading would overlook the more interesting and important point being underscored here. The distinction Kant is making is not one between appointed professors and unaffiliated enlighteners, but a distinction *within* those who are officially appointed to the university's faculty of philosophy. Officially appointed, the latter are nevertheless free professors of right. Notice, however, that if Kant must insist on this distinction, it is because one risks neglecting to grant the freedom from institutional, official constraint that appointment to an institution abrogates, as it does, for example, in the case of the institution of the Church or the army, to recall the earlier examples, or in this text, as it does in the case of appointment to the "higher" faculties of both law and theology within the university. In other words, one risks instating for the professor of philosophy the very division between private reason and public reason that should not exist in that case. And yet, Kant must acknowledge that division even as he insists that it does not affect the free professor's freedom to profess publicly the rights of the public. Once again, we come across the figure of the university (at least as concerns the faculty of philosophy) instituted by a division that does not divide, a division that is or is supposed to be a purely formal mark which does not set anything apart from the space of public reason.

That the institution formally demarcated or divided in this way is not restricted by the very division instituting it is made clear by Kant at another point in the same passage we've been reading. This passage occurs in the second part of *The Conflict of the Faculties* (1992), in a section titled "The Difficulty of Maxims Directed Towards the World's Progressive Improvement as Regards their Publicity."[4] The section concerns "popular enlightenment" [*Volksaufklärung*], the public instruction of the people. Now, Kant gives a most interesting analysis of the philosopher's popular instruction which turns on a differentiation in the address of that instruction. The philosopher does not, Kant insists, address his teaching to the people directly, but rather to the State. He writes: "And yet they do not address themselves in familiar tones to the *people* (who themselves take little or no notice of them and their writings), but in *respectful* tones to the state, which is thereby implored to take the rightful needs of the people to heart." That is, the public discourse of the philosophers is not addressed to the public as such, but over the heads of the people, so to speak, to their rulers. At this point, someone might want to say that Kant's free professor of right is elitist, or more precisely paternalistic. That is, he is an *Aufklärer* in the quite specific sense that Kant understands enlightenment: a passage from childhood to adulthood. But the paternalism here defines a conflict with the wishes of the State to rule absolutely over a population that can easily be kept ignorant of its rights. If one restores the context of this passage, it becomes clear that Kant is in fact placing a severe limit on the expectation that State-appointed professors will instruct the people in familiar terms about their duties and obligations to the patriarchal State. But the matter of Kant's paternalism is of less interest here than the effect of an address that is directed elsewhere than to its apparent addressee, that is addressed to the State, which for Kant meant to a King who was able to order, but also to suspend, state censorship. Censorship divides public reason from private reason; it activates, in other words, the very division that, in the case of the institution of public reason that is the university, should remain without effect, without divisive or censoring effect. But how is that possible from the very moment reason institutes itself as reason, that is, by a mark of difference? What is the difference, finally, between reason and censorship? Or between censorship and public instruction? And where is this public instruction supposed to occur if not within the walls constructed by reason?

There are several reasons to bring Kant into the discussion of the university's publicness. First, because enlightenment remains the legacy of the modern, scientific university, and this is perhaps most evident in the heightened concern with diversified representation in all aspects of university activity. That this legacy is also a certain suspicion of legacy, of the sort that has thrived in North American soil for at least two centuries, indicates the historical and not only demographic sense in which nothing perhaps is more American than the multicultural challenge to the notion of a unified, determinant past. But that is only a first and more or less superficial reason to recall Kant's analysis of public instruction in an age of enlightenment (which he distinguishes from an enlightened age; "we have a long way to go," predicted Kant in 1784, "before mankind will have entered an enlightened age"). The second, more important reason is that it seems we are asking with ever more urgency the question Kant addressed in the passage above: What or who is the public of the university? The question recurs, it insists, because it is ever more the case that the people in general "take little or no notice" of professors and their writings, and because it is still the case that, practically or empirically speaking, "public instruction" designates a system of selection or election that effectively closes the classroom door on the vast majority of a population. The enlightened age is still postponed. And in that postponement, the modern, scientific university comes to share a responsibility for having delayed its promise for so long. Yet, even as we indict the university for its failure, we reiterate the demand that the promise be renewed, that the long-overdue letter of public instruction be finally delivered. Perhaps that letter has been misaddressed, or perhaps it has simply been kept circulating within a narrow compass? In asking about the public to whom the university addresses itself, we ask the question of the destination to be reached and to what end. The concept of the university in the age of enlightenment, the modern university, is inseparable from the concept of an end, a destination, a finality.

Let us assume, then, that in recent debates, it is the ends of the university that are at issue, explicitly or more often implicitly. As a minimal indication of this, we can select statements from each of the declared adversaries in one of the first battles of the PC wars to be projected on the large screen of the national media: the university of Texas freshman composition initiative and the editorial response it prompted in *Newsweek*, signed by George Will. In their "Statement of the Black Faculty Caucus," the authors Ted Gordon and Wahneema Lubiano conclude their argument for a multicultural curriculum in these terms: "What we are talking about here is no less than transforming the university into a center of multicultural learning: anything less continues a system of education that ultimately reproduces racism and racists."[5] Here destination is very broadly figured in general terms: the university transformed "into a center of multicultural learning." Whether or not George Will read this "Statement" and its conclusion, his own editorial nevertheless concludes by warning explicitly of the destination toward which Gordon, Lubiano, and their allies are leading the university: "So it goes on many campuses. The troubles at Texas are, as yet, mild. But the trajectory is visible: down. So is the destination: political indoctrination supplanting education."[6] If Will and the authors of the "Statement" can appear to be so firmly locked in mirrored dissent from each other's understanding (for both sides, it is a matter of "political indoctrination" versus "education"),[7] it is because each argues from a notion of destination, an endpoint that can either be attained or missed. This is not to equate the very different sets of references that distinguish these two positions and that make this polemic a struggle for legitimacy (retaining it or gaining it). It is merely to observe that, for both sides, legitimation of the references passes by way of the prior figuration of their legitimate destination, one towards which these references are said to address or destine themselves. This sounds circular, and so it is; nonetheless, this circle of destined reference is what we generally understand by legitimacy: it is, in other words, the legitimated mode of legitimacy.

Without putting in question the necessity or the legitimacy of this struggle, one may also remark something else at work within the scene briefly evoked. The circle of destined reference, the form of legitimate meaning or value, describes a figure of auto- or self-legitimation. The legitimated figure of legitimacy, in other words, is a circle of auto-destination, a kind of self-addressed envelope. What is missing from this circle of self-address is an addressee who is not already a figure of the addressor, an addressee, that is, who is other than the addressor. So, it is here, within this circle, that the question of a destination *not already comprised* by the space of legitimated knowledge arises. But how can that question arise *within* the circle? Unless an opening has been left, a space wherein the auto- or the self- of destination *dis-closes* itself? Unless the dis-closure of the circle opens up a space that is neither within the legitimated domain nor simply outside it, but along the edge where the two divide? To call it a space, of course, is to have recourse to a figure and to the very figure of a bordered extension that is being dis-closed. This is not just a problem of nomination or figuration, but also of legitimation because to the extent that this dis-closure of the circle along its unfigurable edge lets one challenge the legitimacy that is conferred by circular destination, it can be seen to arise as an illegitimate question, as falling outside the realm of legitimate reason. And this despite the fact that, as already suggested, the question can only be posed because that realm itself in effect produces the question of its limit at its limit. If the circle had effectively realized or completed its closure, there would be nothing to dis-close, nothing to discuss, nothing to say—nothing. And manifestly that is not the case. The legitimacy that concerns us most—the legitimacy of the very figure of legitimacy—is open to question and to challenge only in a space opened *within* the circle, but which is therefore not part of that figure. It is within without being a part of the circle and as such it is the very possibility of the figure's reconfiguration.

Now, I have been using the term dis-closure, spaced with a hyphen, in order to bring out the pairing of two effects at work here: on the one hand, the effect of a certain repetition or retracing that discloses, i.e., brings into view, the circular outline; on the other, the effect of this dis-closed or un-closed figure, that is, of a figure that does not complete itself, that does not completely return to itself. The term dis-closure, however, has been standing in for another, apparently more familiar term: deconstruction. Before introducing the latter word, I wanted to survey somewhat the ground on which the current debate over legitimacy has been waged. This deferral was a strategic attempt to keep a critical space open that, in the context we are discussing, risks being closed down as soon as one invokes deconstruction by name. This risk of closure is an institutional effect, the effect of an instituted name that works to dispel a referential uncertainty. Concerning the institution that is the university put in question by the PC debate, the term "deconstruction" is most often presumed to refer to a theory, a method, a school, perhaps even a doctrine, in any case, some identifiable or localizable thing that can be positioned—posed and opposed—within that institution, but also that can be excluded from this defined enclosure. What is interesting, however, is less the imaginable reasons for this kind of positioning and opposing of names, than the disclosed movement in an unfigurable space between names and between positions, the space for different kinds of effects.

We may take a brief example here. In the summer of 1991, the well-known American historian C. Vann Woodward wrote a review for the *New York Review of Books* of Dinesh D'Souza's *Illiberal Education* (1991), the book that, along with Roger Kimball's *Tenured Radicals* (1990), called neoconservatives to arms against, in D'Souza's phrase, "the politics of sex and race on campus." Woodward's review was in the main sympathetic to D'Souza's argument while making numerous assertions that other university historians and scholars found inaccurate or objectionable. Two months later, the NYRB published some of these objections, along with a long response to them by Woodward. One of the letters-to-the-editor was signed by Clyde de L. Ryals, who identified himself as a Professor of English at Duke university. As the letter is short, I will quote it *in extenso:*

In his review of Dinesh D'Souza's *Illiberal Education,* Professor Vann Woodward refers to Duke university's recruitment of "superstars leading the then fashionable school of critics of the humanities who were known as deconstructionists." Since a number of observers of the current academic scene seem to share Professor Woodward's belief that the humanities departments here are filled with deconstructionists, I hope that you will allow me to correct this misapprehension.

So far as I know, there is not one deconstructionist in the Duke English Department or in the Program in Literature. There are persons interested in gender, sexuality, Marxism, reader-reception, new-historicism, canonicity, popular culture, and many other types of criticism and theory, but to my knowledge there is no one here who identifies him/herself as a practitioner of the kind of deconstructionist criticism associated with Jacques Derrida.[8]

This objection will be answered by Professor Woodward, but before quoting that reply, let me make just a few remarks about Professor Ryals' letter. Its point is to underscore Woodward's confusion or conflation of the many sorts of critical activities actually espoused and represented by name within Duke's English department or its Program in Literature with the single name, deconstructionism, which Professor Ryals reports, perhaps not without some pride, is totally absent from their ranks. But for whatever reason Ryals may be riled up over that confusion, his rhetorical demeanor remains quite careful, although insistent: "So far as I know," he writes, "there is not one deconstructionist . . . to my knowledge, there is no one here who identifies him/herself . . . " By means of this repetition of a similar limiting construction within one two-sentence paragraph, Ryals seems to imply that there may be some authentic deconstructionists among his colleagues, but their association has not been revealed to him, as if, at Duke at least, the "deconstructionist criticism associated with Jacques Derrida" had become a kind of secret society in which only initiated members can be sure to recognize one another. This implication, which may remind one of other, more sinister contexts, doubtless does not correspond to Professor Ryals' own notion of his own intention. It nevertheless appears as soon as that intention is published, a fact that Professor Woodward in his reply does not fail to remark. He writes:

Professor Ryals assures us that "there is not one deconstructionist in the Duke English Department or in the Program in Literature." This comes as no surprise. In fact the term deconstruction has, for various reasons, become to some at least something of an embarrassment. That is not, however, to retract my suggestion that its one-time rhetoric helped smooth the path for multicultural innovations, some of which are of doubtful value.[9]

Woodward easily flushes out the problem with Ryals' assertion, although as an historian, and a professed liberal, he ought to have been more on guard against echoing a certain question that once upon a time began "Are you now or have you ever been . . .?" But it is not this echo that should interest us as much as the fact that these two academics, each for apparently quite different reasons, question the legitimacy of understanding the work of the university (or at least that part of the university that is invested with so much cultural capital: the English Department) in terms of deconstruction. For Woodward, as well as for the neoconservatives whose assessments he relies on, deconstruction is simply an umbrella name for "multicultural innovations . . . of doubtful value," when they are not downright harmful. This denomination is justified in Woodward's view because deconstruction's rhetoric "helped smooth the path" for these innovations (which, let it be said in passing, is hardly a discriminating criterion since one could say the same thing for many, vastly heterogeneous factors). For Ryals, on the other hand, who speaks for colleagues "interested in gender, sexuality, Marxism, reader-reception, new-historicism, canonicity, popular culture, and many other types of criticism and theory," it is important to discriminate and to call a new historicist a new historicist and so forth, to use, that is, a plurality of names. For it is less the names as such than their virtually endless plurality—the list concludes with "many other types of criticism and theory"—that provides the legitimating function here. Ryals' unintentional parody offers itself as proof that the historian is incorrect since it *just so happens* that this list does not include the designation "deconstructionist." Beneath this dispute, however, is a profound agreement: deconstruction is the name of something that *has no place* in the university, either in Woodward's prescriptive sense that it should have no place or in Ryals' empirical sense that in fact it does not.

In order to reach that agreement, the parties to the dispute (whom I am treating here, no doubt unfairly, as typical of the sides opposed in a larger debate) must be able to invoke with some assurance, explicitly or implicitly, an idea of what the university is or should be, in other words, its destination. Even Ryals' brief *mise au point* must intimate such an idea: it is a plurality of co-existing "interests" that complement one another within the larger, overriding interest of *universitas*. The problem with this harmonious picture of pluralism is that it is invoked in order to establish, somewhat triumphantly, the absence of one of "many other types of criticism and theory." Pluralism, at Duke at least, has a limit, and that limit has a name: "deconstructionism." The marked absence of the latter functions to bring the pluralized elements together within a kind of unity, because a limited plurality is always, finally, a unity.

For Woodward, a version of this same idea is made explicit in the concluding paragraph of his reply, which I quote for its appeal to the "mission" and "purpose" of the university as well as for its exceptional incoherence:

We desperately need to go beyond the defensive to the positive, to what we have in common. We must seek agreement on the ideals, mission, purpose, and character of the academy—what the university means. One way to say what we are is to agree on what we are not. I do not think the university is or should attempt to be a political or a philanthropic or a paternalistic or a therapeutic institution. It is not a club or a fellowship to promote harmony and civility, important as those values are. It is a place where the unthinkable can be thought, the unmentionable can be discussed, and the unchallengeable can be challenged.

Notice the abrupt shift from a definition by means of exclusion ("One way to say what we are is to agree on what we are not") to a definition that would have to include what has just been excluded ("It is a place where the unthinkable can be thought, the unmentionable can be discussed, and the unchallengeable can be challenged"). This last rhetorical flourish sounds admirable until one realizes that Professor Woodward has in mind an already limited definition of the unthinkable, unmentionable, and unchallengeable, which definition "we" would agree not to think about, mention, or challenge. Or one could also wonder how the appeal to "what we have in common" and the imperative to "seek agreement" could be followed by the assertion that the university "is not a club or fellowship to promote harmony." What this series of disjunctive sentences discloses, besides the historian's evident disregard for his own language, is the difficulty that gets in the way of the project to pose "what the university means," or "to say what we are," a difficulty that arises because prescriptive definition slips from under its ontological mask in the very process of its articulation. To say what we are as institution, that is, as a nonnatural, cultural invention or artifact, is to say what we should be, what we are *meant* to be, or what we *will have been* in a future past from which the deferred moment of arrival at destination is seen as already included in the present of the definition. It is to attempt to circle back from this already comprised destination in order to pose a presence-to-itself that includes an always deferred *meaning* ("what the university means") in *being* ("what we are"). Woodward's incoherence is but the marker left by this circle's failure to close completely on itself, or, in this case, even to come close.

I have attempted to make several points with this example. In conclusion, I will reiterate what they are and then try to take each one a little further.

1) When Vann Woodward takes "deconstructionism" to be the generic name of the brand of thinking that has, as he put it, smoothed the path for multicultural innovations of doubtful value, he is merely repeating the gesture of so many other journalists who have, deliberately or not, made themselves the spokespersons of an old political reflex to seek a clearly identifiable enemy. What is rather remarkable in this identification, however, and what can be gauged in Ryals symptomatic response, is that almost none of those singled out as suspect of "political correctness" would accept being called a "deconstructionist"; they can even be rather hostile to those of us for whom this label is not problematic, at least not for the reasons alleged here. Although the press, of course, cannot be concerned with this kind of distinction, which is deemed by them to be too subtle, its identification of "deconstruction" as the enemy nevertheless allows a crack to appear that traverses the whole field of political discourse, from left to right and from the interior to the exterior of the university institution. Between the two sides of the present confrontation is this thing called "deconstruction," which one side wants to get rid of as much as the other. This rejection thus forms a kind of secret and unavowable liaison between the two sides, even as it destabilizes the terms of their opposition. It is, in other words, a deconstructive effect that will have occurred and that will have indicated the limit, by exceeding it, of the most recognizable political and analytical discourses.

2) By deconstructive effect is meant a shifting of apparent divisions, in this case, the dividing lines that are supposed to set off an institution like the university and its defining discourses from, to use Woodward's phrase, "what we are not." The fact that this effect shows up around the use of the term "deconstruction" to name a referentially stable unit that can be either inside or outside that institution is not incidental, although it perhaps complicates the analysis. The exchange between Woodward and Ryals (but here we could have taken other examples as well) can be read on one level as a dispute about referential value, which is possible

only because each assumes the indisputably referential value of his own use of a term. Beyond this level of initial paradox, however, which could be illustrated just as well with any other term, "deconstruction" here is both the name in dispute and a name—more or less conventional, more or less instituted—for what happens when instituted, referential boundaries shift. Which means that what I earlier called the profound agreement between the parties to this dispute—deconstruction is the name of something that *has no place* in the university—is reached by reinscribing a deconstructive shift in the very space of a proscription of that name.

3) That this shift can occur without regard to what we are being told to think about the place of deconstruction *in* the university should lead us to reverse the terms and speak of the university in deconstruction. "The university is in deconstruction": Such an affirmation is not an announcement of something that has overtaken this institution recently and from without, as various accounts would have it, something that would have come either from the radicals whose '60s ideology has taken refuge in tenure or from the imported writing of a few European thinkers, mostly French.[10] Such pseudo-historical fables cannot dis-close how it is that, already in its Kantian form, the university divides itself, not only into internal divisions, departments, or faculties, nor within these into warring schools of thought, but divides the very division by which it is set apart and instituted over against all that "we are not." The earlier brief reading of the two texts of Kant, led us to pose an apparently paradoxical figure, that of an institution without instituted difference, without division between its inside and its outside but which nevertheless divides itself off from or within the society. This means it is possible that a division be not a division, or the other way around, that the non-division be nevertheless a division. It is possible, in other words, for division to divide itself in its very mark. This possibility, indeed, is the general possibility of the mark as institution, as instituted sign, for example. And by the same token, the instituted mark, institution in general cannot exclude the essential demark-ing or division that structures it. An instituted difference cannot, in other words, exclude what it is meant to exclude.

4) If, like any institution, the university is in deconstruction, it has also been a place, particularly in the United States, in which that deconstruction comes to be at least partially formalized and theorized. Only "partially" because this work of formalization or theorization, for the same reasons just mentioned, cannot formally exclude nonformalizable, nontheorizable—i.e., practical or pragmatic—elements. What this means in practice is that, as theory, deconstruction will have had effects that do not in any simple sense belong to or return to its formal structure. Vann Woodward and other journalists implicitly recognize this when they see deconstruction as responsible for a vast array of institutional realignments, most of which, of course, they deplore. Despite this tendentious and hopelessly misinformed account, one may be tempted to find it closer to some truth than an opposing account of deconstruction's effect in or on the institution, or rather its lack of effect because it is, I quote no one in particular, "too theoretical," "not political." The fact that deconstruction can be positioned as at once too political and not political at all, as both PC and not PC, signals that the terms in which the political is posed in this debate are inadequate to account for all the effects being produced.

To name these other effects deconstructive does not imply that they return in any simple sense to the theoretical formation called deconstruction as to their cause. Rather, they are so named because they mobilize the division within the institutionalized trait. Whatever returns does not return to any one, to any one thing. Which leads to a final point: it concerns a public address that is always necesssarily divided, not in the sense that Kant set out when he evoked the "free professor of right" who speaks to the King even as he appears to address the people. No, it is an address divided precisely by the absence of any King, real or symbolic, which is to say by the absence of any figure who can stand in for the final destination of public discourse.

Notes

1. *In Kant's Political Writings*, ed. Hans Reiss (Cambridge: Cambridge University Press, 1970), p.55.

2. That the use of reason according to Kant is never unrestricted or uncensored has been argued in detail by Jacques Derrida in "Languages and Institutions of Philosophy" (*Recherches Semiologiques/Semiological Inquiry*, 4, 2), pp.128ff.

3. "An Old Question Raised Again: Is the Human Race Constantly Progressing?" in *The Conflict of the Faculties*, trans. Mary J. Gregor (New York: Abaris Books, 1979), p.186.

4. I have discussed this passage at greater length in "The University Founders," in *Logomachia: The Conflict of the Faculties in America*, ed. Richard Rand (Lincoln: University of Nebraska Press, 1992).

5. In Paul Berman, ed., *Debating P.C.: The Controversy over Political Correctness on College Campuses* (New York: Dell, 1992), p.257. The "Statement" originallly appeared in a different form in the *Daily Texan*, May 3, 1990.

6. *Debating P.C.*, p.261. The editorial was first published in *Newsweek*, Sept. 16, 1990.

7. On this distinction, cf. my "University Founders," op. cit.

8. *The New York Review of Books*, Sept. 26, 1991, p.74.

9. Ibid., p.76.

10. This figure of "importation" from France runs throughout Berman's introductory essay, and this foreign influence is made responsible for all the excesses of PCism. The latter, Berman implies, would have been avoided if the American left liberal tradition had not encountered French "cynicism": "Political correctness in the 1990s . . . is the fog that arises from American liberalism's encounter with the iceberg of French cynicism" (op. cit., p.24).

III

The Politics of Singularity

7

Possibilizations, in the Singular

Rodolphe Gasché

Undoubtedly, deconstruction has invited us to reconceive the relation between philosophy and literature as it had been understood througout the tradition, by philosophers and, in their wake, by literary critics. But are we truly prepared to accept that invitation? The dominant trend among literary critics who have looked favorably on deconstruction seems to prove that we are not. By claiming that philosophy is literature, or that literature is philosophy, we already have missed the challenge that deconstruction represents. This is also the case where literature becomes construed as the more primordial genre, and philosophy sees itself restricted to a mere province within the wider domain of the literary. Nor is the challenge met where literature is simply declared to be the "Other" of philosophy. Indeed, when we neutralize the difference between philosophy and literature, the problem of their relation does not pose itself anymore; by making literature into the dominant genre, we do not rethink the traditional view on how philosophy and literature relate. We only invert it; and, when literature is turned into the Other of philosophy, either a highly conventional, and unquestioned conception of literature, or an obscurantist mystification of it, usually serves to fill in the blank space of the Other. The thought of the relation of philosophy to an Other such as literature does not even get a chance to begin

115

to address that relation according to the terms that come with the notion of Otherness.

For a number of reasons, Derrida has not made it easy for us to address the question concerning the relation between literature and philosophy without ambiguity and without immediately falling prey to understanding that relation from the already constituted poles of that difference. If one believes that philosophy and literature are positive givens, and that one knows already what they are, then one can think of the relation between both only in terms of the differents themselves; in other words, either philosophy or literature dominates, embraces the Other, or subserviently yields to its Other. Or, one thinks of the relation as a more or less harmonious and reciprocal exchange, as having the form of an unrelenting struggle, and, finally, as a dialectical interplay of sublation. If deconstruction represents an invitation to rethink the relation between philosophy and literature, it does so by calling our attention to the relation itself as a relation of constitution. The question with deconstruction is no longer whether literature or philosophy is primordial, more essential, or broader, whether one side is made to tremble by its its richer, more plentiful or more abyssal Other, and the like, but of how philosophy and literature become—more precisely, begin to become—what they are in their respective difference. A deconstructive focus on the relation between philosophy and literature not only requires that both be taken seriously in their irreducible difference, but also that that difference is seen as resting on an infinite bringing forth of itself and its differents. For deconstruction, the difference between philosophy and literature is not an established, positive given. On the contrary, what makes philosophy philosophy, and literature literature, takes place in a constituting "process," in which philosophy calls upon literature as *an* (rather than *its*) Other so as to be able to demarcate itself, and be what it is in difference from something like literature. Literature, for its part, is also not without such an address to an Other upon whose response depends the possibility for literature to be what it is. An Other must always be invented for something to be, but by the same token, such inevitable invention also means that no being can ever be taken for granted, for being what it *is*.

There are still other reasons to be evoked here that explain the difficulties of a deconstructive assessment of the relationship between philosophy and literature. The first is that to date, Derrida has not given one, but several answers to the question of how philosophy and literature relate. Since what might be called Derrida's "performative turn," such plurality appears to be inevitable. The answers provided to that question are not only context bound, but are also, and especially in so far as they have the structure of answers, always singular. Intimately combining categorial statement and idiomatic singularity, Derrida's elaborations allow for no easy generalization, and hence, no application. Indeed, what follows from deconstruction's concern with accounting in a radically "genetic" mode for the surge of philosophy in difference from literature, and vice-versa, is that a response to that demand must each time be invented anew.

From what I have said so far, it should be clear that a deconstructive treatment of the relation between philosophy and literature is, of necessity, an investigation of what in philosophy are called "conditions of possibility." Indeed, I wish to claim that what is so provocative, and if you will, philosophically decisive, about Derrida's elaborations on the commerce between philosophy and literature, is that they put to work the traditional concept of a "condition of possibility" in an entirely different way. To understand deconstruction as suggesting a priority of the literary over the philosophical, or of philosophy being literature, and literature philosophy, is irremediably to miss the chance of encountering this philosophical debate with the notion of the condition of possibility.

Hereafter I wish to discuss Derrida's treatment of the relation between literature and philosophy from such an angle, and will do so on the basis of an analysis of a text by Derrida entitled "Before the Law."[1] Within the constraints of this essay, this analysis has to be quite brief, and very schematic, and cannot hope to take up any of the many hints that this text contains, for instance, Derrida's repeated reference to Kant's Second Critique. "Before the Law", is, as you know, a text on Kafka's parable of the same name. One of the several issues discussed by Derrida in this text is whether Kafka's story belongs to literature, and what such belonging implies and means. After having evoked in his concluding remarks, the peculiar relation between Kafka's insular parable and *The Trial*, of which it is also a part, Derrida raises the possibility that everything he has developed about the parable might well be included *en abyme* by the novel, and hence have to be relativized. I shall, however, in the following, leave that possibility aside. If I do so it is not only because Derrida has suggested ,in addition, that "Before the Law" might do "the same thing through a more powerful ellipsis which itself would engulf *The Trial*, and us along with it"(217) but also because what Derrida says in this reading of the parable about the relation between literature and the law, literature and philosophy, and so forth, contains already *in nuce*, structurally as it were, the possibility of such a *mise en abyme*.

Derrida's essay is an inquiry into "what and who ... decides that *Before the Law* belongs to what we think we understand under the name of literature"(187). Even though this inquiry is framed by the repeated allusions to a seminar on the moral law and the notion of respect in Kant, Heidegger, and Freud, in which the Kafka story was first discussed, the thrust of the inquiry in question is not philosophical in a general sense, for two reasons. First, and this is, of course, not unimportant, because the philosophical is only invoked under the title of the philosophy of the (moral) law, the philosophy of law, as well as the history of law. Second, even if "it would be tempting, beyond the limits of this reading, to reconstitute this story without story within the elliptic envelope of Kant's *Critique of Practical Reason* or Freud's *Totem and Taboo*, ... we could never explain the parable of a relation called "literary" with the help of semantic contents originating in philosophy or psychoanalyis, or drawing on some other source of knowledge"(209). The question of what and who decides whether Kafka's story belongs to literature is not to be answered in a philosophically and epistemological fashion, for essential reasons we shall see in just a moment. To become aware of these reasons, let me circle back to the previously mentioned seminar on the Second Critique, in which Derrida reports to have been interested in the status of the example, the symbol, and what Kant calls, in distinction from schematism, the typic of pure practical reason, as well as the role of the "as if" in the second formulation of the categorial imperative. Derrida evokes the seminar in the following passage: "I tried to show how it [the "as if"] almost *[virtuellement]* introduces narrativity and fiction into the very core of legal thought, at the moment when the latter begins to speak and to question the moral subject. Though the authority of the law seems to exclude all historicity and empirical narrativity, and this at the moment when its rationality seems alien to all fiction and imagination— even transcendental imagination—it still seems *a priori* to shelter these parasites"(190). What is at stake here is certainly not that the philosophy of law would be literature, and even less that such a philosophy's claim to authority and autonomy would be undermined, or canceled out, by the presence in its core of narrativity and fiction. First of all, with the "as if," narrativity and fiction are only said to be *almost,* more precisely, *virtually* present in the pure and, in principle, irrepresentable law. In other words, they are present as possibilities, but not as actualities. In addition, if Derrida can say that the thought of the pure law seems *a priori* to shelter narrativity and fiction, it is because he understands these possibilities to be conditions, rules, laws without which the thought of pure law becomes impossible. In short then, the pure moral law, or legal thought in general, requires with *a priori* structural necessity that it be inhabited not by narrativity, fiction, or literature, but by their virtual possibility. The philosophical, in the shape of the thought of the moral, must combine, if it is to be possible at all, with the possibility in its core of an Other—that is, here, with the literary. Apart from the fact that we encounter here a novel conception of an *a priori* condition of possibility, a novel concept as well as to how philosophy and literature relate, the dependence of the law on the possibility of fiction and narration also points to a recast conception of the universal and the singular. That this is the case should become clear as I now turn to a highly concise discussion of Derrida's elaborations on the literary status of "Before the Law."

To the question of who and what decides if Kafka's parable belongs to literature, Derrida shall give no direct answer, not, however because of some incompetence or because he would simply hold "that when it comes to literature we cannot speak of a work belonging to a field or class, that there is no such thing as a literary essence"(187). Essential reasons prohibit that the question be answered in general, universal terms, by establishing or invoking a universal law. He admits that in the position of being before "Before the Law" (as a text first of all), he is "less interested in the generality of these laws or these problematical conclusions than in the singularity of a proceeding which, in the course of a unique drama, summons these laws before an irreplacable corpus, before this very text, before *Before the Law*"(187). The essay, then, is concerned with the way such general laws fare before the tribunal of a singular text, and, in particular, before one about the law; and being before the law, more precisely, the essay is concerned with how general laws about the essence of literature—that literature has no essence, that it is not rigorously identifiable, that no criterion exists for it to be demarcated absolutely, that there is no proper name for it, etc.—are in their very generality tied up with a certain singularity. The laws in question, which are to establish the truth about literature, and be it that there is no truth to, of, or about literature, are thus summoned before a unique, irreplacable singular (text), in a proceeding *(procès)* that itself is singular, since the mode of the relating of universality to the singular, is, each time, marked by singularity as well. Derrida writes: "There is a singularity about relationship to the law, a law of singularity which must come into contact with the general or universal essence of the law without ever being able to do so"(187). As should thus be obvious, the emphasis on the inevitably singular relation to the law does not mean that there would be no universal essence of the law, but that singularity is the condition under which there can be something like a law at all, a law that is pure, nonrepresentable, and inaccessible. In "Before the Law," we thus see Derrida inquiring into "a law of singularity" that at once makes the encounter between the order of the universal and the singular possible and impossible, whereby the impossible is not to be understood as the simple negative modality of the possible. It is a law for the "conflict without encounter between law and singularity, [for] this *paradox* or *enigma* of being-before-the-law" (187). It is a law for the law to be pure, nonrepresentable, untouchable, inaccessible, and for oneself to be able to be before its universality in such a mode that it is a singular law, a law that is singular,the law for a singularity as well. As Derrida's invocation of the Greek term *ainigma* reveals, the conflict between universal law and singularity, rather than offering itself to a purely conceptual treatment and, hence, to a universally articulatable truth, has instead a narrative, storylike quality. There is, then, something irremediably singular about the conflictual nature of this relation in general.

Derrida dealt with Kafka's story "Before the Law" in his seminar on morality, not because it would be a philosophical text, but because its narrative "proposes a powerful, philosophic ellipsis," of pure practical reason, in other words, because it contains the virtual possibility of the philosophical thought of the moral law. Whereas the philosophical text of the Second Critique was shown to "contain an element of the fantastic or of narrative fiction," the literary text of "Before the Law" contains something on the order of legal thought. The distinction between the literary and the philosophical remains intact, but what transpires is that the so-called literary text of Kafka contains encrypted within it the possibility of an Other (of it), the possibility, but not actuality, of the philosophical legal discourse. This encrypted possibility of philosophical legal thought is what makes it a "literary" text in distinction from philosophy. It is *from* that encrypted possibility of the philosophical that the literarity of "Before the Law" is engendered. Kafka's text is thus a literary text on condition that it does not entirely belong to literature, but that it also refers, by means of the virtual "presence" within it of the possibility of a philosophy of the moral law, to an Other (of it).

There is no way that I could even come close to doing justice to Derrida's reading of Kafka's parable, and his multilayered analysis of the modes in which the story in question narrates a story whose content has all the allures of a philosophical topos. In order to conclude, I must nonetheless briefly speak of it. First this, however. At the beginning of the essay, Derrida raised a question which, now that we have seen him to have been concerned with understanding the specificity of the philosophical and the literary from the possibility of the Other encrypted in each of them, can be rendered in a clearer fashion. He writes: "What if the law, without being itself transfixed by literature, shared the conditions of its possibility with the literary object"(191). In making the specificity of the literary dependent on the inscription within its core, not of an Other of it, and certainly not of *its* Other, but of the possibility of an Other, Derrida continues and displaces by deepening Heidegger's thought of the relationship between *Dichten* and *Denken*. This happens in a disjoining of *Dichten* and *Denken* as a relation to a priveleged Other, and in particular by refining the way in which the encrypted relation to an Other can be thought. With the question regarding the shared condition of possibility of both literature and the law, Derrida invokes the question of what Heidegger had called the neighborhood (of poetry and thinking) intent on recasting the thought of a common ground for both them. Need I recall that this recasting will not take place in general terms but via a singular nonliterary text and a literary text, in a intimate conjunction of the categorial and the idiomatic.

As Derrida recalls, for the law to be the law, for it to have categorial authority, it "must be without history, genesis, or any possible derivation"(191). To intervene as an absolutely emergent order, the law "cannot be constituted by some history that might give rise to any story"(194). And yet, as Freud's *Totem and Taboo* demonstrates, "the inacessible incites from its place of hiding. One cannot be concerned with the law, or with the law of laws, either at close range or at a distance, without asking where it has its place and whence it comes"(191). Incited by the purely categorial thought of a law without origin, Freud invents the event of the murder of the father to explain the origin of the moral law. As Derrida shows, it is the story of an event in which nothing happens (especially since what originates from it already presupposes the moral law); it is a pure story, one that is only narration, because it narrates nothing. "If there were any history [of the moral law], it would be neither presentable nor relatable: the history of that which never took place,"(194) Derrida claims. Freud's idiomatization of the moral law through the fiction of the murder of the father is precisely this, a fiction called upon, incited by the moral law, but a fiction that annuls itself, the pure fiction of a nonevent. This fiction at the core of categorial thought—mind you, not a narrative or positive fiction, but the "fiction *of* narration as well as fiction as narration: fictive narration as the simulacrum of narration and not only as the narration of an imaginary history" (199)—is not only the origin of law, but as Derrida underlines, the origin of literature as well." With this notion of a pure fiction of a quasi-event, of a fiction in which nothing is narrated, but which the purely categorial calls upon, and thus harbors in its core, Derrida has found—within the singularizing parameters of the texts discussed—the general condition of possibility shared by both the philosophical thought of the law and literature. To share this condition of possibility does not imply that the law would be "itself transfixed (*transie*) by literature," or the other way around. This is so because, on the one hand, this condition of possibility is not yet literature, but only its possibility. On the other hand, as we now shall have to see, literature, in the proper sense, can only stage this pure fiction by simultaneously gesturing in its core toward the law. Rather than being itself this pure fiction in purity, literature, while enacting this fiction, must negotiate with the possible thought of something categorially without origin.

I return to Kafka's parable. According to Derrida, "Before the Law" tells of a law we know neither *who* nor *what* it is. Kafka's text is not a text of philosophy, science, or history. "Here one does not know the law, one has no cognitive rapport with it; it is neither a subject nor an object *before* which one could take a position." Knowing neither *who* nor *what* the law is, "this, perhaps, is where literature begins," Derrida remarks (207). But the story in question in which nothing happens, in which the threshold of the law is never crossed, and which thus seems to recount a nonevent, also relates the origin of the law to the main character's decision to adjourn his entrance into the law. In forbidding himself to pass through the gate, he not only makes the inaccesible law accessible, but also makes the law the law, and becomes a subject of the law. As a result, this seemingly pure story relating an event in which nothing takes place is pregnant with the germ of the philosophical thought of the law. In literature, then, the pure fiction that it shares as a condition of possibility with philosophy cannot not turn into, say, a call for something like the Second Critique.

A pure story, or the fiction of narration, is the condition of possiblity that literature and philosophy (philosophy as moral philosophy, more precisely), share. To quote Derrida: "the fictitious nature of this ultimate story which robs us of every event, of this pure story or story without story, has as much to do with philosophy, science, or psychoanalysis as with literature"(206). In classical terms, one could, if this were indeed possible, call this pure fiction a transcendental narration. It is pure in that it relates nothing, but as a narration it is also the condition for the idiomatization of what, in principle, is cut off from singularity, namely, the categorial. A note of caution, however, is required here. One cannot simply proceed to generalizing what has been set forth in "Before the Law." The pure story we have been told cannot be simply cut off from the texts through which it became elaborated. The question from which Derrida started, a question with a transcendental thrust, namely whether philosophy and the thought of the law share the same condition of possibility, is itself marked by singularity. In conclusion, one final quote therefore: "In order to formulate this question [*aujourd'hui*, today] in the briefest manner, I will speak of an *appearance*, in the legal sense, of the story and the law, which appear together and find themselves summoned one before the other: the story, as a certain type of *relation*, is linked to the law that it relates, appearing, in so doing, before that law, which appears before it."(191)

Notes

1. Jacques Derrida, *Acts of Literature*, ed. D. Attridge (New York: Routledge, 1992), pp.181–220. All references are to this edition.

8

Writing Resistances

Elisabeth Weber

"Tout écrivain qui, par le fait même
d'écrire, n'est pas conduit à penser: je
suis la révolution, seule la liberté me
fait écrire, en réalité n'écrit pas.
— Maurice Blanchot"[1]

In his text "Freud and the Scene of Writing" Jacques Derrida states: "Writing is unthinkable without repression"(*L'écriture est impensable sans le refoulement).* Analyzing Freud's "Note upon the 'Mystic Writing-Pad' ", he comments upon the Freudian notion of censorship:

> It is no accident that the metaphor of censorship should come from the area of politics concerned with the deletions, blanks and disguises of writing, even if, at the beginning of the *Traumdeutung,* Freud seems to make only a conventional, didactic reference to it. The apparent exteriority of political censorship refers to an essential censorship which binds the writer to his own writing. *(L'apparente extériorité de la censure politique renvoie à une censure essentielle qui lie l'écrivain à sa propre écriture.)*[2]

If writing is unthinkable without repression (in the Freudian sense of this word that translates *Verdrängung),* if consequently it is unthinkable without the resistances "which, earlier, made the material concerned into something repressed by rejecting it from the conscious"[3]; if writing is unthinkable without these resistances that earlier produced and now protect repression, then an "essen-

125

tial censorship ... binds the writer to his own writing" and imposes its authority on him or her.[4] In other words, writing would then emerge from another "navel" of the "unknown"[5], from the unknown of something that will *remain* other and resist any analysis. Writing would be, through repression and resistances, that is, through the "essential censorship", necessarily located at an extreme point that could be described with Gilles Deleuze's words as "the outermost edge of one's knowledge":

One writes only at the outermost edge of one's knowledge, at this extreme point that separates our knowledge from our ignorance, and *that changes the one into the other*. It is only in this way that one is determined to write. To remedy ignorance means to postpone writing to tomorrow, rather, to make it impossible. Perhaps this is a relation even more threatening than the one that writing is said to maintain with death, with silence.[6]

Three hypotheses: First, writing emerges at the extreme point of the absence of knowlegde, the extreme unknowable, the extreme of the unknown into which the known may change and out of which it may emerge, because this point is the point of extreme resistance. If the tension between writing and the extreme point of knowledge and ignorance, that is, of resistance, is more threatening than the relation between writing and death or silence, it is, second hypothesis, because this extreme point is located at the navel or the scar of the origin of writing, the scar of this original knot and plot called repression and resistance. The threat or danger of writing lies less in its link to death and silence than in its essential link to repression and censorship, because, third hypothesis, death and silence inhabit writing as residents of a state, residents possibly alien, but declared and legal, and, above all, indispensable for the state's economy, whereas the extreme point of non-knowledge, by concentrating repression and resistance not only gives birth to the constituting borders of the state, but threatens them also from its extremity which is neither outside nor inside. It accumulates on its extremely condensed space the highest concentration of potential explosives, threatening the state's (that is its own) economy and all the economies related to it: the economies of silence, of desire, of lack.

If writing emerges from the "navel" of the "unknown," of what resists analysis (possibly at the same time mobilizing, that is, amplifying or weakening resistance), its effects, stemming from the Other, are consequently incalculable: Nothing will absolutely prevent writing from causing the repression and the resistances of the other to resound, for example, the repression and the resistances of this other that is the reader. Which means that it would mobilize, that is amplify or weaken, his resistances. If writing emerges from that unknown other, if, to come back to Derrida's text, the "origin of the work itself" is "at stake" in the "war and the ruses perpetrated by the author who reads and by the first reader who dictates," namely the war that constitutes *at the same moment* censorship and writing,[7] then nothing can prevent writing from becoming an incalculable threat, an unforeseen aggression.[8] My purpose would be to approach through a series of hypotheses this statement: writing as an aggression.

Let us begin again. It is, as Derrida writes, an "essential censorship which binds the writer to his own writing." The writer is bound to this essential censorship which consequently is the "navel" of his writing: he is bound to it because it makes him write. He is bound to that "scar" that makes him write and that is a "knot that no analysis can resolve," as Derrida writes in his recent text "Résistances".[9] Thus, the writer is absolutely bound to a resistance that cannot be overcome, he would not write outside of it. He would not write outside that other inside him: "Any resistance presupposes a tension, and first of all an internal tension. But since a purely internal tension is impossible, it is an absolute inherence of the other or of the outside in the heart of the internal and auto-affective tension."[10] The danger, the threat, the aggression of writing lies in this strange and constitutive infiltration of internal resistance from the outside, from the extreme outside that constitutes the inside, constituting resistance by attacking it. But inspite of the metaphors of war and guerilla tactics, the aggression is an absolutely subtle, imperceptible one, which however makes it all the more threatening. Maurice Blanchot has described it as follows:

Absent sense (and not the absence of sense or a potential or latent but lacking sense). To write is perhaps to bring to the surface something like absent sense, to welcome the passive pressure which is not yet what we call thought, for it is already the disastrous ruin of thought.[11]

Absent sense, Blanchot writes explicitly, is not a "potential or latent but lacking sense." Absent sense, brought to the surface through writing, is possibly more threatening than writing's relation to death and silence, since it is *not yet* thought and *already* thought's ruin. It is a third term blurring the opposition between presence and absence, since through writing it emerges from the scar, the navel of unknowing without being transformed by writing into "present" sense. My hypothesis would be that it is absent sense that mobilizes by amplifying or by weakening the resistances of the other, for instance the reader. The "disastrous ruin of thought" puts into question the (illusionary) union of power and desire. The scar, the knot of the unknowable navel, the knot of resistances causes, through writing, absent sense that ruins thought as power to emerge. And this is the most frightening threat, the most unacceptable aggression, because it ruins the economy of desire insofar as the latter is defined by power and lack of power. It is surely the most gentle threat, extreme gentleness, extreme *douceur*, but its extremeness is the aggression. The "authority of writing" resides nowhere else than in this extremeness that is aggression. When Maurice Blanchot changes Simone Weil's sentence that says "*there is, in my view, no grandeur except in gentleness*" to "nothing extreme except through gentleness *(douceur)*. Madness through excess of gentleness, gentle madness. To think, to be effaced: the disaster of gentleness,"[12] when he changes Weil's sentence in that way, he obeys an extreme that menaces not only the sovereignty of thought and reason and all their resistances ("gentle madness"), but threatens also the social constructions based on that sovereignty and the order it imposes onto desire. For the "disastrous ruin of thought" that Blanchot characterizes as "thought's patience,"[13] has a social, if not political consequence: "Between the disaster and the other there would be the contact, the disjunction of absent sense—friendship."[14] And he goes on: "An absent sense would maintain 'the affirmation' of a push pushing beyond loss *[poussée au-delà de la perte]*, the pressure of dying *[poussée de mourir]* that bears loss off with it.

Lost loss." The affirmation of an "absent," but not "lacking sense" which would be brought to the surface by writing, is the ruin of thought as presence, the ruin of the "obstinate desire to save presence"[15] and of the obsession to lose presence, the ruin of thought defined as presence and thus as power; it is the disaster of desire defined as power, the ruin of an economy defining desire in terms of power or lack of power, in other words, the ruin of the oedipal economy. My hypothesis would be that the unacceptable aggression of writing is its subtle, irresistible, unbearable aggression against the oedipal economy that for instance determines sons and fathers as rivals, that is, as winners and losers in the struggle for possession of mother's love, and that defines desire in the categories of capitalist competition, in other words, in terms of the family's economy,[16] or, still in other words, in terms of loss and lack. It is undeniable that there is a desire for this economy, there is a desire for this economy's desire, in other words, there is the desire for oedipal desire, there is a desire for the father, and thus for the mother, for their omnipresence, authority, punishment and desire—and this may be even today or perhaps especially today one of the constituents of the navel of the unknown, of the unanalyzable resistance. That's perhaps why Blanchot describes "the contact, the disjunction of absent sense" as "friendship" and not as "desire." Perhaps he does not mention "desire" here because it is poisoned by all the overdeterminations of oedipal wishes and lacks; and because, inside *their* economy, there is, as Freud pointed out, room exclusively for one "libido," namely the male libido that Lacan described as phallic desire, a position towards the other that not only men, but also women can occupy.[17] "Friendship" then could be here the word not for the negation or sublimation of desire, nor for the absence or lack of desire, but for a desire beyond loss and lack, a desire not denying but going beyond its oedipal determinations of never-ending loss: "An absent sense would maintain 'the affirmation' of a push pushing beyond loss, the pressure of dying that bears loss off with it. Lost loss."

Absent, not lacking sense: the space kept free in order to allow us to count to three and beyond, the space kept open that allows us to desire beyond the Oedipus-complex, since "Oedipus" means, in the end, always a love for myself, the fight for mom's or dad's exclusive love for me, my love exclusively for them, in short, an endless mirroring of my love for myself or for those whom I resemble. That is why the open space of absent sense has to be kept open, without occupation, without appropriation.

The oedipal economy is defined by possession and loss, the threat of loss always being a threat of death; the haunting of loss being exorcized by the possession of those who are said to have definitively lost (women) and, since they nonetheless survive, are phantasmatically bestowed the power to put to death. But sometimes, writing, through bringing to the surface "absent sense" or "lost loss," shatters desire as a question of possession and loss and consequently affects and shatters an economy of death governed by the same opposition. "Right from the pledge which binds together two desires, writes Derrida, each is already in mourning for the other, entrusts death to the other as well: if you die before me, I will keep you, if I die before you, you will carry me in yourself, one will keep the other, will already have kept the other from the first declaration."[18] The "absolute certainty" of the fact "that one must die before the other. One of them must see the other die"[19] rules over "the contact, the disjunction" of absent sense and thus of desire. The extreme, unbearable vulnerability, the extreme *douceur* of this mourning for the other "from the first declaration," its extreme gentleness are nothing but affirmation.

"Absent sense" then has to be conceived "without *nostalgia*; . . . it must be conceived outside the myth of the purely maternal or paternal language belonging to the lost fatherland of thought. On the contrary, we must *affirm* it,"[20] as Derrida writes already in *Speech and Phenomena*. Its absence is perhaps located at the empty space of a law that announces an "ethics, converted to silence, through the avenue not of terror, but of desire"[21]. Texts like Derrida's *Glas, The Postcard, Cinders, Circumfession*, but also others make of writing this extremely gentle and thus unbearable aggression that bears witness to the "lost loss," to an "absent", not lacking sense, to the affirmation of another economy of desire. They confront us with resistances, they literally write on resistances; and nothing can guarantee that these—our—resistances will not, some day, explode and suddenly expose a "burning tomb in the middle of grass."[22]

According to Mallarmé, quoted by Blanchot,"*[t]here is no explosion except a book.*"[23] There is no explosion except writing.

Notes

1. "Every writer who through the mere fact of writing does not think 'I am the revolution, nothing but freedom makes me write', in fact does not write." Maurice Blanchot, "La littérature et le droit à la mort", in: *La part du feu*, Paris, Gallimard, 1949, p. 311.
2. *Writing and Difference*, trans. by Alan Bass, The University of Chicago Press, 1978, p. 226.
3. Sigmund Freud, "The Unconscious", in: *The Standard Edition of the Complete Psychological Works of Sigmund Freud*, trans. under the general editorship of James Strachey (SE), vol. XIV, London: The Hogarth Press and the Institute of Psycho-Analysis 1957, p. 166. Cf. also SE vol. XVI (1916–1917): *Introductory Lectures on Psycho-Analysis* (part III), London 1963, Lecture XIX: "Resistance and Repression", p. 293–294.
4. This juxtaposition of "resistance" and "censorship" requires some explanation. In his *Seminar, Book II* (*The Ego in Freud's Theory and in the Technique of Psychoanalysis* 1954–1955, trans. by S. Tomaselli, New York, London: W. W. Norton 1988), Jacques Lacan claims that "censorship has nothing to do with resistance". According to Lacan, "the subject's resistance is linked to the ego's register", censorship, on the other hand, is "always related to whatever, in discourse, is linked to the law in so far as it is not understood" (p. 127). A little later however, Lacan has to modify such a strict separation of the two concepts: "The resistance is everything which is opposed, in a general sense, to the work of analysis. Censorship is a special qualification of this resistance." (p. 134) Indeed, in Freud's writings, the distinction between resistance and censorship is not sharply drawn, and it is in fact rather blurred when he speaks for example of the "resistance of the censorship" *("Widerstandszensur")* (SE, vol. V, p. 530) or the "censorship imposed by resistance" *("Widerstandszensur")* (ibid., p. 499, 542, 563). In his *Introductory Lectures on Psycho-Analysis*, Freud describes the repression as the work of a "watchman", who "acts as a censor". "It is the same watchman whom we get to know as resistance when we try to lift the repression by means of the analytic treatment." (SE, vol. XVI, loc. cit., p. 295–6). Many other examples could be given. An even more important point remains to be made. In

"The Unconscious" (SE XIV, loc. cit.), Freud writes (p. 173): ". . . the rigorous censorship exercises its office at the point of transition from the Ucs. to the Pcs. (or Cs.)." P. 180: "We have arrived at the conclusion that repression is essentially a process affecting ideas on the border between the systems Ucs. and Pcs. (Cs.) . . . ." One sees that censorship as well as repression is situated at the same frontier. The difficulty in distinguishing them is possibly due to the fact that this border is also the border of the "translation into words" of the presentations (Vorstellungen). What repression "denies to the presentation is translation into words which shall remain attached to the object. A presentation which is not put into words, or a psychical act which is not hypercathected, remains thereafter in the Ucs. in a state of repression." (p. 202). The censorship could then be described as the action that literally "blacks out" the words (cf. SE, vol. V, p. 529), and the resistance as the force that protects these 'blanks' from becoming legible again. What Derrida calls "essential censorship" would be a blank that cannot be given back to meaning because it has never been "blacked out," but rather belongs to an irreducible "absent sense" (cf. below).

5. Freud uses this famous expression in order to characterize the limits of the interpretation of dreams. Cf. SE, vol. IV and V: *The Interpretation of Dreams*, London 1953, p. 111, footnote, and 525. See also Jacques Derrida, "Résistances", in: *La Notion d'analyse*, Toulouse: Presses Universitaires du Mirail 1992, p. 45 ff.

6. "On n'écrit qu'à la pointe de son savoir, à cette pointe extrême qui sépare notre savoir et notre ignorance, *et qui fait passer l'un dans l'autre*. C'est seulement de cette façon qu'on est déterminé à écrire. Combler l'ignorance, c'est remettre l'écriture à demain, ou plutôt la rendre impossible. Peut-être y a-t-il là un rapport de l'écriture encore plus menaçant que celui qu'elle est dite entretenir avec la mort, avec le silence." Gilles Deleuze, *Différence et répétition*, Paris, P.U.F., 1968, p. 4.

7. *Writing and Difference*, op. cit., p. 227. Derrida emphasizes that this is a war to which any " 'sociology of literature' is blind". Consequently the "origin of the work" is dissiminated, which means that "the 'subject' of writing does not exist if we mean by that some sovereign solitude of the author" (ibid., p. 226).

8. See Gilles Deleuze: "Il appartient au simulacre, non pas d'être une copie, mais de renverser toutes les copies, en renversant *aussi* les modèles: toute pensée devient une agression." (*Différence et répétition*, op. cit., p. 3)

9. "Résistances", op. cit., p. 46.

10. Ibid., p. 58.

11. Maurice Blanchot, *The Writing of the Disaster*, trans. by Ann Smock, Lincoln & London: University of Nebraska Press, 1986, p. 41. I trans-

late "sens absent" with "absent sense" and not as Ann Smock with "absent meaning". Smock however chooses to render one of the occurences of "sens" in the parenthesis with "sense."

12. Ibid., pp. 6–7.
13. Ibid., p. 41.
14. Ibid.
15. Jacques Derrida, *Speech and Phenomena*, trans. David B. Allison, Evanston, Northwestern University Press, 1973, p. 51.
16. See Joseph Vogl's book on Kafka: *Ort der Gewalt. Kafkas literarische Ethik*, Munich: Fink, 1991.
17. Cf. Jacques Lacan, *Le Séminaire, Livre XX: Encore*, Paris, Seuil 1975, p. 67, 70, 74.
18. J. Derrida, "Aphorism Countertime", in J. D., *Acts of Literature*, ed. by Derek Attridge, New York, London: Routledge, 1992, p. 422.
19. Ibid.
20. J. Derrida, *Speech and Phenomena*, op. cit., p. 159.
21. Jacques Lacan, *Écrits*, Paris, Seuil 1966, p. 684, and *Le Séminaire, Livre VII: L'Éthique de la psychanalyse*, Paris, Seuil 1986. It is thus a fundamental misunderstanding to identify the Law with interdiction, with a forbidding, prohibiting agency. As Juranville points out, for Lacan, the Oedipus complex is "Freud's dream" (Alain Juranville, *Lacan et la philosophie*, Paris, second edition, P.U.F. 1988, p. 199). Lacanian theory can certainly be criticized on several accounts, but its crucial notion of the Law can scarcely be reduced to the menace, the instillation of fear that some symbolic despotic agency would exercise on its tortured subjects. In Lacanian terms this interpretation of the law is nothing short of the neurotic interpretation of castration (cf. Juranville, *Lacan et la philosophie*, pp. 206–207). For Lacan, the law is not the paternal or oedipal interdiction (cf. for ex. Lacan, *Le Séminaire, Livre VII: L'Éthique . . .*, p. 358: "L'intériorisation de la Loi, nous ne cessons de le dire, n'a rien à faire avec la Loi," pp.362, 364; see also *Écrits*, p. 826: "Le névrosé se figure que l'Autre demande sa castration"). But this would be the subject of another text.
22. J. Derrida, "Fors", in: Nicolas Abraham and Maria Torok, *Cryptonomie: Le verbier de l'Homme aux loups*, Paris: Aubier Flammarion, p. 73.
23. Stéphane Mallarmé, quoted by Blanchot, *The Writing of the Disaster*, op. cit., p. 7.

9

Presentness and the "Being-Only-Once" of Architecture

Peter Eisenman

In her book, *The Optical Unconscious* (1993), Rosalind Krauss discusses a Jackson Pollock painting in relationship to its position in space. She contends that when a Pollock painting is placed in a horizontal position, that is, on the floor as it was painted, it is a "savage work". But the moment the canvas is taken off of the floor and moved to a vertical position on the wall, Krauss continues, it becomes "naturalized," reinstitutionalized and reinscribed into the discourse of painting.

All of this is said with an uncharacteristic innocence about the possible effect of the floor or the wall on this change in perception. She assumes that one can lift things up and down, off and on, without any discussion of why the relationship between floor or wall, or, for that matter between the floor or the wall and the painting, could cause this to happen. What is clear in Krauss's argument is that the contexts provided by architecture, in this case the floor and the wall, do effect how the subject conceptualizes a painting. Yet the issue of how or why such an effect is possible is not discussed. Such an omission is by no means unique to Krauss's argument. Most of those outside of architecture assume that architectural conventions have a thought to be naturalness with respect to such things as walls and floors. Jacques Derrida even points out that we must be wary of the idea that architecture "is destined for habitation," that the concept of architecture is "a heritage which comprehends us even before we could submit it to thought." Walter Benjamin also attempts to explain this idea of "destined for habitation" in a different way. He says in "architecture, habit determines to a large extent even optical reception. Architecture cannot be understood by optical means alone, that is by contemplation. It is mastered gradually by habit." Thus in one sense the wall is already seen in any specific context by habit. This could be responsible for the naturalizing of the Pollock painting, since it is known that all paintings by force of habit are hung on walls and not on floors. Clearly, the question of habit and the habitual is already predetermined when dwellings are called places of habitation as opposed to say places of occupation. But this assumption of habit alone, it will be argued here, is not enough to account for the naturalizing effect of the wall on the Pollock painting. Nor can the ideas of an a priori destiny or naturalness, the assumption that "this is the way things are," be the only cause of this effect. Clearly something else must be at work. And it is this something else that makes architecture a problematic discourse.

The very conditions that bring about this idea of an a priori destiny or a thought to be naturalness of architecture, and thus what makes architecture problematic, lie initially in the fact that architecture is alone of all the discourses in its particular linking of its iconicity with its instrumentality, its meaning with its objecthood. A wall in architecture is not merely holding something up, it also symbolizes that act of holding up. Architecture, Derrida says, "cannot be without meaning." One cannot have the wall without the sign of the wall and vice versa; architecture will always implicate the wall. When Vitruvius, in his famous dicta on architecture, used the term *firmitas*, he did not mean that buildings should stand up (since, of necessity, all buildings must stand up) but rather that they should look like they stand up. It has been argued that in all disciplines instrumentality in some way affects iconicity; for example, the form of a book, its pagination, type, and binding all affect our reading of the text, but not all texts are necessarily in book form. Yet in architecture there will always be the presence of walls, walls that are both icon and instrument. It is this unique linkage that becomes problematic, because in order to "deconstruct" the meaning of architecture, one must attempt to separate the presence of the wall from the meaning of the wall— what in fact cannot be separated. Thus, unlike any other discourse, architecture both resists and requires the deconstructive impulse. This resistance alone should be of interest to deconstructive thought.

In addition to the strong connection between iconicity and instrumentality, architecture also has a unique relationship to what Jacques Derrida refers to in *The Truth in Painting* (1987) as the "once only" of a work of art. The condition of this "once only" at work in architecture is not the same as it is in painting or in photography. Derrida poses the issue of the "being-only-once" of a work of art as the fault line of deconstruction in its relationship to painting and photography. He cites Walter Benjamin, and says, "as soon as the technique of reproduction reaches the stage of photography a break line and also a new front traverses the whole space of art. The presumed uniqueness of production, the 'being-only-once' of the exemplar and the value of authenticity, is practically deconstructed." Therefore it could be argued that the work of deconstruction has as one of its objects the notion of the displacement of the original, the prior condition of either a painting or a photograph.

In terms of photography, the being-only-once formerly devolved upon the issue of the original photographic plate in relation to the serial print. The plate is manipulated in development to produce a serial work which bears the mark of the hand of the author as well as that of the process. For example, a photograph can be developed with more or less grain, more or less contrast, and more or less light and intensity. Under these circumstances, the value of the photographic object relies both on the quality of the original plate and the quality of the reproduction as well as the limited seriality of the reproduction. The number one-of-ten is of more value to a collector than the number two-of-ten. There is a prior value given to the closeness of the copy in time to the plate which in this case is the being-only-once. The use of the plate and the collection of the plate—whether plates are destroyed or not—

defines the problematic of originality in the era of mechanical reproduction.

When one moves from the mechanical paradigm to the electronic paradigm another issue enters in. Conditions are no longer the same for the photograph (it should be noted that for the sake of this argument only the question of replication in photography and not in painting is at issue). The possibility of an electronically reproduced photograph becomes interesting in this context as it represents the ultimate deconstruction of the original. Now, instead of a plate, a physical negative, there are only electronic impulses, ones and zeros—impulses of light. The object no longer contains being, but only exists as contiguous electronic impulses; there is no longer a being-only-once. This erasure of the being-only-once that is proposed by the digitized photograph has several consequences. At one and the same time it turns the mediation that was present in the photograph from a condition of self-similarity to self-sameness. For it is possible to digitize a photograph in such a way as to reproduce it so that even an expert cannot tell if it was the first instance or the second. In digitized reproduction the self-same characteristic is so strong that it is impossible to discern the difference even with a so-called expert mediating eye. In other words, all of the potential subjective characteristics of the being-only-once are erased. But equally, the converse is true.

Formerly, one was able to trust a photograph for documentary evidence. For example, if one wanted to buy a Rembrandt, verifying that the Rembrandt was authenticated by a signature could be done through a photograph. Therefore, a self-same photograph would become the most objective record that one could have. But the digitized photograph—the new self-same record—is now most open to mediation, and thus to being manipulated. It is possible to change a photograph of an original painting, an original that did not have a Rembrandt signature, by putting in such a signature without anyone being able to detect that the photograph had been doctored. It would thus appear that the evidence originally there was in fact not. In the digitizing process two things happen. First, there is a collapse of the idea of the being-only-once as the idea of the original or the authentic, and second, the role of the hand of the author, which formerly was a distinguishing characteristic between an objectifying and a subjectifying process, also becomes blurred. These two processes become, as it were, superposed over one another; time and space as the limits of difference are erased. In fact, it can be argued that they deconstruct one another because there is no longer the possibility that the photograph can be relied on for objective truth. But equally the digitized photograph bears no trace of its process, and thus it is no longer possible to tell if there was any authorial mediation. In fact the digitized photograph becomes simultaneously subject to the most mediation and to the least mediation.

This produces a condition whereby the mediation of the author is seen within a different spectrum. It either takes place, on the one end, as the traditional art object, with its value in presence, or, at the other, as the nihilistic gesture of the erasure of the object and the authorial trace. This spectrum of discourse, it can be argued, is only possible in print media—that is, where the possibility of repetition and replication is at issue. This is not the case with architecture.

The discourse of replication, and thus the question of the original, would seem not to be at issue in built architecture. That a building is always a unique instance would be the argument of conventional wisdom. But before this can be assumed, one must first put aside the unique relationship that built work has to its drawing (which in its more general consequences is a broader issue that will not be discussed here). Often times the drawing of architecture is more of an original than the work of architecture: as when Palladio redraws all of his buildings as they were designed to be, rather than as they were built; or when Daniel Libeskind in his Micromegas Project draws an architecture that is not intended to be built; or when Piranesi draws, in his Carceri series, architectures that could never be built. In each of these examples the drawing of architecture becomes an original instance, and thus questions the simplistic view of building as an example of a being-only-once. But it is not the instance of building that is intended here as the reference for this unique being-only-once of architecture. While in one sense the built work, in its site and programmatic specificity, is always a unique instance, this is again an overly determined answer, one that does not speak to a condition that can be considered unique in architecture.

Derrida himself comes closer to defining this unique condition when he says that architecture is more like the idea of an event, which "reinvents architecture in a series of 'only onces' which are always unique in their repetition." This idea overlays replication with the idea of the unique, that architecture can be replicated, and that this replication is always unique. This quality of the unique is brought about by the fact that architecture always demands presence. While it is possible to challenge the idea of the presence of an object with regard to works of photography, and clearly to works of other written, mediated discourses on tape or on film, it is not as simple to challenge in architecture.

While deconstruction seems to take into consideration the idea that architecture, unlike painting and photography, is a highly conventionalized system; and while it may be possible to loosen architecture's relationship to its instrumentality, that is, to loosen the relationship between form and function, it is impossible to deny architecture's metaphysics of presence. Even in a condition of virtual reality, architecture is conventionalized as the metaphysics of presence; within virtual reality, architecture is still imagined as a physical body. It is this metaphysics of presence which dominates any discussion of architecture. Therefore, in order to propose a deconstruction of architecture it is necessary to propose something that can overcome this dominance of presence.

It will be argued here that this unique conventionality of architecture, which links its iconicity and instrumentality, already contains the capacity to open up and separate its condition of presence from its meaning. This opening up creates a possibility for another condition of being-only-once. That is, once the separation of the thought to be natural and normative conditions of architecture is proposed, there is the possibility of another being-only-once, which can be seen as the opposite of the deconstruction of the being-only-once in painting. And it is the deconstruction of this natural relationship that puts into place another being-only-once that is unique to architecture. This condition can be properly called *presentness*.

Presentness can be defined in several different ways. First, the term should not be confused with Michael Fried's use of a term with the same name. According to Rosalind Krauss, presentness for Fried is a "reinscribing of modernism within a historic metaphysic." For Fried, presentness was a moment which collapsed time into the inexorable present, where there was no difference between thinking and experience. For Derrida, experience is something outside of, or different from, this time frame. The event for Derrida, i.e., the time frame of the moment, requires the "writing of a space," a mode of spacing which distinguishes the space of the event from the time of the event. My use of the term *presentness* also begins from an idea of spacing, a spacing which is required in the loosening of the relationship of the architectural object from its thought-to-be natural condition of instrumentality. Thus in one sense, *presentness*, as I conceive it, is precisely the opposite of the Fried definition. As Krauss points out, the central concept of the phenomenology of self-presence requires an undivided unity of a temporal present, that is, between the object and the sign. Precisely because this relationship is so predetermined in architecture, the term *presentness* offers a means to loosen the inexorable relationship of the architectural object from its thought to be natural condition of instrumentality.

If *presentness* is such an occupied term, why the insistence on its use? More than any other term it combines both the idea of time in presence, of the experience of space in the present, while at the same time its suffix *-ness* causes a distance between the object as presence, which is a given in architecture, and the quality of that presence as time, which may be something other than mere presence. This creates the idea of a spacing between presence and the quality of presentness. However, this does not in any way implicate two other characteristics of presentness: that is, its quality of an already given and its capacity to render that already given as necessarily subversive. These latter two characteristics, unique to architecture, also distinguish *presentness* from Derrida's use of the term *maintenant,* which in many respects may be seen as similar. Maintenant, while implicating both time and space, in its idea of maintaining does not demand the quality of subversion as a prior condition to any transformation, which, it is argued here, is a necessary condition of architecture. It is precisely the subversion of the type and the norm, of the thought to be natural relationship between icon and instrument that creates architecture's being-only-once. As long as the instrumentality of architecture is seen to be its form and its function—whether that function is its site, program, or structure, and its form is its aesthetic, style, or iconography—and as long as this thought to be natural condition is seen as a two-term system, it represses the possibility of presentness.

The importance of presentness as a term for architecture is that it distinguishes a writing from an instrumentality of aesthetics and meaning. Presentness as a writing is the possibility of a subversion of the thought to be convention of type in architecture; that architecture has within it an insidedness which is an already existing possibility for the subversive. Presentness is both the possibility of, if not the need for, architecture to stabilize itself through the reabsorption of the transformation of type brought about by this subversion, and the simultaneous resistance to this reabsorption. This insidedness as a writing is both a trace of this already given and the possibility to experience this trace in space. Trace is the possibility of the subversion of a primordial type, which itself is constantly being transformed over time to become, at any given time in the history of architecture, the then existing convention of type. To achieve this subversion, architecture must always overcome the normative typological and social gestures that, at any given time, attempt to maintain its status quo. Architecture only continues and maintains itself precisely because of this subversive impulse to produce its being-only-once. For example, in Michelangelo's Laurentian Library there is a subversion of the type-form of the then existing library type. Because to this day this subversion has not been absorbed into the library type, that is, the library type has not transformed itself to include the subversion of the more general type manifest in the specific instance of presentness in the Laurentian Library, it still retains the same affective charge, the presentness of its being-only-once, that it had in the 16th century. Thus while part of this idea of presentness obviously deals with the condition of the new and the time of the new, it also deals with the time of duration, that is, with the subversion of presence as trace. Clearly when Michelangelo sub-

Figure 1. Le Corbusier, Chapel at Ronchamp, France.

verted the type-form of the library in his Laurentian project, it was a subversion also of the existing style of architecture, and in that sense it was also new. The fact that today one experiences this duration of presentness (and this is a condition of experience and not so much of drawing) means that the subversion has been a continuous one that has not been absorbed into the conventional instrumentality of architecture.

This idea of presentness as a being-only-once unique to architecture, that is, as a subversion of type, can also be seen if one takes two late projects by Le Corbusier, the chapel at Ronchamp (Fig. 1) and the monastery at La Tourette (Fig. 2), both of which contained at the time of their building a presentness. It could be argued that Ronchamp only contained a presentness of the new, that is, that it was theatrical and performative. While it affected experience because of its newness, it did nothing to displace the instrumentality of type in the notion of the church. It is precisely

Figure 2. Le Corbusier, La Tourette Monastery at Arbresle, France.

the theatricality of the gestures of Ronchamp that have been reabsorbed in architecture, so that today the presentness of Ronchamp is no longer what it was. However, at La Tourette presentness was brought about by the subversion of both typeform and icon. There was a new idea of what it was to be a monastery. At La Tourette this condition of presentness remains in place today because the dislocation of the type has not been reabsorbed in the conventional idea of the monastery type. It still remains a displacement, a subversion of the condition of the type that had formerly existed. This same idea could also be argued in my own work, for example in the Wexner Center (Fig. 3) in Columbus, Ohio, and in the Convention Center (Fig. 4) in the same city. The Wexner Center is an example of presentness precisely because it subverts the instrumentality and iconicity of the museum, whereas the Columbus Convention Center is more theatrical and does not involve the subversion of type (in fact, it involves the

Figure 3. Peter Eisenman, Wexner Center for the Visual Arts, Columbus, Ohio.

maintenance of type), and therefore will be less articulate in the future as a condition of presentness.

If architecture is a unique condition of discourse where the sign and the signified are more closely linked than in any other discourse, presentness is a way of opening up what is repressed in architecture's assumed to be natural instrumentality of form and function, or of meaning and function. Presentness requires the constant subversion of this instrumentality in order to write an architecture as a trace of presence within presence. This becomes particularly critical within the terms of an electronic paradigm, where the former boundaries that maintained any discourse are blurred. As in contemporary physics and biology, where the hegemony of cause and effect has been undermined, so too the cause and effect of architecture, form and function, presence and absence, could be opened up by a condition of presentness.

Architecture can neither merely return to a dialectic of the

Figure 4. Peter Eisenman, Greater Columbus Convention Center, Columbus, Ohio.

metaphysics of presence nor return to a nihilism which denies presence. Presentness is an alternative term that does not force a choice between these two. It could be argued that, since presentness is an already given of architecture, it has always been potentially active in the problematic of architecture, but, because of the bond between icon and instrument, presentness has tended to be repressed by these. It could further be argued that the resistance of architecture to, and its simultaneous need for, a being-only-once would allow deconstruction to think its discourse through architecture in a way that it could not in other modes of being. This would allow one to say that architecture, in its resistance to deconstruction, also requires deconstruction, and that architecture provides a space different from the space of language, literature, or painting that could be an effective means for deconstruction to rethink itself today.

IV

The Performance of Difference

10

Burning Acts: Injurious Speech[1]

Judith Butler

The title of J. L. Austin's *How to Do Things With Words* poses the
question of performativity as what it means to say that "things
might be done with words." The problem of performativity is thus
immediately bound up with a question of transitivity. What does
it mean for a word not only to name, but also in some sense to
perform and, in particular, to perform what it names? On the one
hand, it may seem that the word—for the moment we do not
know which word or which kind of word—enacts what it names;
where the "what" of "what it names" remains distinct from the
name itself and the performance of that "what." After all, Austin's
title questions how to do things *with* words, suggesting that words
are instrumentalized in getting things done. Austin, of course,
distinguishes between illocutionary and perlocutionary acts of
speech, between actions that are performed by virtue of words,
and those that are performed as a consequence of words. The
distinction is tricky, and not always stable. According to the perlocutionary view, words are instrumental to the accomplishment of
actions, but they are not themselves the actions which they help
to accomplish. This form of the performative suggests that the
words and the things done are in no sense the same. But according
to his view of the illocutionary speech act, the name performs
itself, and in the course of that performing becomes a thing done;
the pronouncement is the act of speech at the same time that it is

149

the speaking of an act. Of such an act, one cannot reasonably ask for a "referent," since the effect of the act of speech is not to refer beyond itself, but to perform itself, producing a strange enactment of linguistic immanence.

The title of Austin's manual, *How to Do Things With Words*, suggests that there is a perlocutionary kind of doing, a domain of things done, and then an instrumental field of "words," indeed, that there is also a deliberation that precedes that doing, and that the words will be distinct from the things that they do.

But what happens if we read that title with an emphasis on the illocutionary form of speech, asking instead what it might mean for a word "to do" a thing, where the doing is less instrumental than it is transitive. Indeed, what would it mean for a thing to be "done by" a word or, for that matter, for a thing to be "done in by" a word? When and where, in such a case, would such a thing become disentangled from the word by which it is done or done in, and where and when would that conjunction between word and thing appear indissoluble? If a word in this sense might be said to "do" a thing, then it appears that the word not only signifies a thing, but that this signification will also be an enactment of the thing. It seems here that the meaning of a performative act is to be found in this apparent coincidence of signifying and enacting.

And yet, it seems that this "act-like" quality of the performative is itself an achievement of a different order, and that de Man was clearly on to something when he asked whether a trope is not animated at the moment when we claim that language "acts," that language posits itself in a series of distinct acts, and that its primary function might be understood as this kind of periodic acting. Significantly, I think, the common translation of Nietzsche's account of the metaleptic relation between doer and deed rests on a certain confusion about the status of the "deed." For even there, Nietzsche will claim that certain forms of morality require a subject and institute a subject as the consequence of that requirement. This subject will be installed as prior to the deed in order to assign blame and accountability for the painful effects of a certain action. A being is hurt, and the vocabulary that emerges to moralize that pain is one which isolates a subject as the intentional originator of an injurious deed; Nietzsche understands this, first, as the moralization by which pain and injury are rendered equivalent and, second, as the production of a domain of painful effects suffused with conjectured intention. At such a moment the subject is not only fabricated as the prior and causal origin of a painful effect that is recast as an injury, but the action whose effects are injurious is no longer an action, the continuous present of a doing, but is reduced to a 'singular act.'

The following citation from *On the Genealogy of Morals* is usually read with an emphasis on the retroactive positing of the doer prior to the deed; but note that simultaneous with this retroactive positing is a moral resolution of a continuous "doing" into a periodic "deed": "there is no 'being' behind doing, effecting, becoming; 'the doer' is merely a fiction added to the deed—the deed is everything". ". . . es gibt kein 'Sein' hinter dem Tun, Wirken, Werden; 'der Täter' ist zum Tun blos hinzugedichtet—das Tun ist alles." In the German, there is no reference to an "act"—*die Tat*—but only to *a doing*, "das Tun," and to the word for a culprit or wrong-doer, "der Täter," which translates merely as a "doer."[2] Here the very terms by which "doing" is retroactively fictionalized *(hinzugedichtet)* as the intentional effect of a "subject," establishes the notion of a "doer" primarily as a wrong-doer. Furthermore, in order to attribute accountability to a subject, an origin of action in that subject is fictively secured. In the place of a "doing" there appears the grammatical and juridical constraint on thought by which a subject is produced first and foremost as the accountable originator of an injurious deed. A moral causality is thus set up between the subject and its act such that both terms are separated off from a more temporally expansive "doing" that appears to be prior and oblivious to these moral requirements.

For Nietzsche, the subject appears only as a consequence of a demand for accountability; a set of painful effects is taken up by a moral framework that seeks to isolate the "cause" of those effects in a singular and intentional agent, a moral framework that operates through a certain economy of paranoid fabrication and efficiency. *The question, then, of who is accountable for a given injury*

precedes and initiates the subject, and the subject itself is formed
through being nominated to inhabit that grammatical and juridical
site.

In a sense, for Nietzsche, the subject comes to be only within
the requirements of a moral discourse of accountability. The requirements of blame figure the subject as the "cause" of an act. In
this sense, there can be no subject without a blameworthy act,
and there can be no "act" apart from a discourse of accountability
and, according to Nietzsche, without an institution of punishment.

But here it seems that Nietzsche's account of subject-formation
in *On the Genealogy of Morals* exposes something of its own impossibility. For if the "subject" is first animated through accusation,
conjured as the origin of an injurious action, then it would appear
that the accusation has to come *from* an interpellating performative that precedes the subject, one that presupposes the prior
operation of an efficacious speaking. Who delivers that formative
judgment? If there is an institution of punishment within which
the subject is formed, is there not also a figure of the law who
performatively sentences the subject into being? Is this not, in
some sense, the conjecturing by Nietzsche of a prior and more
powerful subject? Nietzsche's own language elides this problem
by claiming that the " 'der Täter' is zum Tun blos hinzugedichtet."
This passive verb formation, "hinzugedichtet," poetically or fictively added on to, appended, or applied, leaves unclear who or
what executes this fairly consequential formation.

If, on the occasion of pain, a subject is belatedly attributed to
the act as its origin, and the act then attributed to the subject as
its effect, this double attribution is confounded by a third, namely,
the attribution of an injurious consequence to the subject and its
act. In order to establish injurious consequence within the domain
of accountability, is it necessary not only to install a subject, but
also to establish the singularity and discreteness of the act itself
as well as the efficacy of the act to produce injury? If the injury
can be traced to a specifiable act, it qualifies as an object of
prosecution: it can be brought to court and held accountable. But
this tracing of the injury to the act of a subject, and this privileg-
ing of the juridical domain as the site to negotiate social injury,

does this not unwittingly stall the analysis of how precisely discourse produces injury by taking the subject and its spoken deed as the proper place of departure? And when it is words that wound, to borrow Richard Delgado's phrase, how are we to understand the relation between the word and the wound? If it is not a causal relation, and not the materialization of an intention, is it perhaps a kind of discursive transitivity that needs to be specified in its historicity and its violence? What is the relation between this transitivity and the power to injure?

In Robert Cover's impressive essay, "Violence and the Word," he elaborates the violence of legal interpretation as "the violence that *judges* deploy as instruments of a modern nation-state."[3] "Judges," he contends, "deal pain and death," "for as the judge interprets, using the concept of punishment, she also acts— through others—to restrain, hurt, render helpless, even kill the prisoner" [note the unfortunate implication of liberal feminism when it decides to legislate the feminine as the universal]. Cover's analysis is relevant to the question of prosecuting hate speech precisely because it underscores the power of the *judiciary* to enact violence through speech. Defenders of hate speech prosecution have had to shift the analysis to acknowledge that agents other than governments and branches of government wield the power to injure through words. Indeed, an analogy is set up between state action and citizen action such that both kinds of actions are understood to have the power to deny rights and liberties protected by the Equal Protection Clause of the Constitution. Consequently, one obstacle to contemporary efforts to legislate against hate speech is that the "state action doctrine" qualifies recourse to the Equal Protection Clause in such instances, presuming as it does that only governments can be the agents of harmful treatment that results in a deprivation of rights and liberties.[4] To argue that citizens can effectively deprive *each other* of such rights and liberties through words that wound requires overcoming the restrictions imposed by the state action doctrine.[5]

Whereas Cover emphasizes the *juridical* power to inflict pain through language, recent jurisprudence has shifted the terms away from the interpretive violence enacted by nation-states and toward the violence enacted by citizen-subjects toward members of minority groups. In this shift, it is not simply that citizens are said to act like states, but the power of the state is refigured as a power wielded by a citizen-subject. By "suspending" the state action doctrine, proponents of hate speech prosecution may also suspend a critical understanding of state power, relocating that power as the agency and effect of the citizen-subject. Indeed, if hate speech prosecution will be adjudicated by the state, in the form of the judiciary, the state is tacitly figured as a neutral instrument of legal enforcement. Hence, the "suspension" of the state action doctrine may involve both a suspension of critical insight into state power and state violence in Cover's sense, but also a displacement of that power onto the citizen, figured as a kind of sovereign, and the citizenry, figured as sovereigns whose speech now carries a power that operates like state power to deprive other "sovereigns" of fundamental rights and liberties.[6]

In shifting the emphasis from the harm done by the state to the harm done by citizens and non-state institutions against citizens, a reassessment of how power operates in and through discourse is also at work. When the words that wound are not the actions of the nation-state—indeed, when the nation-state and its judiciary are appealed to as the arbitor of such claims made by citizens against one another—how does the analysis of the violence of the word change? Is the violence perpetrated by the courts unwittingly backgrounded in favor of a politics that presumes the fairness and efficacy of the courts in adjudicating matters of hate speech? And to what extent does the potential for state violence become greater to the degree that the state action doctrine is suspended?

The subject as sovereign is presumed in the Austinian account of performativity; the figure for the one who speaks and, in speaking, performs what she/he speaks, is the judge or some other representative of the law. A judge pronounces a sentence and the pronouncement is the act by which the sentence first becomes binding, as long as the judge is a legitimate judge and the conditions of felicity are properly met. The performative in Austin maintains certain commonalities with the Althusserian notion of interpellation, although interpellation is never quite as "happy" or "effective" as the performative is sometimes figured in Austin. In Althusser, it is the police who hail the trespasser on the street: "Hey you there!" brings the subject into sociality through a life-imbueing reprimand. The doctor who receives the child and pronounces—"It's a girl"—begins that long string of interpellations by which the girl is transitively girled; gender is ritualistically repeated, whereby the repetition occasions both the risk of failure and the congealed effect of sedimentation. Kendall Thomas makes a similar argument that the subject is always "raced," transitively racialized by regulatory agencies from its inception.[7]

If performativity requires a power to effect or enact what one names, then who will be the "one" with such a power, and how will such a power be thought? How might we account for *the injurious word* within such a framework, the word that not only names a social subject, but constructs that subject in the naming, and constructs that subject through a violating interpellation? Is it the power of a "one" to effect such an injury through the wielding of the injurious name, or is that a power accrued through time which is concealed at the moment that a single subject utters its injurious terms? Does the "one" who speaks the term *cite* the term, thereby establishing his or herself as the author while at the same time establishing the derivative status of that authorship? Is a community and history of such speakers not magically invoked at the moment in which that utterance is spoken? And if and when that utterance brings injury, is it the utterance or the utterer who is the cause of the injury, or does that utterance perform its injury through a transitivity that cannot be reduced to a causal or intentional process originating in a singular subject?

Indeed, is iterability or citationality not precisely this: *the operation of that metalepsis by which the subject who "cites" the performative is temporarily produced as the belated and fictive origin of the performative itself?* The subject who utters the socially injurious words is mobilized by that long string of injurious interpellations: the subject achieves a temporary status in the citing of that utterance, in performing itself as the origin of that utterance. That subject-effect, however, is the consequence of that very citation; it is derivative, the effect of a belated metalepsis by which that invoked legacy of interpellations is dissimulated as the subject as "origin" of its utterance. If the utterance is to be prosecuted, where and when would that prosecution begin, and where and when would it end? Would this not be something like the effort to prosecute a history that, by its very temporality, cannot be called to trial? If the function of the subject as fictive origin is to occlude the genealogy by which that subject is formed, the subject is also installed in order to assume the burden of responsibility for the very history that subject dissimulates; the juridicalization of history, then, is achieved precisely through the search for subjects to prosecute who might be held accountable and, hence, temporarily resolve the problem of a fundamentally unprosecutable history.

This is not to say that subjects ought not to be prosecuted for their injurious speech; I think that there are probably occasions when they should. But what is precisely being prosecuted when the injurious word comes to trial and is it finally or fully prosecutable?

That words wound seems incontestably true, and that hateful, racist, misogynist, homophobic speech should be vehemently countered seems incontrovertibly right. But does understanding from where speech derives its power to wound alter our conception of what it might mean to counter that wounding power? Do we accept the notion that injurious speech is attributable to a singular subject and act? If we accept such a juridical constraint on thought—the grammatical requirements of accountability— as a point of departure, what is lost from the political analysis of injury when the discourse of politics becomes fully reduced to juridical requirements? Indeed, when political discourse is fully collapsed into juridical discourse, the meaning of political opposition runs the risk of being reduced to the act of prosecution.

How is the analysis of the discursive historicity of power unwittingly restricted when the subject is presumed as the point of departure for such an analysis? A clearly theological construction, the postulation of the subject as the causal origin of the performative act is understood to generate that which it names; indeed, this divinely empowered subject is one for whom the name itself is generative. According to the biblical rendition of the performative, "Let there be light!," it appears that by virtue of *the power of a subject or its will* a phenomenon is named into being. Although the sentence is delivered in the subjunctive, it qualifies as a 'masquerading' performative in the Austinian sense. In a critical reformulation of the performative, Derrida makes clear in relation to Austin that this power is not the function of an originating will, but is always derivative:

> Could a performative utterance succeed if its formulation did not repeat a "coded" or iterable utterance, or in other words, if the formula I pronounce in order to open a meeting, launch a ship or a marriage were not identifiable as *conforming* with an iterable model, if it were not then identifiable in some way as a "citation"? ... [i]n such a typology, the category of intention will not disappear; it will have its place, but from that place it will no longer be able to govern the entire scene and system of utterance *[l'énonciation]*.[8]

To what extent does discourse gain the authority to bring about what it names through citing the linguistic conventions of authority, conventions that are themselves legacies of citation? Does a subject appear as the author of its discursive effects to the extent that the citational practice by which he/she is conditioned and mobilized remains unmarked? Indeed, could it be that the production of the subject as originator of his/her effects is precisely a consequence of this dissimulated citationality?

If a performative provisionally succeeds (and I will suggest that "success" is always and only provisional), then it is not because an intention successfully governs the action of speech, but only because that action echoes prior actions, and *accumulates the force of authority through the repetition or citation of a prior and authoritative set of practices*. It is not simply that the speech act takes place *within* a practice, but that the act is itself a ritualized practice. What this means, then, is that a performative "works" to the extent that *it draws on and covers over* the constitutive conventions by which it is mobilized. In this sense, no term or statement can function performatively without the accumulating and dissimulating historicity of force.

When the injurious term injures (and let me make clear that I think it does), it works its injury precisely through the accumulation and dissimulation of its force. The speaker who utters the racial slur is thus citing that slur, making linguistic community with a history of speakers. What this might mean, then, is that precisely the iterability by which a performative enacts its injury establishes a permanent difficulty in locating accountability for that injury in a singular subject and its act.

In two recent cases, the Supreme Court has reconsidered the distinction between protected and unprotected speech in relation to the phenomenon of "hate speech." Are certain forms of invidious speech to be construed as "fighting words," and if so, are they appropriately considered to be a kind of speech unprotected by the First Amendment? In the first case, *R.A.V. v. St. Paul*, 112 S. Ct. 2538, 120 L. Ed. 2d 305 (1992), the ordinance in question was one passed by the St. Paul City Council in 1990, and read in part as follows:

Whoever places on public or private property a symbol, object, appellation, characterization or graffiti, including, but not limited to, a burning cross or Nazi swastika, which one knows or has reasonable grounds to know arouses anger, alarm, or resentment in others on the basis of race, color, creed, religion or gender commits disorderly conduct and shall be guilty of a misdemeanor.[9]

A white teenager was charged under this ordinance after burning a cross in front of a black family's house. The charge was dismissed by the trial court but reinstated by the Minnesota State Supreme Court; at stake was the question whether the ordinance itself was "substantially overbroad and impermissably content-based." The defense contended that the burning of the cross in front of the black family's house was to be construed as an example of protected speech. The State Supreme Court overturned the decision of the trial court, arguing first that the burning of the cross could not be construed as protected speech because it constituted "fighting words" as defined in *Chaplinsky v. New Hampshire*, 315 U.S. 568, 572 (1942), and second, that the reach of the ordinance was permissable considering the "compelling government interest in protecting the community against bias-motivated threats to public safety and order." *In Re Welfare of R.A.V.*, 464 N.W.2d 507, 510 (Minn. 1991).

The United States Supreme Court reversed the State Supreme

Court decision, reasoning first that the burning cross was not an instance of "fighting words," but an instance of a "viewpoint" within the "free marketplace of ideas" and that such "viewpoints" are categorically protected by the First Amendment.[10] The majority on the High Court (Scalia, Rehnquist, Kennedy, Souter, Thomas) then offered a *second* reason for declaring the ordinance unconstitutional, a judicially activist contribution which took many jurists by surprise: the justices severely restricted the doctrinal scope of "fighting words" by claiming it unconstitutional to impose prohibitions on speech solely on the basis of the "content" or "subjects addressed" in that speech. In order to determine whether words are fighting words, there can be no decisive recourse to the content and the subject matter of what is said.

One conclusion on which the justices appear to concur is that the ordinance imposed overbroad restrictions on speech, given that forms of speech *not* considered to fall within the parameters of fighting words would nonetheless be banned by the ordinance. But while the Minnesota ordinance proved too broad for all the justices, Scalia, Thomas, Rehnquist, Kennedy and Souter took the opportunity of this review to severely restrict any future application of the fighting words doctrine. At stake in the majority opinion is not only when and where "speech" constitutes some component of an injurious act such that it loses its protected status under the First Amendment, but what constitutes the domain of "speech" itself.

According to a rhetorical reading of this decision—distinguished from a reading that follows established conventions of legal interpretation—the court might be understood as asserting its state-sanctioned linguistic power to determine what will and will not count as "speech" and, in the process, enacting a potentially injurious form of juridical speech. What follows, then, is a reading which considers not only the account that the court gives of how and when speech becomes injurious, but considers as well the injurious potential of the account itself as "speech" considered in a broad sense. Recalling Cover's claim that legal decisions can engage the nexus of language and violence, consider that the adjudication of what will and will not count as protected speech will itself be a kind of speech, one which implicates the state in the very problem of discursive power that it is vested within the authority to regulate, sanction, and restrict such speech.

In the following, then, I will read the "speech" in which the decision is articulated against the version of "speech" officially circumscribed as protected content in the decision. The point of this kind of reading is not only to expose a contradictory set of rhetorical strategies at work in the decision, but to consider the power of that discursive domain which not only produces what will and will not count as "speech," but which regulates the political field of contestation through the tactical manipulation of that very distinction. Furthermore, I want to argue that the very reasons that account for the injuriousness of such acts, construed as speech in a broad sense, are precisely what render difficult the prosecution of such acts. Lastly, I want to suggest that the court's speech carries with it its *own* violence, and that the very institution that is invested with the authority to adjudicate the problem of hate speech recirculates and redirects that hatred in and as its own highly consequential speech, often by coopting the very language that it seeks to adjudicate.

The majority opinion, written by Scalia, begins with the construction of the act, the burning of the cross; and one question at issue is whether or not this act constitutes an injury, whether it can be construed as "fighting words" or whether it communicates a content which is, for better or worse, protected by first amendment precedents. The figure of burning will be repeated throughout the opinion, first in the context in which the burning cross in construed as the free expression of a viewpoint within the marketplace of ideas, and second, in the example of the burning of the flag, which could be held illegal were it to violate an ordinance prohibiting outside fires, but which could not be held to be illegal if it were the expression of an idea. Later Scalia will close the argument through recourse to yet another fire: "Let there be no mistake about our belief that burning a cross in someone's front yard is reprehensible." "But," Scalia continues, "St. Paul has sufficient means at its disposal to prevent such behavior without adding the First Amendment to the fire." *R.A.V. v St. Paul*, 112 S. Ct. at 2550, 120 L. Ed. 2d at 326.

Significantly, Scalia here aligns the act of cross-burning with those who defend the ordinance, since both are producing fires, but whereas the cross-burner's fire is constitutionally protected speech, the ordinance maker's language is figured as the incineration of free speech. The analogy suggests that the ordinance itself is a kind of cross-burning, and Scalia then draws on the very destructive implications of cross-burning to underscore his point that the ordinance itself is destructive. The figure thus affirms the destructiveness of the cross-burning that the decision itself effectively denies, the destructiveness of the act that it has just elevated to the status of protected verbal currency within the marketplace of ideas.

The Court thus transposes the place of the ordinance and the place of the cross-burning, but also figures the First Amendment in an analogous relation to the black family and its home which in the course of the writing has become reduced to "someone's front yard." The stripping of blackness and family from the figure of the complainant is significant, for it refuses the dimension of social power that constructs the so-called speaker and the addressee of the speech act in question, the burning cross. And it refuses as well the racist history of the convention of cross-burning by the Ku Klux Klan which marked, targeted, and, hence, portended a further violence against a given addressee. Scalia thus figures himself as quenching the fire which the ordinance has lit, and which is being stoked with the First Amendment, apparently in its totality. Indeed, compared with the admittedly "reprehensible" act of burning a cross in "someone's" front yard, the ordinance itself appears to conflagrate in much greater dimensions, threatening to burn the book which it is Scalia's duty to uphold; Scalia thus champions himself as an opponent of those who would set the constitution on fire, cross-burners of a more dangerous order.[11]

The lawyers arguing for the legality of the ordinance based their appeal on the fighting words doctrine. This doctrine, formulated in *Chaplinsky v. New Hampshire*, 315 U.S. 568, 572 (1942), argued that speech acts unprotected by the constitution are those which are not essential to the communication of ideas: "such utterances are no essential part of any exposition of ideas, and are of such slight social value as a step to truth that any benefit that may be derived from them is clearly outweighed by the social interest in order and morality." Scalia takes this phrasing to legitimate the following claim: "the unprotected features of the words are, despite their verbal character, essentially a 'nonspeech' element of communication." *R.A.V. v. St. Paul*, 112 S. Ct. at 2545, 120 L. Ed. 2d at 319. In his effort to protect all contents of communication from proscription, Scalia establishes a distinction between the content and the vehicle of that expression; it is the latter which is proscribable, and the former which is not: he continues, "Fighting words are thus analogous to a noisy sound truck." *Id.* What is injurious, then, is the sound, but not the message; indeed, "the government may not regulate use based on hostility—or favoritism—towards the underlying message expressed." *Id.*

The connection between the signifying power of the burning cross and Scalia's regressive new critical distinction between what is and is not a speech element in communication is nowhere marked in the text.[12] Scalia assumes that the burning cross is a message, an expression of a viewpoint, a discussion of a "subject" or "content"; in short, that the act of burning the cross is fully and exhaustively translatable into a *constative* act of speech; the burning of the cross which is, after all, on the black family's lawn, is thus made strictly analogous—and morally equivalent—to an individual speaking in public on whether or not there ought to be a 50 cent tax on gasoline. Significantly, Scalia does not tell us what the cross would say if the cross could speak, but he does insist that what the burning cross is doing is expressing a viewpoint, discoursing on a content which is, admittedly, controversial, but for that very reason, ought not to be proscribed. Thus the defense of cross-burning as free speech rests on an unarticulated analogy between that act and a public constation. This speech is not a doing, an action or an injury, even as it is the enunciation of a set of "contents" that might offend.[13] The injury is thus construed as one that is registered at the level of sensibility, which is to say that it is an offense that is one of the risks of free speech.

That the cross burns and thus constitutes an incendiary destruction is not considered as a sign of the intention to reproduce that incendiary destruction at the site of the house or the family; the historical correlation between cross-burning and marking a community, a family, or an individual for further violence is also ignored. How much of that burning is translatable into a declarative or constative proposition? And how would one know exactly what constative claim is being made by the burning cross? If the cross is the expression of a viewpoint, is it a declaration as in, "I am of the opinion that black people ought not to live in this neighborhood" or even "I am of the opinion that violence ought to be perpetrated against black people," or is it a perlocutionary performative as in imperatives and commands which take the form of "Burn!" or "Die!"? Is it an injunction that works its power metonymically not only in the sense that the fire recalls prior burnings which have served to mark black people as targets for violence, but also in the sense that the fire is understood to be transferable from the cross to the target that is marked by the cross? The relation between cross-burning and torchings of both persons and properties is historically established. Hence, from this perspective, the burning cross assumes the status of a direct address and a *threat* and, as such, is construed either as the incipient moment of injurious action *or* as the statement of an intention to injure.[14]

Although Justice Stevens agreed with the decision to strike down the Minnesota ordinance, he takes the occasion to rebuke Scalia for restricting the fighting words doctrine. Stevens reviews special cases in which conduct may be prohibited by special rules. Note in the following quotation how the cross burning is nowhere mentioned, but the displacements of the figure of fire appear in a series of examples which effectively transfer the need for protection *from racist speech,* to the need for protection *from public protest against racism.* Even within Steven's defense of proscribing conduct, a phantasmatic figure of a menacing riot emerges:

Lighting a fire near an ammunition dump or a gasoline storage tank is especially dangerous; such behavior may be punished more severely than burning trash in a vacant lot. Threatening someone because of her race or religious beliefs may cause particularly severe trauma or touch off a riot, and threatening a high public official may cause substantial social disruption; such threats may be punished more severely than threats against someone based on, say, his support of a particular athletic team. *R.A.V. v. St. Paul,* 112 S. Ct. at 2561, 120 L. Ed. 2d at 340.

Absent from the list of fires above is the burning of the cross in question. In the place of that prior scene, we are asked first to imagine someone who would light a fire near a gas tank, and then to imagine a more innocuous fire in a vacant lot. But with the vacant lot, we enter the metaphor of poverty and property, which appears to effect the unstated transition to the matter of blackness[15] introduced by the next line, "threatening someone because of her race or religious beliefs . . .": *because* of her race is not the same as "on the basis of" her race and leaves open the possibility that the race causally induces the threat. The threat appears to shift mid-sentence as Stevens continues to elaborate a second causality: this threat "may cause particularly severe trauma or touch off a riot" at which point it is no longer clear whether the threat which warrants the prohibition on conduct refers to the "threatening someone because of her race or religious belief" or to the riot that might result therefrom. What immediately follows suggests that the limitations on rioters has suddenly become more urgent to authorize than the limitation on those who would threaten this "her" "because of her race. . . ." After "or touch off a riot," the sentence continues, "and threatening a high official may cause substantial social disruption . . . ," as if the racially marked trauma had already led to a riot and an attack on high officials.

This sudden implication of the justices themselves might be construed as a paranoid inversion of the original cross-burning narrative. That original narrative is nowhere mentioned, but its elements have been redistributed throughout the examples; the fire which was the original "threat" against the black family is relocated first as a incendiary move against industry, then as a location in a vacant lot, and then reappears tacitly in the riot which now appears to follow from the trauma and threaten public officials. The fire which initially constituted the threat against the black family becomes metaphorically transfigured as the threat that blacks in trauma now wield against high officials. And though Stevens is on record as endorsing a construction of "fighting words" that would include cross-burning as *un*protected speech, the language in which he articulates this view deflects the question to that of the state's right to circumscribe conduct to protect itself against a racially motivated riot.[16]

The circumscription of content explicitly discussed in the decision appears to emerge through a production of semantic excess
in and through the metonymic chain of anxious figuration. The
separability of content from sound, for instance, or of content
from context, is exemplified and illustrated through figures which
signify in excess of the thesis which they are meant to support.
Indeed, to the extent that, in the Scalia analysis, "content" is
circumscribed and purified to establish its protected status, that
content is secured through the production and proliferation of
"dangers" from which it calls to be protected. Hence, the question
of whether or not the black family in Minnesota is entitled to
protection from public displays such as cross-burnings is displaced onto the question of whether or not the "content" of free
speech is to be protected from those who would burn it. The fire is
thus displaced from the cross to the legal instrument wielded by
those who would protect the family from the fire, but then to the
black family itself, to blackness, to the vacant lot, to rioters in Los
Angeles who explicitly oppose the decision of a court and who
now represent the incendiary power of the traumatized rage of
black people who would burn the judiciary itself. But of course,
that construal is already a reversal of the narrative in which a
court delivers a decision of acquittal for the four policemen indicted for the brutal beating of Rodney King, a decision that
might be said to "spark" a riot which calls into question whether
the claim of having been injured can be heard and countenanced
by a jury and a judge who are extremely susceptible to the suggestion that a black person is always and only endangering, but never
endangered. And so the High Court might be understood in its
decision of June 22, 1992, to be taking its revenge on Rodney King,
protecting itself against the riots in Los Angeles and elsewhere
which appeared to be attacking the system of justice itself. Hence,
the justices identify with the black family who sees the cross
burning and takes it as a threat, but they substitute themselves
for that family, and reposition blackness as the agency behind the
threat itself.[17]

The decision enacts a set of metonymic displacements which
might well be read as anxious deflections and reversals of the
injurious action at hand; indeed, the original scene is successively

reversed in the metonymic relation between figures such that the fire is lit by the ordinance, carried out by traumatized rioters on the streets of Los Angeles and threatens to engulf the justices themselves.

Mari Matsuda and Charles Lawrence also write of this text as enacting a rhetorical reversal of crime and punishment: "The cross burners are portrayed as an unpopular minority that the Supreme Court must defend against the power of the state. The injury to the Jones family is appropriated and the cross burner is cast as the injured victim. The reality of ongoing racism and exclusion is erased and bigotry is redefined as majoritarian condemnation of racist views."[18]

Significantly, the Justices revisited *R.A.V. v. St. Paul*, in a more recent decision, *Wisconsin v. Mitchell*, 113 S. Ct. 2194, 14 L. Ed. 2d 436 (1993), in which the court unanimously decided that racist speech could be included as evidence that a victim of a crime was intentionally selected because of his/her race and could constitute one of the factors that come into play in determining whether an enhanced penalty for the crime is in order. *Wisconsin v. Mitchell* did not address whether racist speech is injurious, but only whether speech that indicates that the victim was selected on the basis of race could be brought to bear in determining penalty enhancement for a crime which is itself not a crime of speech, as it were. Oddly, the case at hand involved a group of young black men, including Todd Mitchell, who had just left the film, "Mississippi Burning." They decided to "move on" some white people, and proceeded to beat a young white man who had approached them on the street. Rehnquist is quick to note that these young men were discussing a scene from the film, one in which "a white man beat a young black boy who was praying." Rehnquist then goes on to quote Mitchell whose speech will become consequential in the decision: "Do you all feel hyped up to move on some white people?" and later, "You all want to fuck somebody up? There goes a white boy: go get him." *Wisconsin v. Mitchell*, 113 S. Ct. at 2196–7, 120 L. Ed. 2d at 442 (citing Brief for Petitioner). Now, the irony of this event, it seems, is that the film narrates the story of three civil rights workers (two white and one black) who are murdered by Klansmen who regularly threaten with burning crosses and firebombs any townspeople who appear to help the Justice Department in their search for the bodies of the slain civil rights activists and then their murderers. The court system is first figured within the film as sympathetic to the Klan, refusing to imprison the murdering Klansmen, and then as setting improper restraints on the interrogation. Indeed, the Justice Department official is able to entrap the Klansman only by acting against the law, freely brutalizing those he interrogates. This official is largely regarded as rehabilitating masculinity on the side of what is right over and against a liberal "effeminization" represented by judicial due process. But perhaps most important, while the effective official acts in the name of the law, he also acts against the law, and purports to show that his unlawfulness is the only efficacious way to fight racism. The film thus appeals to a widespread lack of faith in the law and its proceduralism, reconstructing a lawless white masculinity even as it purports to curb its excesses.

In some ways, the film shows that violence is the consequence of the law's failure to protect its citizens, and in this way allegorizes the reception of the judicial decisions. For if the film shows that the court will fail to guarantee the rights and liberties of its citizens, and only violence can counter racism, then the street violence that literally follows the film reverses the order of that allegory. The black men who leave the film and embark upon violence in the street find themselves in a court that not only goes out of its way to indict the film—which is, after all, an indictment of the courts—but implicitly goes on to link the street violence to the offending representation, and effectively to link the one through the other.

The court seeks to decide whether or not the selection of the target of violence is a racially motivated one by quoting Todd Mitchell's speech. This speech is then taken to be the effect of having watched the film, indeed, to be the very extension of the speech that constitutes the text of the film. But the court itself is implicated in the extended text of the film, "indicted" by the film as complicit with racial violence. Hence, the punishment of Mitchell and his friends—and the attribution of racially selective motives to them—reverses the "charges" that the film makes against the court. In *R.A.V. v. St. Paul*, the court makes a cameo appearance in the decision as well, reversing the agency of the action, substituting the injured for the injurer, and figuring itself as a site of vulnerability.

In each of these cases, the court's speech exercises the power to injure precisely by virtue of being invested with the authority to adjudicate the injurious power of speech. The reversal and displacement of injury in the name of "adjudication" underscores the particular violence of the "decision," one which becomes both dissimulated and enshrined once it becomes word of law. It may be said that all legal language engages this potential power to injure, but that insight supports only the argument that it will be all the more important to gain a reflective understanding of the specificities of that violence. It will be necessary to distinguish between those kinds of violence that are the necessary conditions of the binding character of legal language, and those kinds which exploit that very necessity in order to redouble that injury in the service of injustice.

The arbitrary use of this power is evidenced in the contrary use of precedents on hate speech to promote conservative political goals and thwart progressive efforts. Here it is clear that what is needed is not a better understanding of speech acts or the injurious power of speech, but the strategic and contradictory uses to which the court puts these various formulations. For instance, this same court has been willing to countenance the expansion of definitions of obscenity, and to use the very rationale proposed by some arguments in favor of hate crime legislation to augment its case to exclude obscenity from protected speech.[19] Scalia refers to *Miller v. California* (1973) as the case which installs obscenity as an exception to the categorical protection of content through recourse to what is "patently offensive," and then remarks that in a later case, *New York v. Ferber*, 458 U.S. 747 (1982), in exempting child pornography from protection, there was no "question here of censoring a particular literary theme." *R.A.V. v. St. Paul*, 112 S. Ct. at 2543, 120 L. Ed. 2d at 318. What constitutes the "literary" is thus circumscribed in such a way that child pornography is excluded from both the literary and the thematic. Although it seems that one must be able to recognize the genre of child pornography, to identify and delimit it in order to exempt it from the categorical protection of content, the identifying marks of such a product can be neither literary nor thematic. Indeed, the court appears in one part of its discussion to accept the controversial position of Catharine MacKinnon, which claims that certain verbal expressions constitute sex discrimination, when it says "sexually derogatory 'fighting words' . . . may produce a violation of Title VII's general prohibition against sexual discrimination in employment practices" *Id.* at 2546, 120 L. Ed. 2d at 321. But here the court is clear that it does not prohibit such expressions on the basis of their content, but only on the basis of the effects that such expressions entail. Indeed, I would suggest that the contemporary conservative sensibility exemplified by the court and right-wing members of Congress is also exemplified in the willingness to expand the domain of obscenity and, to that end, to enlarge the category of the pornographic and to claim the unprotected status of both, and so to position obscenity to become a species of "fighting words," that is, to accept that graphic sexual representation is injurious. This is underscored by the rationale used in *Miller v. California* in which the notion of "appealing to prurience" is counterposed to the notion of "literary, artistic, political, or scientific value." Here the representation that is deemed immediately and unobjectionably injurious is excluded from the thematic and the valuable and, hence, from protected status. This same rationale has been taken up by Jesse Helms and others to argue that the National Endowment for the Arts is under no obligation to fund obscene materials, and then to argue that various lesbian performers and gay male photographers produce work that is obscene and lacking in literary value. Significantly, it seems, the willingness to accept the nonthematic and unobjectionably injurious quality of graphic sexual representations, when these representations cannot be said to leave the page or to "act" in some obvious way, must be read against the unwillingness to countenance the injuriousness of the burning cross in front of the black family's house. That the graphic depiction of homosexuality, say, can be construed as nonthematic or simply prurient, figured as a sensuousness void of meaning, whereas the burning of the cross, to the extent that it communicates a message of racial hatred, might be construed as a sanctioned point in a public debate over admittedly controversial issues suggests that the rationale for expanding the fighting words doctrine to include unconventional depictions of sexuality within its purview has been strengthened, but that the rationale for invoking fighting words to outlaw racist threats is accordingly weakened. This is perhaps a way in which a heightened sexual conservatism works in tandem with an increasing governmental sanction for racist violence, but in such a way that whereas the "injury" claimed by the viewer of graphic sexual representation is honored as fighting words, the injury sustained by the black family with the burning cross out front, not unlike the injury of Rodney King, proves too ambiguous, too hypothetical to abrogate the ostensible sanctity of the First Amendment.[20] And it is not simply that prohibitions against graphic sexual representation will be supported by this kind of legal reasoning, whereas racist injury will be dignified as protected speech, but that racially marked depictions of sexuality will be most susceptible to prosecution, and those representations that threaten the pieties and purities of race and sexuality will become most vulnerable.

Two remarks of qualification: first, some critical race theorists such as Charles Lawrence will argue that cross burning is speech, but that not all speech is to be protected, indeed, not all speech is protected, and that racist speech conflicts with the Equal Protection Clause because it hinders the addressed subject from exercising his/her rights and liberties. Other legal scholars in critical race studies, such as Richard Delgado, will argue for expanding the domain of the "fighting words" restriction on First Amendment rights. Matsuda and MacKinnon, following the example of sex discrimination jurisprudence, will argue that it is impossible to distinguish between conduct and speech, that hateful remarks *are* injurious actions. Oddly enough, this last kind of reasoning has reappeared in the recent policy issued on gays in the military, where the statement, "I am a homosexual" is considered to be a "homosexual act." The word and the deed are one, and the claim "I am a homosexual" is considered to be not only a homosexual act, but a homosexual offense.[21] According to this policy, the act of coming out is effectively construed as fighting words. Here it seems that one must be reminded that the prosecution of hate speech in a court runs the risk of giving that court the opportunity to impose a further violence of its own. And if the court begins to decide what is and is not violating speech, that decision runs the risk of constituting the most binding of violations.

For, as in the case with the burning cross, it was not merely a question of whether the court knows how to read the threat contained in the burning cross, but whether the court itself signifies along a parallel logic. For this has been a court that can only imagine the fire engulfing the First Amendment, sparking the riot which will fray its own authority. And so it protects itself against the imagined threat of that fire by protecting the burning cross, allying itself with those who would seek legal protection from a spectre wrought from their own fantasy. Thus the court protects the burning cross as free speech, figuring those it injures as the site of the true threat, elevating the burning cross as a deputy for the court, the local protector and token of free speech: with so much protection, what do we have to fear?

Postscript

MacKinnon herself understands this risk of invoking state power, but in her recent book, *Only Words* (1993), she argues that state power is on the side of the pornographic industry, and that the construction of women within pornography in subordinate positions is, effectively, a state-sanctioned construction.

MacKinnon has argued that pornography is a kind of hate speech, and that the argument in favor of restricting hate speech ought to be based on the argument in favor of restricting pornography. This analogy rests upon the assumption that the visual image in pornography operates as an imperative, and that this imperative has the power to realize that which it dictates. The problem, for MacKinnon, is *not* that pornography reflects or expresses a social structure of misogyny, but that it is an institution with the performative power to bring about that which it depicts. She writes that pornography not only substitutes for social reality, but that that substitution is one which creates a social reality of its own, the social reality of pornography. This self-fulfilling capacity of pornography is, for her, what gives sense to the claim that pornography *is* its own social context. She writes,

Pornography does not simply express or interpret experience; it substitutes for it. Beyond bringing a message from reality, it stands in for reality.... To make visual pornography, and to live up to its imperatives, the world, namely women, must do what the pornographers want to 'say.' Pornography brings its conditions of production to the consumer.... Pornography makes the world a pornographic place through its making and use, establishing what women are said to exist as, are seen as, are treated as, constructing the social reality of what a woman is and can be in terms of what can be done to her, and what a man is in terms of doing it.

In the first instance, pornography substitutes for experience, implying that there is an experience which is supplanted, and supplanted thoroughly, through pornography. Hence, pornography takes the place of an experience and thoroughly constitutes a new experience, understood as a totality; by the second line, this second-order experience is rendered synonomous with a second-order "reality," which suggests that in this universe of pornography there is no distinction between an experience of reality and reality, although MacKinnon herself makes clear that this systemic conflation of the two takes place within a reality which is itself a mere substitution for another reality, one which is figured as more original, perhaps one which furnishes the normative or utopian measure by which she judges the pornographic reality that has taken its place. This visual field is then figured as speaking, indeed, as delivering imperatives, at which point the visual field operates as subject with the power to bring into being what it names, to wield an efficacious power analogous to the divine performative. The reduction of that visual field to a speaking figure, an authoritarian speaker, rhetorically effects a different substitution than the one that MacKinnon describes. She substitutes a set of linguistic imperatives for the visual field, implying not only a full transposition of the visual into the linguistic, but a full transposition of visual depiction into an efficacious performative.

When pornography is then described as "constructing the social reality of what a woman is," the sense of "construction" needs to be read in light of the above two transpositions: for that construction can be said to work, that is, "to produce the social reality of what a woman is," only if the visual can be transposed into the linguistically efficacious in the way that she suggests. Similarly, the analogy between pornography and hate speech works to the extent that the pornographic image can be transposed into a set of efficacious spoken imperatives. In MacKinnon's paraphrase of how the pornographic image speaks, she insists that that image says, "do this," where the commanded act is an act of sexual subordination, and where, in the doing of that act, the social reality of woman is constructed precisely as the position of the sexually subordinate. Here "construction" is not simply the doing of the act—which remains, of course, highly ambiguous in order perhaps to ward off the question of an equivocal set of readings— but *the depiction* of that doing, where the depiction is understood as the dissimulation and fulfillment of the verbal imperative, "do this." For MacKinnon, no one needs to speak such words because the speaking of such words already functions as the frame and the compulsory scripting of the act; in a sense, to the extent that the frame orchestrates the act, it wields a performative power; it is conceived by MacKinnon as encoding the will of a masculine authority, and compelling a compliance with its command.

But does the frame impart the will of a preexisting subject, or is the frame something like the derealization of will, the production and orchestration of a phantasmatic scene of willfulness and submission? I don't mean to suggest a strict distinction between the phantasmatic and the domain of reality, but I do mean to ask, to what extent does the operation of the phantasmatic within the construction of social reality render that construction more frail and less determinative than MacKinnon would suggest? In fact, although one might well agree that a good deal of pornography is offensive, it does not follow that its offensiveness consists in its putative power to construct (unilaterally, exhaustively) the social reality of what a woman is. To return for a moment to MacKinnon's own language, consider the way in which the hypothetical insists itself into the formulation of the imperative, as if the force of her own assertions about the force of pornographic representation tends toward its own undoing: "pornography establish[es] . . . what women are said to exist *as*, are seen *as*, are treated *as* . . ."

Then, the sentence continues: "constructing the social reality of what a woman is"; here to be treated as a sexual subordinate is to be constructed as one, and to have a social reality constituted in which that is precisely and only what one is. But if the "as" is read as the assertion of a likeness, it is not for that reason the assertion of a metaphorical collapse into identity. Through what means does the "as" turn into an "is," and is this the doing of pornography, or is it the doing of the very *depiction* of pornography that MacKinnon provides? For the "as" could also be read as "as if," "as if one were," which suggests that pornography neither represents nor constitutes what women are, but offers an allegory of masculine willfulness and feminine submission (although these are clearly not its only themes), one which repeatedly and anxiously rehearses its own *un*realizability. Indeed, one might argue that pornography depicts impossible and uninhabitable positions, compensatory fantasies that continually reproduce a rift between those positions and the ones that belong to the domain of social reality. Indeed, one might suggest that pornography is the text of gender's unreality, the impossible norms by which it is compelled, and in the face of which it perpetually fails. The imperative "do this" is less delivered that "depicted," and if what is depicted is a set of compensatory ideals, hyperbolic gender norms, then pornography charts a domain of unrealizable positions that hold sway over the social reality of gender positions, but do not, strictly speaking, constitute that reality; indeed, it is their failure to constitute it that gives the pornographic image the phantasmatic power that it has. In this sense, to the extent that an imperative is "depicted" and not "delivered," it fails to wield the power to construct the social reality of what a woman is. This failure, however, is the occasion for an allegory of such an imperative, one that concedes the unrealizability of that imperative from the start, and which, finally, cannot overcome the unreality that is its condition and its lure. My call, as it were, is for a feminist reading of pornography that resists the literalization of this imaginary scene, one which reads it instead for the incommensurabilities between gender norms and practices that it seems compelled to repeat without resolution.

In this sense, it makes little sense to figure the visual field of pornography as a subject who speaks and, in speaking, brings about what it names; its authority is decidedly less divine; its power, less efficacious. It only makes sense to figure the pornographic text as the injurious act of a speaker if we seek to locate accountability at the prosecutable site of the subject. Otherwise, our work is more difficult, for what pornography delivers is what it recites and exaggerates from the resources of compensatory gender norms, a text of insistent and faulty imaginary relations that will not disappear with the abolition of the offending text, the text that remains for feminist criticism relentlessly to read.

Notes

1. I greatly appreciate the thoughtful readings given to this paper in an earlier form by Wendy Brown, Robert Gooding-Williams, Morris Kaplan, Robert Post, and Hayden White. Any inaccuracies and all misreadings are, of course, my responsibility alone. I thank Jane Malmo for help with preparing the manuscript.
2. This criminal sense of an actor is to be distinguished both from the commercial and theatrical terms (*Handlerin* and *Schauspielerin*, respectively).
3. Robert M. Cover, "Violence and the Word," 95 *Yale Law Journal* 1595, 1601 n 1 (1986).
4. "The [state action] doctrine holds that although someone may have suffered harmful treatment of a kind that one might ordinarily describe as a deprivation of liberty or a denial of equal protection of the laws, that occurrence excites no constitutional concern unless the proximate active perpetrators of the harm include persons exercising the special authority or power of the government of a state." Frank Michelman, "Conceptions of Democracy in American Constitutional Argument: The Case of Pornography Regulation," 56 *Tennessee Law Review* 291, 306 (1989).
5. Charles Lawrence III, "If He Hollers Let Him Go: Regulating Racist Speech on Campus," *Words that Wound: Critical Race Theory, Assaultive Speech and the First Amendment*, eds. Mari J. Matsuda, Charles R. Lawrence III, Richard Delgado, and Kimberlè Williams Crenshaw, Boulder: Westview Press, 1993, p.65.
6. I thank Robert Post for this last analogy, suggested to me in conversation.
7. Kendall Thomas, University of Virginia Law Review, forthcoming.
8. Jacques Derrida, "Signature, Event, Context" in *Limited, Inc.*, ed. Gerald Graff, tr. Samuel Weber and Jeffrey Mehlman (Evanston: Northwestern University Press, 1988), p.18.

9. St. Paul Bias Motivated Crime Ordinance, Section 292.02 Minn. Legis. Code (1990).
10. Charles R. Lawrence III argues that "it is not just the prevalence and strength of the idea of racism that make the unregulated marketplace of ideas an untenable paradigm for those individuals who seek full and equal personhood for all. The real problem is that the idea of the racial inferiority of nonwhites infects, skews, and disables the operation of a market" in "If He Hollers Let Him Go: Regulating Racist Speech on Campus," in *Words that Wound*, p.77.
11. The lawyers defending the application of the ordinance to the cross-burning episode made the following argument:

   ...we ask the Court to reflect on the 'content' of the 'expressive conduct' represented by a 'burning cross.' It is no less than the first step in an act of racial violence. It was and unfortunately still is the equivalent of [the] waving of a knife before the thrust, the pointing of a gun before it is fired, the lighting of the match before the arson, the hanging of the noose before the lynching. It is not a political statement, or even a cowardly statement of hatred. It is the first step in an act of assault. It can be no more protected than holding a gun to a victim['s] head. It is perhaps the ultimate expression of 'fighting words.'

   R.A.V. v. St. Paul, 112 S. Ct. at 2569–70, fn. 8, 120 L. Ed. 2d at 320 (App. to Brief for Petitioner).
12. The new critical assumption to which I refer is that of the separable and fully formal unity that is said to characterize a given text.
13. All of the justices concur that the St. Paul ordinance is overbroad because it isolates "subject-matters" as offensive, and (a) potentially prohibits discussion of such subject-matters even by those whose political sympathies are with the ordinance, and (b) fails to distinguish between the subject-matter's injuriousness and the context in which it is enunciated.
14. Justice Stevens, in a decision offered separately from the argument offered by the majority, suggests that the burning cross is precisely a threat, and that whether a given "expression" is a threat can only be determined *contextually*. Stevens bases his conclusion on *Chaplinsky*, which argued that "one of the characteristics that justifies" the constitutional status of fighting words is that such words "by their very utterance inflict injury or tend to incite an immediate breach of the peace." *Chaplinsky v. New Hampshire*, 315 U.S. 568, 572 (1942).

   Here Stevens argues, first, that certain kinds of contents have always been proscribable, and, second, that the fighting words doctrine has depended for its very implementation on the capacity to discriminate among kinds of contents (i.e., political speech is more fully protected than obscene speech, etc.), but also, third, that fighting words that are construed as a threat are in themselves injurious, and that it is this injurious character of speech, and not a separable "content" that is at issue. As he continues, however, Stevens is quick to point out that whether or not an expression is injurious is a matter of determining the force of an expression within a given context. This determination will never be fully predictable, precisely because, one assumes, contexts are also not firmly delimitable. Indeed, if one considers not only historical circumstance, but the historicity of the utterance itself, it follows that the demarcation of relevant context will be as fraught as the demarcation of injurious content.

Stevens links content, injurious performativity, and context together when he claims, objecting to both Scalia and White, that there can be no categorical approach to the question of proscribablity: "few dividing lines in First Amendment laws are straight and unwavering, and efforts at categorization inevitably give rise only to fuzzy boundaries . . . the quest for doctrinal certainty through the definition of categories and subcategories is, in my opinion, destined to fail." *R.A.V. v. St. Paul,* 112 S. Ct. at 2561, 120 L. Ed. 2d, at 346. Furthermore, he argues, "the meaning of any expression and the legitimacy of its regulation can only be determined in context." *Id.*

At this point in his analysis, Stevens cites a metaphoric description of "the word" by Justice Holmes, a term which stands synecdochally for "expression" as it is broadly construed within First Amendment jurisprudence: the citation from Holmes runs as follows: "a word is not a crystal, transparent and unchanged, it is the skin of a living thought and may vary greatly in color and content according to the circumstances and the time in which it is used" (11–12). We might consider this figure not only as a racial metaphor which describes the "word" as a "skin" that varies in "color," but also in terms of the theory of semantics it invokes. Although Stevens believes that he is citing a figure which will affirm the historically changing nature of an "expression's" semantic "content," denoted by a "skin" that changes in color and content according to the historical circumstance of its use, it is equally clear that the epidermal metaphor suggests a living and disembodied thought which remains dephenomenalized, the noumenal quality of life, the living spirit in its skinless form. Skin and its changing color and content thus denote what is historically changing, but they also are, as it were, the signifiers of historical change. The racial signifier comes to stand not only for changing historical circumstances in the abstract, but for the specific historical changes marked by explosive racial relations.

15. Toni Morrison remarks that poverty is often the language in which black people are spoken about.

16. The above reading raises a series of questions about the rhetorical status of the decision itself. Kendall Thomas and others have argued that the figures and examples used in judicial decisions are as central to its semantic content as the explicit propositional claims that are delivered as the conclusions of the argumentation. In a sense, I am

raising two kinds of rhetorical questions here, one has to do with the "content" of the decision, and the other with the way in which the majority ruling, written by Scalia, itself delimits what will and will not qualify as the content of a given public expression in light of the new restrictions imposed on fighting words. In asking, then, after the rhetorical status of the decision itself, we are led to ask how the rhetorical action of the decision presupposes a theory of semantics that undermines or works against the explicit theory of semantics argued for and in the decision itself.

Specifically, it seems, the decision itself draws on a distinction between the verbal and non-verbal parts of speech, those which Scalia appears to specify as "message" and "sound." *R.A.V. v. St. Paul,* 120 L. Ed. 2d 305, 319–21. For Scalia, only the sound of speech is proscribable or, analogously, that sensuous aspect of speech deemed inessential to the alleged ideality of semantic content. Although Justice Stevens rejects what he calls this kind of "absolutism," arguing instead that the proscribability of content can only be determined in context, he nevertheless preserves a strict distinction between the semantic properties of an expression and the context, including historical circumstance, but also conditions of address. For both Scalia and Stevens, then, the "content" is understood in its separability from both the non-verbal and the historical, although in the latter case, determined in relation to it.

17. The decision made in the trial of the policemen in Simi Valley relied on a similar kind of reversal of position, whereby the jury came to believe that the policeman, in spite of their graphic beating of King, were themselves the endangered party in the case.

18. Matsuda and Lawrence, "Epilogue," *Words that Wound,* p.135.

19. *Chaplinsky* makes room for this ambiguity by stipulating that some speech loses its protected status when it constitutes "no essential part of any exposition of ideas." This notion of an inessential part of such an exposition forms the basis of a 1973 ruling, *Miller v. California,* 413 U.S. 15, extending the unprotected status of obscenity. In that ruling the picture of a model sporting a political tattoo, construed by the court as "anti-government speech," is taken as *un*protected precisely because it is said, "taken as a whole to lack serious literary, artistic, political, or scientific value". Such a representation, then, is taken to be "no essential part of any exposition of ideas." But here, you will note that "no essential part" of such an exposition has become "no valuable part." Consider then Scalia's earlier example of what remains unprotected in speech, that is, the noisy sound truck, the semantically void part of speech which, he claims, is the "nonspeech element of communication." Here he claims that only the semantically empty part of speech, its pure sound, is unprotected, but that

the "ideas" which are sounded in speech most definitely are protected. This loud street noise, then, forms no essential part of any
exposition but, perhaps more poignantly, forms no valuable part.
Indeed, we might speculate that whatever form of speech is unprotected will be reduced by the justices to the semantically empty
sounding title of "pure noise." Hence, the film clip of the ostensibly
nude model sporting an anti-government tattoo would be nothing but
pure noise, not a message, not an idea, but the valueless soundings of
street noise.

20. Kimberlè Crenshaw marks this ambivalence in the law in a different
way, suggesting that the courts will discount African-American forms
of artistic expression as artistic expression and subject such expression to censorship precisely because of racist presumptions about
what counts as artistic. On the other hand, she finds the representation of women in these expressions to be repellent, and so feels herself
to be "torn" between the two positions. See "Beyond Racism and
Misogyny: Black Feminism and 2 Live Crew," in *Words That Wound*.

21. Note the subsumption of the declaration that one is a homosexual
under the rubric of offensive conduct: "Sexual orientation will not be
a bar to service unless manifested by homosexual conduct. The military will discharge members who engage in homosexual conduct,
which is defined as a homosexual act, a statement that the member is
homosexual or bisexual, or a marriage or attempted marriage to
someone of the same gender." "The Pentagon's New Policy Guidelines
on Homosexuals in the Military," *The New York Times*, July 20, 1993,
p. A14.

Bibliography

R.A.V. v. St. Paul, 112 S. Ct. 2538, 120 L. Ed. 2d 305 (1992).

Wisconsin v. Mitchell, 113 S. Ct. 2194, 124 L. Ed. 2d 436 (1993).

Austin, J. L., *How to Do Things With Words*, eds. J. O. Urmson and Marina Sbisa, Cambridge: Harvard University Press, 1962.

Berger, Fred, *Freedom, Rights, and Pornography*, Boston: Kluwer Pub., 1991.

Berger, Fred, "Bringing Hate Crime into Focus: The Hate Crime Statistics Act of 1990," *Harvard Civil Rights and Civil Liberties Law Review*, Vol. 26, no. 1, Winter, 1991, pp. 261–294.

Cornell, Drucilla, *The Philosophy of the Limit*, Routledge, 1992.

Cover, Robert, "Violence and the Word," *The Yale Law Journal*, Vol. 95: 1595, 1986, pp. 1601–1629.

Derrida, Jacques, "Signature, Event, Context," *Limited, Inc.*, Evanston: Northwestern University Press, 1977.

Gunther, Gerald and Lawrence, Charles, "Speech that Harms: An Exchange," *Academe*, bulletin of the AAUP, Vol. 76, no. 6, November 1990.

Heins, Marjorie, "Banning Words: A Comment on 'Words that Wound,'" *Harvard Civil Rights-Civil Liberties Law Review*, vol. 18, (1983), pp. 585–592.

Jost, Kenneth, "Hate Crimes," *The CQ Researcher*, Vol. 3, no. 1, Jan. 8, 1993, pp. 1–24.

MacKinnon, Catharine, *Toward a Feminist Theory of the State*, Cambridge: Harvard University Press, 1989.

MacKinnon, Catharine, *Only Words*, Cambridge: Harvard University Press, 1993.

Matsuda, Mari, "Voices of America," *Yale Law Journal*, 1991, 100: 1329–1407.

Matsuda, Mari, "Public Response to Racist Speech," 87 *Michigan Law Review* 2320 (1989); reprinted in *Words that Wound: Critical Race Theory, Assaultive Speech, and the First Amendment* (Boulder: Westview Press), 1993.

Michelman, Frank, "Conceptions of Democracy in American Constitutional Argument: The Case of Pornography Regulation," 56 *Tennessee Law Review* 291, 306, (1989).

Nietzsche, Friedrich, *On the Genealogy of Morals*, tr. Walter Kaufmann, (New York: Viking), 1967; *Werke in Drei Bände, Band II*, (Munich: Hanser Edition), 1981.

Post, Robert C., "Racist Speeech, Democracy, and the First Amendment," 32, *William and Mary Law Review*, p. 267 (1991).

Post, Robert C., "Cultural Heterogeneity and Law: Pornography, Blasphemy, and the First Amendment," 76 *California Law Review* 297 (March, 1988).

Sunstein, Cass, "Pornography and the First Amendment," *Duke Law Journal*, 589, 615, n. 146, (1986).

Wright, George R., *The Future of Free Speech Law*, Quorum, 1990.

Colloquium: "Language as Violence v. Freedon of Expression: Canadian and American Perspectives on Group Defamation." *Buffalo Law Review*, Vol. 37, no. 2, Spring 1988/89, pp. 337–373.

11

Republic, Rhetoric, and Sexual Difference[1]

Barbara Vinken

The feminism of the last four decades spans two poles that could somewhat schematically be labeled identity versus difference; Simone de Beauvoir and Luce Irigaray are their most obvious representatives. For Beauvoir the emancipation of women consists in becoming men, i.e., self-reliable subjects, capable of speaking not only in the name of the particular and therefore necessarily marginal, but in the name of the general, the universal. When Irigaray claims that she is not a feminist, she means this kind of feminism that is concerned with the Subject. The feminism of Irigaray is twofold; in a first step, she deconstructs the western discourse of the subject from Plato to Freud. This discourse constitutes the male subject by functionalizing the difference of the sexes for the identity of the male subject. Woman is turned into a negative reflection of the male. In a second step that is often misunderstood as some new essentialism, she sets out to reconfigure the feminine as a figure of difference. The differentiality of the feminine does not found a new female identity, but deconstructs the reigning scheme of the human-male identity by withdrawing the negative reflections of the feminine, indispensable for that human-male identity's constitution.

Beauvoir saw the feminine in both its historical-social and in its biological manifestation as a state of self-alienation that should in principle be overcome. Women have to be freed so as to be able to function in the given society like men. Irigaray on the contrary has a stake in an essential modification that will definitively change the current state of affairs. She sees the feminine as the subversive element per se, one that reveals the self-identical male subject as a narcissistic illusion; the political fantasies built on that illusion can and should collapse through subversive feminity. Her project consists in a revolution through the feminine.

I begin with a somewhat abrupt confrontation of the positions of Beauvoir and Irigaray because I would like to propose a doubtlessly hybrid mediation. For the sake of brevity I propose the following denominator: decomposition of identity through imitation. I would like to plead for Beauvoir's strategy in order to support Irigaray's goal; women should in fact become human beings like men. Such a mimesis of the human-male not only reveals that the implicit standard of the human is the male; more important: the imitation of the male role reveals that men are not men, but that they too play a role and that they imitate "men." Through the female impersonation of the male role, the masculine turns out to be a mimickry. Whether this parodistic effect is produced intentionally or comes about unintentionally does not matter in the end. That it comes about is important.

This cunning of reason is the positive formulation of what is negatively conceived of as the danger of "woman" and the feminine. That danger cannot be quelled for good reason as long as our republics still fundamentally rely on a segregation of the sexes. This sexual-political configuration of the modern state can be traced back to the 18th century. The sexual-political implications of the discourses of Enlightenment, although central have generally been "overlooked," i.e., not thematized. The fathers of the Republic, Montesquieu and Rousseau, not only charted a new social contract but also a new relation between the sexes that turns out to be the very condition of the new political order: the condition of the *res publica* is the cleansing, the purging of the feminine from the public sphere. The *res publica* is presented in these texts as a *res masculina;* this pure masculinity guarantees the incorrubtibility, the military potential and the order of the modern state. The true ennemy is therefore not the foreign military forces, but an intimate ennemy that resides within. It is femininity, which does not destroy with arms, but which, corrupted by sweet talk, corrupts through flattery. This collective neurosis structures modern thought on the state. It is the lullaby of our young republics. The conception of the *res publica* as a space that is cleansed of the feminine became successful with the French Revolution and has dominated the European idea of the state far into our century—if not until now.

The specter that haunts Europe since the Enlightenment is less the specter of communism, than the specter of the confusion of the sexes, and it is informed by gender anxiety. Men threaten to be not real men, women not real women. The warding off of an "unnatural" confusion of the sexes is motivated by the fear of a loss of masculinity, the anxiety of an emasculation by means of a perverted femininity, or through femininity as perversion. For if women are no longer women, men cannot be men. "Unable to make themselves into men the women make us into women," writes Rousseau, who will be my main witness in the analysis of the relation among sexual difference, rhetoric, and republic.[2]

The political discourse of the 18th century is at bottom a discourse on the relation of the sexes. The political forms are firmly tied to the order of the sexes. The constitution of the state depends—that is very evident from Montesquieu to Kant—on the relation of the sexes. The antimonarchical discourse opposes aristocracy and femininity to the masculinity of the upright republic, inhabited by free citizens. Monarchy, like femity, spoils morals by refining taste, it renders manliness effeminate and makes virtue as masculinity, *virtus*, impossible. The antimonarchical discourse is therefore an implicitly misogynistic discourse. Following Rousseau, who echoes Montesquieu's *De l'esprit des lois*, a king needs subjects whose sex matters little whereas a republic needs free men.

In a new renaissance of the Roman republic, a pure, immaculate, virtuous, martial male society is opposed to a highly cultivated, overcivilized, courteous, effeminate, scheming, vain monarchy. The republic, one might argue is less a revolutionary than a restorative enterprise: it restores patriarchal society and threatened masculinity along with the Roman republic.

The highest republican virtue is a clean separation of the sexes;

women, "restrained by manners," as Montesquieu says, are banned from the political, public sphere and are confined to reproduction within the house so that men can consecrate themselves solely to the "common interest" and the "common good."[3] Passion, gallantry and courtesy are natural enemies of this new state. Montesquieu proposes the English model as an alternative to the virtuous Roman republic; as far as heroic male martial purity is concerned this model evidently cannot compare with its illustruous predecessor, but it is a thousand times more preferable to the French model of courteous gallantry. In England, according to Montesquieu, the women produce children, chastely withdrawn to the confines of the home. The men, when overcome by natural urges, visit the brothels so that their minds uninhibited by passions are free for the relentless turning of ciphers.

First of all what monarchy has corrupted is masculinity; it is to be restored in a republic through equality of all men and fortified by a renewal of patriarchal relations. Of what precisely did the corruption of monarchy consist? Here is Montesquieu on the reversal of all values through courteous gallantry, which must be abolished in the spirit of good laws:

They [sage legislators] have banished even all commerce of gallantry—a commerce that produces idleness, that renders the women corrupters, even before they are corrupted, that gives a value to trifles, and debases things of importance: a commerce, in fine, that makes people act entirely by the maxims of ridicule, in which the women are so perfectly skilled.[4]

The reversal of all values is a reversal of the very difference that could establish them, i.e., a reversal of being and appearing. This difference is abolished in monarchy. In the discourse of gallantry everything becomes nothing, and nothing everything. Appearance, vain appearance, reigns and sheer nothingness is in command. Empty appearance is the very essence of women and when it reigns with and through them, the essence of men—their virtue— is corrupted. The danger of femininity, as it surfaces in Montesquieu's and later in Rousseau's texts, does not so much consist in women manipulating men through the sheer power of the beguiling word; the female danger lies in the fact that with women rhetoric reigns so absolutely that the very distinction between the improper and the proper, between being and appearance collapses. Masculinity, *virtus*, depends on the possibility of a public, clear distinction between being and appearance. So that men can remain men without being stained by femininity, women should not appear in public.

The eighteenth century conceived of the passage from nature to civilization as a radical break in structural correspondence to the paradise myth. This break is provoked by a rhetorical act of woman. She says "no" and refuses herself to men. The female "no" is an undecidable "no." The treshold to civilization, crossed by female *Triebverzicht*, marks a change in the natural power relation of the sexes. Kant agrees with Diderot, Montesquieu with Rousseau, that in the state of civilization woman manages by her natural art—an art, that though natural, does not manifest itself in the state of nature—to "master man's desire for her." By strategically deploying her weakness, she manages to become as strong as he:

Therefore in anthropology the nature of feminine characteristics, more than those of the masculine sex, is a subject for study by philosophers. Under adverse natural conditions one can no more recognize those characteristics than the characteristics of crab apples or wild pears, which disclose their potential only through grafting or innoculation. Civilization does not establish these feminine characteristics, it only causes them to develop and become recognizable under favorable circumstances.[5]

This balance of power, where woman transforms her weakness into strength by appearing cold in love and making the man passionate through her very virtue, is quite precarious. If civilization becomes too refined—and this state of affairs has been reached according to general agreement among the philosophers in the eighteenth century—it brings about a confusion of the sexes. Either women do not say "no" anymore or men know that women mean "yes" when they say "no." The "no" has lost its ambiguity. This lacking *Triebverzicht* shows that the woman wants to be a man: "Whenever the refinement of luxury has reached a high point, the woman shows herself well-behaved only by compulsion, and makes no secret in wishing that she might rather be a man, so that she could give larger and freer latitude to her inclinations; no man, however, would want to be a woman" (221).[6] And since she does not manage to become a man, she turns men into women. Women bring about the collapse of the order of society when they turn male, that is, libertine. If women turn libertine, Diderot sees that not only as a menace to the patriarchal family, but to any form of ordered society.[7] *Pater semper incertus*—this incertainty can only be banned in the bosom of the family.

The conservation of morals and the existence of the state depend on a rhetorical act. According to Rousseau and Montesquieu, even the survival of men depends on it. Men would otherwise be mercilessly hunted to death by women's formidable sexual insatiability—"especially" adds Rousseau, again echoing Montesquieu "in the southern countries." Through this rhetorical act, natural weakness is transformed by a quasi "natural" art, which only manifests itself in the state of civilization into power. This art consists in appearing cold and in saying "no" even if one eventually means "yes." The equivalence of women and rhetoric is perhaps best described by Nietzsche. In contrast to the philosophers of the 18th century, who keep up the difference between being and appearance, rhetoric is for Nietzsche the ultimate truth. Nothing is perhaps hidden behind the veil: "Vita femina. . . . But perhaps this is the most powerful magic of life: it is covered by a veil interwoven with gold, a veil of beautiful possibilities, sparkling with promise, resistance, bashfulness, mockery, pity and seduction. Yes, life is a woman."[8] For Nietzsche woman remains unreadable even in making love. He cannot decide between the proper and the improper: "That they 'put on something' even when they take off everything—Daß sie 'sich geben', selbst noch, wenn sie—sich geben . . . Woman is so artistic."[9] She is "so artistic" because even in giving herself, she can still put on an act and not give "herself." No wonder that the fathers of the republic have to secure its foundation—i.e., the distinction between the proper and the improper and the merely rhetorical—at any cost; masculinity, properly speaking, depends on it. This is why they wanted to banish not only the poets, but also women from their pure, all male republic. They almost managed with the French Revolution, when, to quote from Schiller's *Ode to Joy*, "all men became brothers."

In this rhetorical context, Rousseau's strong tendencies towards regression fantasies, centering around a unisex society, can be put into perspective. His groundbreaking influence in the French Revolution is due in large part to these fantasies. Such fantasies of a retreat into the homeland of true men appear when the influence of fiction, of rhetoric, and of feminity becomes overpowering. In his very efforts to contol this influence, Rousseau offers the most faithful testimony to its power. His fantasies turn around ancient Sparta or the Roman republic—around the constitution of a male, martial, homosocial body politics. This body politics is a blood brotherhood, since it has its basis in the willingness of every member to shed his blood for his state. The only passion that inhabits this body is love for the fatherland. The figure that keeps it together is the similarity and therefore equality of all men by virtue of their male sex. This is the figure of metaphor. The intervention of women into this male cosmos entails another rhetorical figure: contagion, or contamination, and thus metonymy.

The danger of femininity as difference is highlighted in the *Letter à d'Alembert*, less a letter on the theater than a position paper on the relation among rhetoric, republic and sexual difference. It is also central in the *Solitaires*, the supplement to Rousseau's novel on education, *Émile*. After an almost paradisiac "marriage d'amour" Émile leaves his fallen wife, who became pregnant by another man in the Babel that is Paris. He turns his back on women and the problems they unfailingly bring about even in the best of all worlds. He goes off to fight in the colonies against slavery, for the equality of all men.

In *Émile*, Rousseau presents his ideal of a free, autonomous male individual and his female pendant. The reception of Rousseau's work has often curtailed his throries considerably, resulting in two major reducitons. The first reduction states that Rousseau proclaims the idea of natural man, uncorrupted by society, and that his pedagogy promotes the full unfolding of this natural, and naturally good, human being. Humanists have greatly admired and acclaimed him for the putative ideal of a natural, free, self-determined, autonomous man. According to the second reduction of his theories, Rousseau was the most determined exponent of the concept of the complementarity of the sexes. And while most of his male interpretors have not wasted a word on this idea, he has been critized for this construct by feminists.[10]

It is undeniable that on the one hand Rousseau proclaims the free, self-determined man who somehow gains back his lost nature as second nature, while, on the other hand he aims at a segregation and complementarity of the sexes. But it is also undeniable that against the grain of his intention, his text shows that things are not that simple. His text reveals that the very condition of the self-sufficient man is a specific kind of feminity. It is through woman that the figure "man" is established and that this very establishment is at the same time obliterated. It is thanks to her, thanks to her art and to her rhetoric that the figure "man" does not seem to be a figure, but "the proper." Woman thus is not a complement, but a supplement.

The ideal of natural man, proclaimed by Rousseau, is anything but natural: man has to aquire this ideal nature as his second nature. It is within this process of acquisition and recuperation of his first nature, that his true human nature becomes manifest. In order to put nature in the state of the desired natural, original nature has to be replaced by some kind of secondary "originality." Only this reproduced originality carries the hallmark of innocence, attached to the natural. The true origin is the product of the substitution for the origin. It is essential that the creation of the second as first nature leaves no traces and produces the illusion of the natural, of nonconstructedness. Natural man is thus a rhetorical product, whose rhetoricity must be completely obliterated.

Let us turn to the first reduction of Rousseau's theory, to the ideal of the autonomous man, who relies solely on himself and his own forces. He turns out to be, without having the faintest awareness of it, absolutely dependent. Few relationships in Western literature are as manipulative as the relationship between Émile and his mentor. This mentor does not introduce his pupil to the world as it is, but as it should be. He arranges the world, as if it were unrhetorical, proper; he gives a rhetorical mise en scène of the proper. Émile's unmeditated relation to the objects of this world, his reliance upon his own forces, his self-conscious freedom from *amour propre*, his independence based on *amour de soi*—all these are effects of a gigantic staging, where the mentor, invisible like God, pulls the strings and manipulates Émile as a puppet. Émile's love life, to take only one example, is not only planned down to the smallest practical details, it is carefully staged with great intertextual refinement, following literary pretexts to the letter. Like all great art, this staging appears to be completely spontaneous. Even those who unwittingly play the leading roles have no suspicion that they are merely reciting a prewritten script. The texts consulted—Homer's *Odyssey* and Fénélon's *Télémaque*—already contain an ingenious poetics of *imitatio*, which uncannily doubles the "real" encounter between Sophie and Émile. Émile's naturalness and his freedom are therefore pure illusion, the effect of a rhetoric that is effective to the extent that it never reveals itself. His self-reliance is nothing but a narcissistically fullfilling fantasy, due to the rhetorical skills of the mentor. This mentor has altogether unsettling similarities with women; and that maybe is why he is the only man in the whole book who sees through them and their artifice.

Let us now turn to the second reduction, the complementarity of women. In contrast to men, women are not supposed to have any immediacy or unmediatedness. Properly, one cannot speak of woman proper. The only thing she is interested in even, as a little girl, is the effect she has on others. She receives the gift of manipulation—that is, a rhetorical gift insofar as one manages to get something without saying it properly—in her cradle. To judge her utterances according to the criterion of truthfulness would be utterly mistaken. Effect is the only thing that counts. Woman has no *être en soi*, but only an *être pour autrui;* she therefore has no *amour de soi*, but only an *amour propre*. And it is precisely through that *amour propre* that Rousseau tries to guide her to virtue, while it is precisely *amour propre* that precludes any virtue in a man. Women never *is*, she always appears. She is a medium, pure performative. This unsettling female power for absolute performance is characterized by Rousseau by a divine attribute: that of the unmoved mover. Like God, woman is—almost— motionless. Like him, she moves the whole world. But unlike him, to move the world, she must use her tongue.

It is not within female nature to be autonomous, immediate,

proper and without rhetoric—that would, on the contrary put man's life—due to her unlimited lustfulness—into mortal danger. From women, Rousseau therefore expects a certain type of rhetoric what he calls "pudeur." Clothes are, for good reason the figure for rhetoric; and it is through female fashion that Rousseau, alias St. Preux, explains in his letters from Paris the good and the bad rhetoric of femininity. "Natural" feminity consists in a process of double veiling. A woman should hide her charms and let the beholder guess and allow his fantasy play. What she should hide even more carefully is the act of producing femininity; a woman should by no means show that she has made herself up and she should never look as if she is looking for an effect. The protestant bourgeois rhetoric of the unobtrusive and unadorned has here one of its paradigmatic instances. Emerging from this mise en scène that claims to be sheer naturalness, is a definition of woman whose impact on the ideal of the bourgeois protestant woman should not be underestimated: values like modesty and bashfulness turn out to be code names for a very specific relation of the female self to herself.

The fate of woman is sealed in the relation the little girl has to her doll. Femininity consists from the very beginning in an identification with oneself as somebody else: "She is entirely in her doll, and she puts all her coquetry into it. She will not always leave it there. She awaits the moment when she will be her own doll."[11] The very same woman that sees herself as her own doll—fully capable of seeing herself with other eyes—has to mask carefully this capacity to gain her innocence. This second nature, by no means natural, is the height of acculturation. To become the object for men is her calling. In the fullfillment of this social contract she gains her innocence and thereby her true femininity. Female beings have to dress as women and must then pretend to be incapable of reflecting this process in order to guarantee its effectiveness.

Parisian women immediately come to mind as the counterexample to this "good" feminity. Rousseau concedes from the start that they are the best dressed women in the world. But their adroitness is a bitter necessity: they need this skill to compensate for their natural shortcomings, which are much more significant than in other women. Up to this point, everything is fine. The problem with the Parisians is, however, that they do not conceal the process of making themselves up and try not to pretend it is nature; they openly expose their art as art. So that they cease to be—a truly amazing conclusion—women. Instead of lowering their eyes under the male gaze, and blushing bashfully, they look straight back into mens' eyes to control and test the effect they have as women.

The least feminine women are the aristocrats. And this not despite, but because they generously expose their female charms, overexposing their femininity, so to speak. Femininity here shows its true face: far from being natural, it turns out to be a masquerade. They wear too much rouge, paint their breasts, have vertiginous plunging décolletés; their shamelessness is such that Rousseau shrinks from describing them to his bashful Julie. Exposed femininity does not signify "woman," but "aristocrat.": "Thus, they cease to be women out of fear of being confounded with other women; prefering their rank to their sex they imitate whores so as not to be imitated."[12] The Parisian aristocrats not only make themselves up all too evidently as women; in addition they reflect the process by which they become objects of desire—two unveilings too much, for Rousseau's taste. Since femininity consists in this double veiling, there is little left of it among the women of the *beau monde*. For Rousseau, art consists in hiding art: *Ars adeo latet arte sua*, as Ovid already knew. Parisian women have unfortunately forgotten all about it. Art, which hides itself and its own doing, is necessary however to establish male subjectivity.

Therefore, according to Rousseau, woman is not the complement but rather the very condition of the male subject. It is the condition for his belief in literal properness, for the establishment of the figure of "man" and its concealment. The supplement, to quote Derrida, floods the being. The artful erasure of the female self—Rousseau does not tire to assure us—is in the very best interest of women. The more unmediated they appear, the greater their effect. Their rhetorical skills should only be used so that the man learns to play his *"rôle d'homme."* Woman should erase herself so that man can learn to know and love himself in others—*"ses semblables,"* says Rousseau—and these others are always the same: men.

The self-erasure of feminity, which should function only as medium, as pure performative, should turn man into a good citizen. As soon as his passion is directed toward woman and he desires to please, Rousseau fears for the "*rôle d'homme.*" Because that means entering the realm of rhetoric: not to be, but to appear—and therefore entering into effeminacy. This is why man should please woman only as someone who does not want to please. Woman, instead of usurping the particularity and uniqueness of man's passion, should bring him to the love of humanity. Woman is thus a pure medium for the sake of the homosociality that is the very cement of the republic.

If the constitution of the sexes is without problem in the state of nature it is because, in the absence of society, Rousseau thinks he can examine man as an isolated being, unthreatened by sexual difference. Rousseau's paradise is like the angels' unisex. In the state of culture, banished from paradise, sexual difference proves to be by no means natural, but a highly complicated construct. "Man" is nothing that is naturally given, but a rhetorical figure. To make this figure appear natural—i.e., not constructed—is the ultimate aim of Rousseau's writings on society and politics. The corruption of society therefore is not a corruption of nature, but a corruption of this rhetorical figure—namely of the male body politic. The agent of this corruption is woman: "Never has a people perished from an excess of wine; all perish from the disorder of women." [13]

The disorder of women consists in revealing the rhetoricity of what should appear natural. Man is the figure of the proper, women the figure of figuration; her lack of being, her sheer rhetoricity can be hidden by her art, by her very rhetoric. Man becomes man proper by the mediation of women. But she might also expose the figure of man for what it is, a figure, and thereby corrupt men and society irremediably. For Rousseau, the mythical fall from paradise consists in sexual difference that can only be redeemed by functionalizing this difference for the consolidation of the one sex.

"Do you want to know men? Study women" writes Rousseau in the *Lettre à d'Alembert* (82). But the less you learn in this study the better it is for men. The less women are talked about, the less you see of them, the better it is for the people. Women remain for the people of men an agent of corruption, of decomposition, of subversion—some kind of drug, whose danger should not be underestimated. The biggest favor women can do men therefore is to agree to a segregated society that banishes them from the scene that is the world. As long as they do nothing with men, women can do what they want. Contact between men and women leads to man's subjugation and domestication, to the destruction of the masculine. If distance and difference are abolished, the masculine is extinquished. The icon of this horrible vision is the perverted harem: "and every woman at Paris gathers in her apartment a harem of men more womanish than she" (101). Rousseau's gender anxiety, whose classical formula is the fear that men be turned into women, is linked to a claustrophobic space, tinged with orientalism. This foreign, oriental, confined space is opposed to the open air and the healthy exercises to strengthen the body that are linked to Greek and Roman antiquity. The hallmark of this orientalism is a perverted relation of the sexes. This space, dominated by women, is a space of inverted prostitution, where men, unable to move, are kept indolent prisoners, and where all they have to do is to please. The only service not demanded of these "vile slaves" is to have sex "à la manière des orientaux," that is to make love when ordered to do so. To be turned into an object of pleasure that has to perform at command provokes another fear: being unable to stand the test. The spectre that comes to Rousseau's mind is what Stendhal would call man's fiasco. Men in contact with women are in danger of turning oriental, of becoming impotent slaves of female lust, of losing their mastery, of becoming infected with femininty and thus counterfeited men:

On my last trip to Geneva, I already saw several of these young ladies [young men, B.V.] in jerkins, with white teeth, plump hands, piping voices, and pretty green parasols in their hands, rather maladroitly counterfeiting men. (112)

No wonder that Rousseau shudders when thinking about the possible effects of this all-powerful female rhetoric that transforms men into women who in turn, ape, parody, counterfeit the original man. It is, by the way, a paradox à la Rousseau that men turned into women do not counterfeit women, but men. The most devastating effect consists of the exposure of femininity, of a reflection of rhetoric. This happens in the fashion of the Parisians, who overexpose femininity and test as subjects the effect they have as objects in the male eye. Only the theater is more devastating. The *Lettre à d'Alembert sur les spectacles* is, not only as the title indicates, a letter to a man concerning the establishment of a theater in Geneva, but also a manifesto against a certain form of representation, whose adressees are men in general.

Theater alienates the *individuelle Allgemeine*, which turns out to be precisely—masculinity. What constitutes man? It is not the recognition of oneself as an incommensurable individual, nor is it the complete identification with someone else as other. It is rather the recognition of oneself as part of a universal, generic being: resemblence as similarity that is guaranteed in the male sex. Rousseau therefore opposes resemblence to identification, because one alienates onself in identification (like the girl in her doll and later in herself), whereas one recognizes oneself through similarity with the other. Paul de Man has spoken of a generalized metaphor in his Rousseau interpretations.[14]

I will not go into the *Lettre à d'Alembert's* retroping of the contemporary aesthetic discussion. It is nevertheless interesting that Rousseau was the first to use sexual difference to conduct a polemic against Aristotelian aesthetics. Rousseau translates the danger of the passions into a threat of generalized effeminization. The problem of passion, since Augustine and a fortiori in the interpretation of Port-Royal, has been a problem of figuration. In Rousseau's text, the protestant obsession with the literal, with the proper meaning and the proper sense, becomes manifest through the assertion of man as literal, as properly man. In order to reformulate that obsession in a more "catholic" or a more medieval perspective, one could say that man becomes the figure that denies figurality, whereas woman becomes the figure that incarnates figurality. In the new binary, non-allegorical order this can only mean perversion.

The *Letter* shows men how the adressee, "man," is threatened by women and the theater. The text that illustrates this threat works against its own semantic assertion. While it claims "man" to be natural, it discloses him as a rhetorical figure. While Rousseau pretends to protect "man" against the perverse decomposition that theater accomplishes, his text works de facto as theater and as the bad female rhetoric: what it stages is "man" as a figure that appears disfigured in the aesthetic experience of the theater. Contrary to the "spectacles", theater is the place where the construct "man" is not only exposed as a figure, but deconstructed in its metaphorical figurality. And that is precisely what Rousseau's text accomplishes.

The actor who gives up on the most noble of all roles, the role of man, is no longer a real man. He does not play a generalizable role as "man", his *"rôle d'homme"* since he has to dissolve in the representation of the particular, the individual. The actor loses himself so completely in the other that he keeps nothing proper, whereas the other remains so particular and individual that no common "man" unites them. This kind of identification is an *"oublie de soi,"* that, characterized by self-forgetting, is at the same time man-forgetting. Rousseau opposes a spectacle to this corrupting theater, in which the community stages itself under the open sky in war and love games, so that everybody can learn to recognize and love himself in the others (260). The similarity of the others is guaranteed in the male sex that, reflected in female eyes, achieves its full luster. Women have to extinguish their sexual difference in order to consolidate the one sex. In the theater, however, one never sees people who resemble oneself, but always people who are different: "and we always see beings other than our own kind in the theatre" (27).

The staged representation of the feminine destroys the similarity of men that guarantees the solidarity of the citizens and therefore the stability of the state. The group of citizens is particularized in single male lovers. A group of lovers is a group of singularized concurrents. They are identical and antagonistic— and must, in their rivalry, try to please. Since they court the love of a woman, she has, by holding power over any one of them, power over all of them. Love, which should only be a supplement to the other passions, engulfs them all—first and foremost the most noble of all virtues, patriotism. "Titus can very well remain a Roman; he is the only one on his side; all the spectators have married Bérénice" (53).

Even if the individual fates are as similar as two peas, the male collective is nevertheless destroyed. Rousseau criticises in the theater a certain kind of mediality; by showing herself, woman also shows how she shows herself and thus destroys her "invisibility," which consists in being nothing but a reflection of sameness. She stages the very effect she has. So much for feminity and rhetoric. Let us turn to Rousseau's own rhetoric. Rousseau goes to great length to explain and to excuse his fictional writings such as the *Nouvelle Héloise.* In his non-fictional texts he disclaims the use of rhetoric. He did not take the pen, he points out, to write well; his poor skills could in any case not compete with the brilliant rhetoric of D'Alembert. He knows on the contrary that he will displease and yet he does not shrink from lending his voice to "truth and justice"—the first duties of men, and to humanity and fatherland—his first emotions.

But Rousseau fatally commits the very mistake he blames Parisian women for; he uses not only rhetorical figures—that is inevitable—he overexposes his rhetorical gestures. The "*Lettre*" could be read as a classical treatise on rhetoric put into praxis. Take for example the triple anaphora "*mais il fallait plaire,*" echoing the Shakespearean speech of Marc Antony, one of the best-known pieces of rhetorical craftmanship. Although vehemently condemming the desire to please, Rousseau is not exempt from this very fault. Nothing makes the point better than the rhetorical form of the reproach. Because one wants to please, one cannot tell the hard truth and one must betray the cause of virtuous masculinity to rhetoric and femininity—which at this point have virtually merged. Rousseau's text cannot help but commit this same betrayal. Against the grain of the author's intention that most of his readers have read with satisfaction, the text reveals that man is not a natural essence, but a figure, one that has to be produced by a rhetoric, which is qualified as feminine. The text unveils this rhetoric; it exposes it and, through its vainly disclaimed desire to please, betrays the cause of masculinity that Rousseau holds up with a radicality happily uncommon.

To return to the beginning, I make a jump into the present. I depart from the thesis that our republics—democracies that claim their republicain heritage with pride—are still informed by the background-metaphor of a male body politic. This male bond is no longer grounded in the willingness of all of its members to spill their blood for their country, but in the shared consciousness of participating in a war of economy and authority. Within this male body, power, influence, and money are traded. Women who manage to get power, money, or authority confirm as exceptions the rule of its male constitution.

The very permanence of this structure—despite the womens' movement and its partial successes—proves that the modern state is a defense mechanism against male gender anxiety; one is tempted to say that the modern state *is* this generalized gender anxiety. The modern state fends off a general fear of contamination, the fear of becoming contaminated with the feminine. The dark and threatening knowledge that it is clothes that make the man, and therefore men are women, has to be covered up. The cover-up of that dimly perceived truth is the concept of the sexes' naturalness. Gender is seen as nothing but the natural expression of sex. It is not understood as the process, or figuring, that creates the meaning of biological sex—a sex, when on its own, entirely lacking in meaning. It is through gender that sex acquires its proper meaning. If women take the male role, the fiction that gender is nothing but the expression of sex cannot work any longer. The "naturalness" of sex and its "proper meaning" is exposed as figure, as an effect of rhetoric. Impersonating man should stop the endless reaffirmation that a man is a man is a man is a man.

This is why I want to plead for Beauvoir's praxis in order to achieve Irigaray's aim. Women should become like men. But they/ we should not do that to be in the end self-identical subjects; that was Beauvoir's ideal. They should become men so that this imitation can expose male self-identical subjecthood as an illusion. By parodying masculinity intentionally or unintentionally, women decompose the illusion of male identity. By mimicking masculinity, they introduce ironic distance. They disfigure the figure of referentiality, the congruence of biological sex and social role. It is in this difference that an ironical play can be staged, an intentionally theatrical comedy of the sexes in which both parts play their role with greater distance, more self-irony, and in the end with more power for women and, for both sexes, more pleasure.

The emphasis on pleasure and play should not delude us about the amount of work entailed in the undertaking of such a double strategy. As Judith Butler most recently has made clear: "it is necessary to learn a double movement: to invoke the category [of, say, 'woman'] and, hence, provisionally to institute an identity and at the same time to open the category as a site of permanent political contest."[15] To do this "at the same time" is what the play is about. To play it as a "political contest" may be congenial in coping with American style "affirmative action." What is crucial however, is to keep the game open and the play of difference a pleasure. In forcing the comedy into the pathos of tragedies no particular contest is to be won but a politics of confrontation that instead, forecloses the field to be opened in this parodistic praxis. There is no fixed identity to be reached and no exclusions are to be tolerated, but the singularity of provisional ironies is to be maintained. That it may be fun to take up the self-serving identity politics of self-declared policemen of pleasure enforces rather than depoliticizes a politics of feminism.

Notes

1. The German text of this talk was elaborated on several occasions, particularly in a seminar given in the Post-Graduate Program on Sexual Difference at the University of Munich in January 1993, from which this last version is derived, as printed in Lendemain, no 71/72 (1993), pp.112–124. —For help with the English version and valuable commentary I would like to thank Michèle Lowrie, New York University.
2. Jean-Jacques Rousseau, Lettre à d'Alembert sur les spectacles, hereafter Rousseau, Politics and the Arts, trans. Allan Bloom (Ithaca, NY: Cornell University Press, 1968), p.100.
3. For a general evaluation of women in Montesquieu see Jeanette Geffriaud Rosso, Montesquieu et la feminité (Pisa: 1977).
4. Montesquieu, The Spirit of the Laws, VII, 8, trans. Thomas Nugent (New York, NY: Hafner, 1949), pp.101–102.
5. Immanuel Kant, "The Character of the Sexes," Anthropological Characterization, 2 part, p. 216.
6. See Sarah Kofman, Le respect des femmes: Kant et Rousseau (Paris:

Galilée, 1982); Kofman sees as the true motive for gender anxiety, especially in Rousseau, a desire to be a woman.

7. Denis Diderot, *Sur les femmes*, quoted after *Qu'est-ce qu'une femme?* ed. Elizabeth Badinter (Paris: 1989), pp. 181–183.

8. Friedrich Nietzsche, *The Gay Science*, trans. Walter Kaufmann (New York: Vintage, 1974), pp. 273–274.

9. Nietzsche, *The Gay Science*, pp. 361, 317. See Jacques Derrida, *Spurs: Nietzsche's Styles*, trans. Barbara Harlow (Chicago: University of Chicago Press, 1978).

10. See Christine Garbe, *Die weibliche List im männlichen Text: Jean Jacques Rousseau in der feministischen Kritik* (Stuttgart: Metzler, 1992).

11. Jean-Jacques Rousseau, *Emile or On Education*, V, trans. Allan Bloom (New York: Basic Books, 1979), p.367.

12. Rousseau, *Julie ou la Nouvelle Héloïse* II,21, *Oeuvres complètes* II (Paris: Gallimard, 1964), pp.267–268, my translation.

13. Rousseau, *Letter to M. D'Alembert on the Theater*, p.109.

14. See Paul de Man, *Allegories of Reading* (New Haven: Yale University Press, 1979), p.275.

15. Judith Butler, *Bodies That Matter* (New York: Routledge, 1993), 222.

12

The Test Drive

Avital Ronell

Wasted a fair bit of patriotic young flesh in
order to test some new technology.
>   (William Gibson, *Neuromancer*)

>   Attunement
There was once a man: he had learned as a child that beautiful tale of
how God tried Abraham, how he withstood the test, kept his faith and
for the second time received a son against every expectation. . . . This
man was no thinker, he felt no need to go further than faith. . . . This
man was no learned exegete, he knew no Hebrew; had he known Hebrew then perhaps it might have been easy for him to understand the
story of Abraham.
>   (Søren Kierkegaard, *Fear and Trembling*)

Testing 1

A peculiar feature in the legacy of the *Gay Science* lies in the fact
that the *scientificity* of Nietzsche's use of "science" has not yet been
examined. This fact is not to be ascribed simply to some contin-
gent prejudice in reading or to another, equally fugitive, form of
blindness. If we have been unable to read Nietzsche's word on the
scientificity of science in contemporary terms, this may be so
because his reach is so far ahead of the limits of understanding
that our scanners are eluded by it. In fact, Nietzsche's science has
eluded commentators not only because of the unprecedented leaps

and bounds on which his writing prides itself thematically, but also because of the strange terms of prediction that it posits, and which seem linked to whatever it is that Nietzsche means by *la gaya scienza*. In this context "gay," as Walter Kaufman is careful to point out, does not necessarily mean "homosexual," though such rights of nonreproductive association by pleasure and thought pattern, are certainly extended by the terms of the contract that Nietzsche draws up. What is a science that predicates itself on gaiety without losing its quality of being a science? And how does Nietzsche open the channels of a scientificity that, without compromising the rigor of inquiry, would allow for the inventiveness of science fiction, experimental art and, above all, a highly stylized existence?

If Nietzsche had discovered something like the essence of future science, it may be the case that it exposed itself to him in the way great discoveries are made, namely, when thought "catches it in flight without really knowing what it has caught." The scientificity which concerns Nietzsche, and which can be seen to dominate the technological field in which we moderns exist, embraces the qualities both of destructive and artistic modes of production, involving an ever elusive and yet at the same time tremendously potent force field. Our being has been modalized by the various technologies in ways that are beginning to receive serious attention in the fields of ontology, ethics, political theory, cybernetics, and artificial intelligence. Yet, there is something that belongs neither inside nor outside any of these fields but has nonetheless infiltrated their very core—something, indeed, that Nietzsche's Gay Sci first articulated. Nietzsche variously motivates the scientific premise of his work by terms that indicate the activities of testing, which include experimentation, trial, hypothetical positing, retrial, and more testing. If anything, Gay Sci signals to us today the extent to which our rapport to the world has undergone considerable mutation by means of our adherence to the imperatives of testing. The consequences are considerable, involving, to say the least, our relation to explanatory and descriptive language, truth, conclusiveness, result, probability, process. Henceforth everything will have to stand the test of time, which is to say, it must be tried and proven, and ever provisional, it is structurally regulated by the destruction of a hypothesis that holds it together. (If it weren't too sudden, one could say that Nietzsche laid the groundwork for affirming Popper's theory of falsifiability.)

Nietzsche marvels at a science that, like a warrior, can go out and test itself repeatedly. If today's world is ruled conceptually by the primacy of testing, then this is coextensive with Nietzsche's recognition of the modern experimental disposition. The experimental disposition, as we now know it from a history of flukes, successes, and near misses, in its genesis and orientation, travels way beyond good and evil. This is perhaps why experimentation is a locus of tremendous ethical anxiety. But Nietzsche's itinerary itself is inflected by the tests that he and his work had to endure or, to put it more gaily, the experiment which they, in every walk of life and writing, attempt. There is always the question of Nietzsche's scandalous itinerary, not the least stage of which was his prediction that his name would one day be associated with the greatest catastrophe in history. What does science have to do with this predictive utterance? Nietzsche would show prediction to be the very essence of science, related as it is to the future, which it is always preparing. Prediction, as a promise that can only ironize itself (only time will tell), is the genealogical test par excellence, linking futurity to language. In this regard it is important to note that Nietzsche names in "Preludes of science" the importance of magicians, astrologers and witches—figures who created a taste and hunger for hidden, forbidden powers but who also make us recognize that "infinitely more had to be promised than could ever be fulfilled" (240). Thus prediction and science, however occult their origins (and only a few things are more spooky than futural ghosts such as prophesy and invention), are rooted in the irony of promise. The noncoincidence of scientific promise and its fulfillment is what we call the Test.

Lest we succumb to the temptation of turning Nietzsche into a magician, astrologer or witch, we should remember that, while he was a strong medium, his feeling for the future, "a very powerful feeling" (268), is that of "an heir with a sense of obligation, [of] the most aristocratic of old nobles and at the same time the first of a new nobility—the like of which no age has yet seen or dreamed of . . . the oldest, the newest, losses, hopes, conquests, and the victories of humanity . . ."—a paradoxical feeling that includes both aristocratic obligation toward the future and the more American live-for-today spirit of experimentation. Both moments are involved for Nietzsche in a necessarily prophetic science. The mood of such a scientist is that of Dionysian pessimism, what Nietzsche calls the "pessimism of the future—for it comes! I see it coming!" This premonition and vision "belongs to me as inseparable from me, as my *proprium* and *ipsissimum*." (330) And so, in Book Five of the *Gay Science* Nietzsche explicates "the meaning of our cheerfulness" by situating "us" at our posts; this occurs directly after the announcement of the greatest recent event—that God is dead, that the belief in the Christian God has proven unbelievable, God indeed has failed the test, faith has been undermined: "This long plenitude and sequence of breakdown, destruction, ruin, and cataclysm that is now impending—who could guess enough of it today to be compelled to play the teacher and advance proclaimer of this monstrous logic of terror, the prophet of a gloom and an eclipse of the sun whose like has probably never yet occurred on earth?"(279)

"Even we born guessers of riddles who are, as it were, waiting on the mountains, posted between today and tomorrow, stretched in the contradiction between today and tomorrow, we firstlings and premature births of the coming century, to whom the shadows that must soon envelop Europe really *should* have appeared by now—why is it that even we look forward to the approaching gloom without any real sense of involvement and above all without any worry and fear for ourselves? . . . our heart overflows with with gratitude, amazement, premonitions, expectation. At long last the horizon appears free to us again, even if it should not be bright; at long last our ships may venture out again, venture out to face any danger; all the daring of the lover of knowledge is permitted again. . . ." The permit that we have received is nothing less than a test driver's licence. If it had been revoked, Nietzsche suggests in another passage, this is due to the moral prejudice against science, adventure and deregulated knowledge imposed on us culturally by the couple, Faust and Mephistopheles—true traitors to the cause of godless science. This represents one of the very few swipes that Nietzsche takes at Goethe. It is somewhat of a strange moment, for Nietzsche attacks the literary Goethe for a scientific error. At the same time, it could be argued that the secret hero of Nietzsche's scientific investigations is the Goethe of the *Theory of Color*, whose bold experiments put the experimenter on the line. Goethe prioneered the moment when the body became the test site and not a transcendentalizing consciousness. This is the Goethe that Nietzsche represses when he goes after the Goethe who produced Faust's gradual decathexis of science. But Goethe's doublings and repressions, his Nietzschean mirrorings in art and science, are the subject of another book.

One could argue that, nowadays, since the advent of the Gay Sci, but perhaps not solely because of it, there is nothing that is not tested or subject to testing. We exist under its sway, so much so that one could assert that technology has now transformed world into so many test sites. Among other things, this means that everything we do is governed by a logic that includes as its necessary limit, probability calculation, self-destruction, and interminable trial. Let me focus Nietzsche's unprecedented emphasis on experimentation, which is what I believe provides the crucial access code to the possibility of a gay science.

Testing 1, 2

Nietzsche: the thinker of the test site (from the selective test of the eternal return, to Zarathustra's trials, and the experimental language shots of the aphoristic texts). Nietzsche was always testing one, two, three. The utterence,"*Versuchen wir's!*" (let's put it to the test, let's try it out), circumscribes the space of an unceasing series of audacious experiments:

I would praise any skepsis to which I am permitted to reply: "Let us try [*versuchen*] it!" But I do not want to hear anything any more of all the things and questions which do not permit of the experiment . . . for there courage has lost its rights. [in Kaufmann xerox 67]

One could argue that Nietzsche, in *Human, All-too-Human* (1878), *Dawn* (1881), and *The Gay Science*, sets up a lab in which he performs "the countless experiments on which later theories might be built" (70). Each aphorism is set up as an experiment to be tested, observed and, at times, rescinded. Rescindability is the true test of courage. This has nothing to do with wimping out but with taking the cuts of criticism and basing nothing on faith or merely on durability. It is the mark of the antiparanoiac par excellence. Show me scholars today who have the courage to see their little convictions put to the test. But scholars are cool with Nietzsche, for they demand that prior training and discipline be proven to them—he calls it their unconditional probity (323). Thus, "I bless you, my scholarly friends," writes Nietzsche (323). I bless you "even for your hunched backs. And for despising, as I do, the 'men of letters' and culture parasites. And for not knowing how to make a business of the spirit. And for having opinions that cannot be translated into financial values . . . And because your sole aim is to become masters of your craft, with reverence for every kind of mastery and competence . . ." and so forth. This is one of the rare passages where Nietzsche acknowledges, with only some irony, the relative nobility of the scholar. This is because scholars are on the way to scientificity, that is, they require proof and have undergone the severe conditions of one boot camp or another. Scholars, who, in principal, are not pretenders, are not in it for the money, and they deal with the boss, the university, with some amount of defiance despite themselves. At least they are not writing "for" the university, though they may be teaching for the institution. This is the most positive evaluation of scholars, who are otherwise seen to be ossified in reactivity—they say yes, no, yes, no (usually no, moreover) to everything that is run by them. These lowgrade testers are often called upon to give tests, conduct experiments and come up with research results.

In *Will to Power* (1906) testing is linked to the becoming-active of forces. Active negation or active destruction is the state of strong spirits which "destroy the reactive in themselves, submitting it to the test of the eternal return and submitting themselves to this test even if it entails willing their own decline" (Deleuze, 100). What is the nature of the test? Does it have an essence? Is it sheer relationality? Why is our security—whether or not you are prepared to admit this—based on testability? We *want* everyone and everything tested, and I am not unaware of the sinister resonance of this observation. But since when has a desire signaled by humanity not been pulled by a sinister undertow?

Testing, which our Daseins encounter every day in the form of SAT, GRE, HIV, MCATS, FDA, cosmetics, engines, stress, and arms testing 1-2-3- broadcast systems, and testing your love, testing your friendship, in a word, testing the brakes—was located by Nietzsche mainly in the eternal joy of becoming. Becoming involves the affirmation of passing away and destroying—the decisive feature of a Dionysian philosophy. In the first place (but the place of testing still needs to be secured), testing marks an ever new relation between forces. Ceasing to raise to infinity or finitude, it imposes the inevitability of unlimited finity. This is the temporality we associate with third-generation machines, cybernetics, and information technology. In fact, technology ensures its evolving perpetuation by quietly positing as its sole purpose an infinite series of Testing severed from any empirical function. This suggests that an elliptical circuit has been established between Testing and the Real: a circuit so radically installed—it is irreversible—cancels the difference between the test and the real thing. As activity or object, does the test discover, expose, establish, or even invent something?

Testing, which should be read as the figure par excellence of our modernity, still claims absoluteness (something has been tested and proved; we have test results), but in the form of provisional temporariness. It opens up the site that occurs, Nietzsche suggests, after Christianity has fizzled, arriving with the crisis in the relationship of interpretation to experience. It is no longer a question of interpreting one's own experience as pious people have long enough interpreted theirs, namely, "as though it were providential, a hint, designed and ordained for the sake of the salvation of the soul—all that is *over* now (GS:307). Now we godless ones test, we rigorously experiment. We are the Christian conscience translated and sublimated into a scientific conscience. Converted to scientificity, we still carry a trace of Christianity because what triumphed over the Christian god was Christian morality itself, "the concept of truthfulness that was understood ever more rigorously" (GS:307). As it became more refined, Christianity forced intellectual cleanliness upon us; it came clean by pushing science as the sublimation of its own murkiness. Now man's *conscience* is set against it; it is "considered indecent and dishonest by every more refined conscience." Elsewhere: "So [our dear religious people] experience 'miracles' and 'rebirths' and hear the voices of little angels! But we, we others who thirst after reason, are determined to scrutinize our experiences as severely as a scientific experiment—hour after hour, day after day. We ourselves wish to be our experiments and guinea pigs." (253) Henceforth, reactive positings will have to stand up to the scrutiny of recursive testing.

The experimental disposition, and the provisional logic of testing that accompanies it, occurs, in its technological sense, as an event, after the death of God. It does not arrive on the scene as a barbarian conqueror, but modestly, for it is at once more modest than anything Christianity had proposed—proceeding, namely, by the modesty of hypotheses which are always overturnable. Yet this modesty is split by the spirit of audacity, wielding a strength capable of risk-taking and tremendous courage. It gathers its strength on mistrust. In the Gay Sci Nietzsche, posing as the Dionysian philosopher, writes, "the more distrust, the more philosophy." This is perfectly consistent with the exigencies of testing. Dionysian pessimism can be read along the lines proposed by Paul de Man in *Allegories of Reading* (1979), where we are reminded that "a statement of distrust is neither true nor false: it is rather in the nature of a permanent hypothesis." Thus in the modern sense testing does not lean on the ontotheological notion of creation for its strength—the test creates nothing ex nihilo and yet it is the sin qua non of any possible creation. To be sure, testing did not emerge as an event one day; it did not arise cleanly from the ashes of Judeo-Christian tradition but occupied a place prior to technological dominion; and so, God was always testing his nearest and dearest: Abraham, Job, Christ, and my mother were constantly being tested, and not all of them remained mute about having their patience tried. But here's the hitch prior to technotesting, and Kierkegaard provides the clue: "And yet Abraham was God's chosen, and it was the Lord who put him to this test. All was now surely lost!" (*Fear and Trembling*, 53). Abraham, for his part, must not know it is a test, for this would eliminate the paradox of Abraham's total faith in relation to God's promise to him of a son. If Abraham had known it was a test, the answer would have been easy. God does not announce that "this is a test, this is *only* a test of the emergency broadcast system. If this were a real..." until Abraham has passed it. Abraham cannot know until the test is over, which means that it was and was not a real test, but in any case becomes a test after its question has been effectually answered. Though I am not yet widely recognized as a biblical scholar, even though I have proven definitively that Moses and Aaron were a telephone, I would venture to opine that Job, in the series of God's litmus tests, is locatable at the heart of the undecidable limit between testing and infinite contestation.

Be that as it may, with the spread of technology, testing lost some of its auratic and exceptional qualities and started hitting everyone with its demands, that is, anyone who wanted to gain admission anywhere, and all institutions started testing to let you in—and let you out. If something weird happens, you are taken in for psychiatric testing. Technological warfare belongs to the domain of testing as well, and will do much to support the hypothesis that there is little difference between testing and the real thing. For testing counts as warfare today and thus marks the elimination of boundaries between weapons testing and their deployment. The test is already a signal to the enemy other. What this means, among other things, is that the Cold War *was* a war.

One can show, and I have tried to do so elsewhere, the extent to which the Persian Gulf War was conducted as a field test; but it also, phantasmically, displayed the characteristics of a national AIDS test in which America initially scored HIV-negative, owing to the "bloodless" and safe war (now strange diseases are coming out of their period of latency). The Gulf War proved the hypothesis that no technology will ever exist without being tested; but once it is tested, we are no longer simply talking about a *test*. In the case of the Gulf War weapons were deployed that had been amassed against the Soviet Union but fell under the risk of never being tried out. As clear as the logic of engagement may have seemed with the justificatory chatter of a New World Order, the Gulf War was, strictly speaking (in terms of the essence of technology that is pushing these buttons), little more than a field test. While the unstoppable relation of technology to testing may still require considerable theoretical scrutiny, it comes as no surprise to the so-called military establishment (the distinction between military and civil technologies is blurring by the minute). Nothing will be invented, no matter how stealth, nuclear or "unthinkable," that will not be tested, that is, realized. Thus testing, in addition to raising issues of deployment, is always written into treaties. The necessity of treaties, conventions and regulative discourses in itself proves, in the manner of Kant, Benjamin and Derrida, in their critiques of violence, that testing, like war, has become naturalized, and can only be provisionally suspended by treaties that try to ban them.

In any case, the trade fair held directly after the Gulf War tagged certain weapons as "combat proven" and boosted sales. Finally, war, as it increasingly becomes the technological and teletopical test site par excellence, has lost its metaphysical status as meaningful production. This loss can be measured at least since Hegel, when war was still conceived as a sort of pregnancy test for historical becoming. If we no longer know how to wage war, in other words, how to legitimate and justify its necessity in history's unfolding (we desist at times from calling our interventions war—they have become police actions, missions or humanitarian runs), we still hope that it may yield some test results.

The relation of testing to the question of place is essential. The test site, as protoreal, marks out a primary atopos, producing a "place" where the real awaits confirmation. The test site is not a home (unless you're a homunculus). Linked to a kind of ghostless futurity the site offers no present shelter. This explains perhaps why Nietzsche names the gaya scienza in the same breath that convokes "we who are homeless": "We children of the future, how could we be at home in this today—in this fragile, broken time of transition?" (338). But Nietzsche, being Nietzsche, knows how to affirm the unhinging of home as the preparation for another future, one not rooted in ideologies of the homefront. The logic of the test site that we have not yet understood concerns precisely the relation of the site to *life;* we still know only how to leave the test site uninhabitable, mapping ever more deserts as eco-wasteland, unexploded arsenal, littered terrain, the "third world." The question that Nietzsche presses us on is therefore never merely one of affirming homelessness after metaphysics, but of rendering spaces habitable, multiplying trajectories for life and the living, refiguring the site of experimentation in such a way as to ensure that it is not already the ensepulchered reserve of the living dead. In other words: why have we not yet thought the test site on the side of life? It is important to note that Nietzsche is not, in this phase of this thought, the exhuberant adolescent of old. The Nietzsche who thinks the experiment has come back from the dead several times over; he is formulating his theory of the great health; he has returned once again to health and, like a great convalescent, looks at life with a somewhat ghostly air that dissolves only gradually. Still, he is on the move again, and home-lessness becomes an expression of renewed *vitality*, the overcom-ing of passive destitution. The homelessness that Nietzsche posits is never simply reactive, therefore, but defiant and future-ori-ented. Resembling at moments the crew of Star Trek, "we who are homeless are too manifold and mixed racially. . . . We are not tempted to participate in mendacious self-admiration and racial indecency" (340). Racial indecency is, Nietzsche suggests every-where, the absence of test. It is the untested presumption and would never hold scientific sway. Racial indecency and self-admi-ration go steadily together, for one not only feeds the other but refuses the movement of self-overcoming, which is to say, cease-less self-correction. Nietzsche, however, is by no means setting up a political correctional facility, with human subjects weighted down by punishing chains. To be capable of a long distance will to knowledge one must consistently lighten up. Also: "One has to be very light to drive one's will to knowledge into such a distance and beyond one's time . . . The human being of such a beyond undergoes a test of strength" (343).

A mark of the beyond, or of sending and *envoi*, the test site is an articulation of being-not-at-home, whether this be figured as the desert of nuclear testing, a constellation of the underground, in the lab or, as Nietzsche has it, very happily far away—at a remove from the fatherland, in Italy, where experimental life can be af-firmed. What does Nietzsche say about the age of the experiment?

The capacity to experiment, and its considerable implications, is clearly something of a gift for Nietzsche. This is why Nietzsche cannot stop expressing his gratitude for the dangerously changing aspect of the great health (there are a number of healths, and they often take you under). The possibility of experimentation, the kind that urges the testing of your strength over and over again, presupposes a granting. A gift has been given to which Nietzsche in turn gives his work, offering his gratitude, despite everything, to what has been granted. The gift of starting more or less from scratch, but with a new mistrust, takes as granted the thinker's probity, which is given as a nonressentimental rapport to one's task, affirming time and again that one is free to let go of the very gift that granted the work—a relation to the work which Nietzsche is not loathe to associate with great love. In the section "Against remorse" Nietzsche outlines a high moral code, without imperative, observed by a thinker who exists in the noncontradictory space where action, freedom and noble sensibility inflect thought: "—A thinker sees his own actions as experiments and questions—as attempts to find out something. Success and failure are for him *answers* above all. To be annoyed or feel remorse because something goes wrong—that he leaves to those who act because they have received orders and who have to reckon with a beating when his lordship is not satisfied with the result" (108). The experiment implies, among other things, tenure, freedom, a nobility of taste—if I were to lay another track down, it would circuit the relatedness of experiment to Nietzschean gratitude, as it is expressed throughout the Gay Sci, the question of taste that he links consistently to experiment, in other words, testing and tasting. The relation of the test to taste is crucial, and here I can only indicate the direction in which it points us. The freedom with which Nietzsche associates genuine experimenting has a double legacy. On the one hand, he invokes a freedom by which an experiment answers to no one. Nietzsche's thinking has passed through the crucible of answerability. Yet, accountability will also prompt the most serious ethical questions of the twentieth century. Questions of accountability will organize the way we think about experimentation and testing from the relative innocence, it was thought, of the experiments in free love to animal testing or the genome project. In fact every form of testing is open to ethical anxiety and, in many areas, has contributed significantly to the resurgence of ethics. This still remains, in Nietzsche's sense, a question of taste. Because decency and even justice, for Nietzsche, are matters of taste. (Nietzsche's example goes something like this: I would rather be robbed than see a homeless person suffer. This is a matter of taste.)

Testing and experimentation, related inextricably to acts of negating and affirmation, are conducted in the name of life but also by life itself. Selective testing comes with the eternal return and not in some naive and spontaneous expression of a zest for life. Thus Nietzche's rhetorical embrace of this double affirmation comes by way of the negative: "No, life has not disappointed me [after a long period of illness]. The great liberator came to me: the idea that life could be an experiment of the seeker for knowledge—and not a duty, a calamity, not trickery.—And knowledge itself: let it be something else for others; for example, a bed to rest on, or the way to such a bed, or a diversion or a form of leisure—for me it is a world of dangers and victories in which heroic feelings, too, find places to dance and play.—*Life as a means for knowledge*—with this principle in one's heart one can live not only boldly but even gaily, and laugh gaily, too" (255). That life could be an experiment is a gift of great liberation; that is why it gets named together with the entitling instance of the Gay Sci—the double affirmation of "gaily," which nuances living boldly, for one can be bold and sinister.

Perhaps somewhat surprisingly for us moderns today, who associate experiment with desubjectivation, the experimental imagination, as Nietzsche calls it at one point, implies a strong personality. The lack of personality always takes its revenge, Nietzsche writes in #345, "*Morality as a problem*": "A weakened, thin, extinguished personality that denies itself is no longer fit for anything good—least of all for philosophy. All great problems demand great love, and of that only strong, round, secure spirits who have a firm grip on themselves are capable. It makes the most telling difference whether a thinker has a personal relationship to his problems and finds in them his destiny, his distress, and his greatest happiness, or an 'impersonal' one, meaning that he can do no better than to touch them and grasp them with the antennae of cold, curious thought." Once again, the Nietzschean motif of love determines the strength of thought. Nietzschean science has nothing to do with cold objectivist observation but demands something on the order of a spiritual self-deposit. The encounter of great problems with great love takes place as a result of the scientific curiosity and experimental imagination which secure its possibility. In this regard, love supplants moral valuations, rendering the scientific pursuit irresistible. Why is it, Nietzsche moreover asks in this section, that "I see nobody who ventured a *critique* of moral valuations; I miss even the slightest attempts of scientific curiosity, of the refined, experimental imagination of psychologists and historians that readily anticipates a problem and catches it in flight without quite knowing what it has caught" (284). The experimental imagination is exceptional in several ways. Taking risks but also exercising prudence, practicing, in Nietzsche's famous sense, the art of living dangerously, the experimental spirit is not so much a technobody (equipped with the antannae of cold, curious thought) but, in the first place, a vitality that disrupts sedimented concepts and social values. Society values unchangeability and dependability. It rewards the instrumental nature (the dependable, computable, i.e., someone you can count on) with a good reputation. On the other hand, self-transformation and relearning, making oneself somewhat unpredictable in this regard, are consistently devalued. "However great the advantages of this thinking may be elsewhere, for the search after knowledge no general judgment could be more harmful, for precisely the good will of those who seek knowledge to declare themselves at any time dauntlessly *against* their previous opinions and to mistrust everything that wishes to become firm in us is thus condemned and brought into ill repute. Being at odds with a 'firm reputation,' the attitude of those who seek knowledge is considered *dishonorable* while the petrification of opinions is accorded a monopoly on honor! Under the spell of such notions we have to live to this day" (238). Submitting itself to constant critique and revision, the experimental disposition is capable of leaving any conclusion in the dust when it obsolesces or proves decadent; when a result is "arrived" at, the experimental imagination suspends it in its

provisional pose of hypothesis. The hypothetical statement submitted to critique does not belong to a class of positivistic certainties or objective observations. A truth or probability was,
Nietzsche stresses, formerly loved. The scientific imagination is
cathected on the hypothesis, and itself becomes different as the
"object" changes. While it seems as though reason has prompted a
process of decathexis, it is in fact life and its production of needs
that is responsible for criticism and revision. Thus "In Favor of
Criticism" states the following: "Now something that you formerly
loved as truth or probability strikes you as an error; you shed it
and fancy that this represents a victory for your reason. But perhaps this error was as necessary for you then, when you were still
a different person—you are always a different person—as are all
your present 'truths,' being a skin, as it were, that concealed and
covered a great deal that you were not yet permitted to see. What
killed that opinion for you was your new life and not your reason:
you no longer need it. . . . When we criticize something, this is no
arbitrary and impersonal event; it is, at the very least, very often
evidence of vital energies in us that are growing and shedding
skin. We negate and must negate because something in us wants
to live and affirm—something in us that we do not know or see as
yet.—This is said in favor of criticism" (245–6). The experimental
disposition is somewhat on the run, whether passing through nonknowledge, and catching the unknowable in the outfield of inquiry, or because something within us compels negation and further negation as a condition for living and affirming. Unknowable,
and as yet unseen, something within us could come from the
future because we are molting and the gay science has pledged
itself in so many ways to the future.

Testing 1, 2, 3

To the extent that the experimental disposition emerges from
constant self-differentiation, which is to say also that it can simulate itself, as Nietzsche suggests, and wears many masks, it also
belongs to an experimental site that Nietzsche calls in a crucial
moment of development "America." If I say "development," it is
also because Nietzsche for once offers thanks to Hegel for having

introduced the decisive concept of development into science. The gratitude is shortlived because we learn quickly that Hegel "delayed atheism dangerously by persuading us of the divinity of existence where Schopenhauer's unconditional and honest atheism at least made the ungodliness of existence palpable and indisputable" (307). But America becomes an experimental site because it is the place of acting and role playing—a concept developed by Nietzsche for America or by America for Nietzsche. At this point or place Nietzsche links experimentation with improv techniques—something of which I have availed myself for this presentation. In any case, the dimension of scientificity underscoring the gay science is related to exploration and discovery, though discovery is not seen simply as "inventing" but rather as discovering what was already there, inhabited, which is why Nietzsche has recourse sometimes to the discovery of America—an event, an experiment that did not occur without its risks. The experimentor must give up any secure anchoring in a homeland, allow herself to be directed by an accidental current rather than a preestablished goal. This accidental current nonetheless becomes the groove for a voyage taken without any helmsman, without any commander, Nietzsche insists. And now, to the accidental discovery of America.

There have been ages when men believed with rigid confidence, even with piety, in their predestination for precisely one particular occupation. But there are opposite ages to those of durability ("and duration is a first-rate value on earth"); they are really democratic, and a certain cocky faith advances more and more into the foreground—"the Athenian faith that first becomes noticeable in the Periclean age, the faith of the Americans to day that is more and more becoming the European faith as well: namely, the individual becomes convinced that he can do just about everything and can manage any role, and everybody experiments with himself, improvises, makes new experiments, enjoys his experiments; and all nature ceases and becomes art." The jack-of-all-trades (an American translation of the Renaissance man) is an American symptom rebounding to Europe, the bright flipside of which we could count as the art of improv and experimentation, including performance art and jazz (music was always with science on this point, from at least Bach's *Inventions* to computer synthesizers). Nietzsche's focus is on the individual's incredible conviction that he can manage any role. The refined European profile for role management, by the way, Nietzsche locates in the Jewish people, who have had to rigorously play it as it comes, go with the flow, adjust and associate. The experimentor is at once the experimentee: there is little of that supposed scientific or artistic distance, or just enough to try oneself out. Individuals turn themselves into a test site, produce ever new experiments and, significantly, *enjoy* these experiments. This is not the grim lab for which Dr. Frankenstein became the paradigmatic director, beset as he was with German gravity and remorse over the meaning of his relentless experiments.

There is a price to be paid by the experimental player. One cannot remain detached from the activity but finds oneself subject to morphing. One grows into one's experimental role and becomes one's mask. America's increasing obsession with actors can be connected to Nietzsche's observations on nonsubstantial role playing: "After accepting this role faith—an artist's faith, if you will—the Greeks, as is well known, went step for step through a rather odd metapmorphosis that does not merit imitation in all respects: *They really became actors* . . . and whenever a human being begins to discover how he is playing a role and how he can be an actor, he *becomes an actor* . . . It is thus that the maddest and most interesting ages of history always emerge, when the actors, *all* kinds of actors become the real masters. As this happens, another human type is disadvantaged more and more and finally made impossible; above all, the great 'architects': The strength to build becomes paralyzed; the courage to make plans that encompass the distant future is discouraged; those with a genius for organiztion become scarce: who would still dare to undertake projects that would require thousands of years for their completion? For what is dying out is the fundamental faith that would enable us to calculate, to promise, to anticipate the future in plans of such scope, and to sacrifice the future to them—namely, the faith that man has value and meaning only insofar as he is *a stone in a great edifice*, and to that end he must be *solid* first of all, a 'stone'—and above all not an actor!" (303).

By this passage of paradoxical reversal, experimenting gradually becomes associated with America and the rule of actors. Nietzsche comes to see experimenting in the negative light of project paralysis, inhibiting acts of promising, calculating or anticipation—acts by which the future can be nailed down, as it were, and "sacrificed" to the performatives that bind it. The futural stone age has been compromised, however, by new human flora and fauna, which, Nietzsche asserts, could never have grown in more solid and limited ages. So the experimental disposition is cast in soft metaphors. Watering down the solid reputation, showing the experimentor to be not quite solid as a rock but rather absorbed into a soft present that shies away from distance of future. Nonetheless Nietzsche considers this age as one without limit—of unlimited finity; it is the maddest and most interesting of ages. It is not clear how the loss of this hard rock faith is to be evaluated, because Nietzsche elsewhere tends to emphasize the need for shedding such faith and, taking on new forms spontaneously, becomes somewhat of an American himself. He is attached only to brief habits, to a fluidity that allows him to get to know many things and states: "I love brief habits and consider them an inestimable means for getting to know *many* things and states, down to the bottom of their sweetness and bitternesses. My nature is designed entirely for brief habits even in the needs of my physical health and altogether as far as I can see at all—from the lowest to the highest. I always believe that here is something that will give me lasting satisfaction—brief habits, too, have this faith of passion, this faith in eternity—and that I am to be envied for having found and recognized it; and now it nourishes me at noon and in the evening and spreads a deep contentment all around itself and deep into me so that I desire nothing else, without having any need for comparisons, contempt or hatred. But one day its time is up; the good thing parts from me, not as something that has come to nauseate me but peacefully and sated with me as I am with it—as if we had reason to be grateful to each other as we shook hands to say farewell. Even then something new is waiting at the door, along with my faith—this indestructible fool and sage!—that this new discovery will be just right, and that this will be the last time. That is what happens to me with dishes,

ideas, human beings, cities, poems, music, doctrines, ways of ar-
ranging the day, and life styles"(237). Beyond the motif of farewell
and Nietzschean gratitude, the passage formats the things which
offer themselves to experimentation, testing, and rearrangement,
ranging from dishes and music to Nietzsche's Californian invention of life style. If it is possible however for Nietzsche to say that
one day the time comes for good things to bid him farewell in a
mood of satience and peacefulness, this means that the relation to
things is not one of violent and constant improvisation. Rather, he
admits, "Most intolerable, to be sure, and the terrible par excellence would be for me a life entirely devoid of habits, a life that
would demand perpetual improvisation. That would be my exile
and my Siberia."(237) Carried to extremes, however, the homelessness of experimentation turns into radical exile when it demands non-stop improv. Thus: "Enduring habits I hate. I feel as if
a tyrant had come near me and as if the air I breathe had thick-
ened when events take such a turn that it appears that they will
inevitably give rise to enduring habits; for example, owing to
an official position, constant association with the same people, a
permanent domicile, or unique good health. Yes, at the very bottom of my soul I feel grateful to all my misery and bouts of
sickness and everything about me that is imperfect, because this
sort of thing leaves me with a humdred backdoors through which
I can escape from enduring habits" (237).

The experimental disposition, then, has to dismantle its internal and material lab frequently to keep the punctual rhythm of
the brief habit going—Nietzsche never places the experiment on
the side of monumentality or reliable duration; it cannot be
viewed as a project. Nor is he attached to any particular form of
experiment—this is not the scientist obsessed with an *idée fixe*—
but one capable of uprooting and going, for better or worse,
with the diversifying flow of ever new flora and fauna. This openness, though it does have its limits and points of closure, necessarily invites ambivalence—those moments, for instance, when
Nietzsche stalls, dreaming of immense edifices and the permanence promised by contracts written in stone.

The normative test does not originate knowledge but confirms
it. Yet testing, even at it sets its limits strictly, in accordance with

specific codes or conventions, always checks for the unknown loop which takes it beyond mere passing or failing. The true aim of a test is abysmally to fail. This is when it produces an effect of discovery, which is shown to be linked to accident, chance or luck—what we could call off-track betting. It is to be understood that true failure is not merely of an instrumental nature, such as a defect or mechanical failure. This concerns a type of testing that probes more than workability or conformity to an already regulated norm—more than, say, smog test.

In a limited technological sense, the question of passing or failing may be a trivial one, as the recursive nature of the test determines its generation regardless of discreet results. It is in the nature of testing to be ongoing indefinitely, even when the simulation may pass into the referential world. As simulated and operational orders collapse into one zone (where, for instance, the distinction between real war and field test are blurred), the more interesting questions of cadence, interruption or reinterpretation emerge. Is it possible, in our era, to stop or even significantly to interrupt testing? We have seen the difficulties involved in banning nuclear tests. The successive attempts at banning tests require the intervention of signed treaties. We know from Kant *(A Sketch for Perpetual Peace)*, Walter Benjamin ("Critique of Violence") and Derrida ("Force of Law"), that treaties suspend violence momentarily, artificially. The irony of Kant's unfinished sketch performs the allegory of an impossible peace. Because testing henceforth belongs to the question of violence—involving treaties, conventions, regulations, policing, ethical debate, eco-ontology, and so forth—only a discussion of rhetorical codes strong enough to scan the paradoxical logic of testing can begin to analyze the problem of its unstoppability, if indeed this is for us, today, a problem. The task of reading the links between violence and testing however requires us to pass the test thorugh the crucible of undecidability, to understand it as good and evil, beyond good and evil, if not the very determination of good and evil. Can there be any good prior to the test? Can there be a human being without a test? (One thinks of the endless battery of tests devised for determining the replicant/human difference in *Blade Runner*.) If we were able to get through to the other side of these questions, beyond the ambivalence that the test appears at every juncture to restore, and supposing we decided that it would be best to end with all this testing: would banning or disruption be at all possible?

What Nietzsche means by "personal" has everything to do with the nature of scientificity that he expounds. For scientists are at no point outside the field of experimentation; they cannot extricate themselves from the space of inquiry in the name of some mystified or transcendental project from which the empirical person can be dropped out or beamed up at will. The test site can always blow up in their face. This is an insight that has been tried by Derrida in his analysis, for instance, of Freud's place in the discovery of *fort/da* as well as in the trajectories of Lacan's return to Freud, or Foucault's massive reading of desire and power. Yet it is Derrida who is most often cast in the role of experimentor. Indeed, Derrida's relation to improvisation and invention is something that still needs to be understood *scientifically*, if one can still say so, if only to clear away the blindness that has addressed some of his boldest experiments. For this is the age of experimentation, and we have not yet learned to read its protocols.

V

A New Sense of the Political

13

Ghost Writing

Derek Attridge

I saw a ghost last night. More important, I heard a ghost, I was addressed by a ghost, we were addressed by a ghost.[1]

Was it the ghost of William Shakespeare? The ghost of Karl Marx? The ghost of deconstruction (yet again risen from the dead?). Or of deconstruction in America?

Or even the ghost of Jacques Derrida? One of the many ghosts of Jacques Derrida?[2]

It said many things, but in saying everything that it had to say it also said: "Remember me!"

During yesterday afternoon's session, Philip Lewis posed a question to Hillis Miller, who had been discussing the responsibility entailed in the act of reading.[3] Where does this responsibility come from? he wanted to know. Who lays it upon me? Who *calls* me to be responsible? And *to* whom, *for* whom, *before* whom am I responsible?

Called upon to identify the source of the responsibility that calls upon him when he reads, Miller gave a somewhat evasive answer, talking about fidelity to the original text and his Protestant upbringing. This evasiveness was not surprising; it *is* a discomfiting question, without a single or a simple answer.

Last night, Derrida gave one answer (or reminded us that we already know one answer—if we know the best-known work in English literature).

Responsibility comes from a ghost, or the ghost; the revenant which is also an *arrivant*.[4] The ghost lays me under an obligation to recognize my responsibility. The ghost says to Hamlet, "Remember me"—once in so many words but by implication continuously throughout the play. "Remember me" is an injunction, in this context, to *act*, to kill a man, a "high public official,"[5] a king. It is a call to justice.

The peculiar institution we know as "literature" is haunted by many ghosts, which appear to the living to remind them of their responsibility, to test them, to demand justice. Think only of the ghost in *Beloved*, and what it calls for and recalls. Or the ghostlike figure of Melville's Bartleby, which the narrator terms an "apparition." (Both of these are important texts for "deconstruction in America.")

But not only is it possible to talk about the ghost *in* literature; we can say that the ghost *is* literature (as long as we're cautious about that word "is"). Literature appears to us, calls on us, recalls us to our task, lays us under an obligation. The ghost is *prosopopoeia* and *apostrophe* in their most violent form.[6]

This is not the place to elaborate in detail on the connection between literature and ghosts, but I want to make four points about ghosts which are also points about literature.

1) The ghost is as much *event* as *object* (the word "apparition" holds both of these together). The ghost speaks performatively—it is itself a performative—nothing will be the same again after it has appeared and spoken.

(It is also a citation, of course, or else it would not be recognized as a ghost.)

And it is an event which demands a *response*.

2) It is more than an event demanding a response, however: it is an event *already constituted* by that resonse. Hamlet's response to the ghost's narrative is "Oh my prophetic soul!" (I.v.40). What he has heard is and is not news to him. Although, as literary critics often point out, Shakespeare exteriorizes the ghost in the first scene (in which Hamlet plays no part), the ghost will *speak* only to Hamlet. Its injunction is for Hamlet's ears alone (like the door before which the man from the country waits in Kafka's "Before the Law").

The otherness of the ghost, so powerfully conveyed in the play, is not opposed to its familiarity. The ghost is borderline creature, an insider as well as an outsider. A certain *virtuality*, a *relation* to the other, as Rodolphe Gasché might put it.[7] The ghost is Hamlet, after all, another Hamlet, Hamlet as the other.

So Hamlet's responsibility is not laid upon him by means of a *punctual* injunction, nor is it just a question of accountability or answerability. As Derrida reminded us last night, Hamlet complains that he was *born* to set right the out-of-joint time. One is born, thrown, into responsibility; one inherits it. In "The Politics of Friendship," Derrida observes that the moment I speak I am *"pris, surpris"* by responsibility (634).

The very question "Where does responsibility come from?" arises out of responsibility; responsibility is prior to subjectivity, to questioning.

3.) Hamlet's immediate response is that there is no way of knowing whether this is a good spirit or an evil spirit (a reasonable response in early seventeenth-century Europe):

Angels and ministers of grace defend us!
Be thou a spirit of health or goblin damn'd,
Bring with thee airs from heaven or blasts from hell,
Be thy intents wicked, or charitable...
(I.iii.39)

Nothing is certain here. There are no rules. Hamlet has to read the ghost with no assured codes of reading.

Hamlet has to *judge*, to *decide*; he has to take a *risk*, indeed, to risk everything. In responding to the ghost's summons, he asserts: "I do not set my life at a pin's fee" (I.iv.65). He has to *trust*, and trust is only possible when there are no grounds for it.[8] Trust is always trust in the future, an attitude which Hamlet adopts—or rather finds himself adopted by—towards the end of the play: "If it be now, 'tis not to come; if it be not to come, it will be now; if it be not now, yet it will come—the readiness is all" (V.ii.220).

4.) The ghost comes back. The *arrivant* is also a *revenant*. "Perchance 'twill walk again," says Hamlet to Horatio after hearing about the ghost's appearance, but Horatio is in no doubt: "I warr'nt it will" (I.ii.242). If we fail to remember it, it will remember us. And as we cannot not forget it, it cannot not return.

We have been summoned by many ghosts at this conference—all the talks have been performative events calling for active responses, reminding us of our responsibilities. Their demands have been impossible ones, as all real demands are, since they demand that which is impossible, justice.[9] Derrida's litany of reasons for thinking that our own time is out of joint is a reminder of the scale of the obligations we are under, but his work, and deconstruction in America, deconstruction around the globe, reminds us too that we still have the ghost of a chance—the chance of a ghost.

Notes

1. These comments were made on the second evening of the conference "Deconstruction is/in America," the first evening of which had been taken up by Jacques Derrida's address, partly reprinted in this volume and partly in *Spectres de Marx.* They refer also to several other talks given at the conference and reprinted here.
2. Maud Ellmann (103) recalls that in the film *Ghost Dance* Derrida is interviewed by a woman who enquires whether he believes in ghosts. His reply, roughly translated, is "That's a hard question because, you see, I am a ghost."
3. See Miller, chapter 4.
4. See Derrida, *Aporias*, 33 and *passim.*
5. See Butler, chapter 10.
6. See Chase, chapter 2.
7. See Gasché, chapter 7.
8. This proposition is exemplified in J.M. Coetzee's *Age of Iron;* see my discussion of this novel in "Trusting the Other."
9. See Derrida, "Force of Law."

Bibliography

Attridge, Derek. "Trusting the Other: Ethics and Politics in J. M. Coetzee's *Age of Iron." South Atlantic Quarterly* 93 (1994): 59–82.

Derrida, Jacques. *Aporias.* Trans. Thomas Dutoit. Stanford: Stanford UP, 1993.

———. "Force of Law: The 'Mystical Foundation of Authority.' " *Deconstruction and the Possibility of Justice.* Ed. Drucilla Cornell, Michel Rosenfeld, and David Gray Carlson. New York: Routledge, 1992. 3–67.

———. "The Politics of Friendship." *The Journal of Philosophy* 85 (1988): 632–645.

———. *Spectres de Marx: L'État de la dette, le travail du dueil et la nouvelle Internationale.* Paris: Galilée, 1993.

Ellmann, Maud. "The Ghosts of Ulysses." *The Languages of Joyce*, eds. R. M. Bollettieri Bosinelli, C. Marengo Vaglio, and Chr. van Boheemen. Philadelphia/Amsterdam: John Benjamins, 1992.

14

The Form of Politics

Perry Meisel

I

It is, of course, a deconstructive commonplace to observe that the singular or the unique is the function or the effect of a relation. And yet a political and intellectual climate like ours in America today—a New Sanctimony, if you will, a recall of transcendental categories by Left and Right alike—too often propounds the singular as a value in itself, whether it is ethnicity, gender, or oppression as such. Our climate needs to be reminded of this deconstructive commonplace, not only to explain to Neo-conservatives why and how deconstructive relativism is actually very systematic indeed, but also to distinguish deconstruction from the neo-centrisms of the Left (a self-contradictory description that is itself an example of the problem). These latter impulses, astonishingly enough, reconstitute the binarisms of black/white, male/female, power/oppression that gird tyranny, and that are under presumable siege as categories.

What is perennially misconceived about deconstruction (Harold Bloom's term "weak misreading" well accounts for the surprisingly literal response to Derrida that we all know) is that its procedure for deracinating essences, absolutes, transcendental categories of all kinds is not in the service of an anarchic play of signifiers. Nor is it designed to prioritize the historically repressed or marginalized side of an opposition. Deconstruction is a highly exact mode of reading designed, not to throw texts or the world into chaos, but to show how the world we think we find only gets—and has gotten—made in the shapes and terms that we take for granted as given, self-evident, natural.

American criticism may perhaps wake from its dogmatic slumbers by remembering what Anselm Haverkamp states in his introduction to the conference—that America *is* difference. This is the crucial tie between deconstruction and America despite deconstruction's French (and Germanic) ground of philosophical emergence (here, too, though, we should recall that both America and deconstruction share, after all, a place in the tradition of the Enlightenment despite a difference in the epistemological deposition of the subject that Enlightenment Romanticism was invented to sustain following the first death of God).

As Jonathan Culler points out, the performative or constitutive nature of discourse, together with its chiastic ground-making, is particularly plain in American life; indeed, it is American life's singular virtue. If marginal America constructs itself as a difference from dominant America, we should remember that dominant America constructed itself as an enabling difference from Europe, thereby preparing a common and originary ground for American life at large, based, not on European—read logocentric—notions of identity or sameness, but, in principle if not always or altogether in practice, on difference. This common epistemology of American life ironically guarantees freedom by requiring everyone to deal with influence.

Hence the ease with which we allow ourselves to be swayed by the language of the singular—of the essentiality of the ethnic, the gendered, the this, the that—is precisely what a deconstructive reassessment of the political asks us to question. Without aesthetic theory—I use these terms with Kant in mind—and without a deconstructive reimagination of the categories involved, a dangerous epistemological lassitude will continue despite the need for its correction.

Consider, for example, the category of the ethnic. What is its status as a notion? In 1992, the Poetics Institute of New York University and the Cardozo School of Law sponsored a conference with Jacques Derrida that allowed me to address the problem then. The Greek *ethnos*, I argued at that time, emerges in the Septuagint as a means of translating the Hebrew *goyim*, which has the sense of "heathen"—those who do not believe in the Jewish God. Only in the nineteenth century does the word gain the more specific sense of race with which we associate it still in this century. This way of reading *ethnos* as designating biosemiotic traits, sometimes derived iconically through or from the language a person speaks, well suited nineteenth-century ideological needs, particularly those of nationalism. The less-than-various array of ethnic nationalisms, from Mazzini to Herzl, sought a justifying physicalism familiar in nineteenth-century reasoning from phrenology to ethnography. Ethnography and ethnology alike emerge as disciplines of study contemporary with the growth of nationalist feeling, the first in 1834, the second in 1842. Lexicons record a hazy relation between *ethnos* and *ethos*, too, the latter meaning custom, although the nature of the relation is unclear. This muddy proximity is the very nature of the relation, which motivates what is merely customary among people by divining a mystic bond among them and elevating it, that is, reducing it, to the status of an innate rather than a derived characteristic.

The ethnic as a trope, then, rests, or fails to do so, on a paradox whose structure is a familiar deconstructive site constituted by the play between inclusion and exclusion. That which is without value—those who do not believe, those who are *goyim* or heathen—becomes precisely that which is of, that which is, value—the inherent, often racially construed trait that assigns and defines one at a presumably fundamental level. The ethnic or racial—that denigration or impropriety that defines *goyim*—is also the trope designed to signify the pure, the essential, the very opposite of the unclean or the improper that it originarily signifies in the history of its usage. It should be noted, too, that *ethnos* also originarily signifies the notion of "one's own"—of what is, properly speaking, proper to one—a notion whose like paradoxical structure has also long been familiar to us. Curiously enough, then, the otherness that structures the heathen or the unruly—the excluded—is also the properness, the inherence that structures what is included.

If a narrative were to be constructed from this play of the

trope's senses, it would find its *telos* in the scientific racism and eugenics of the Nazi era, even if it might also find an epistemological counterpart in soil-Zionism, African-American separatism, or feminism of the essentialist variety. Democratic thinking, by contrast, describes the truth of the universality it declares by virtue of its erasure. Freedom of worship, for example, has as its implication that which guarantees the possibility of its emergence: a constitutional indifference to the very religions that it frees.

Any contemporary articulation of the ethnic rolls and rocks on the lip of this paradox. Its negation is the repressed that returns late in the twentieth century with the revalorization of those ethnic categories that the century's civil and human rights revolutions, especially in the United States, supposedly put in question. The rise of multiculturalism in the United States and the end of the socialist ideal in the Soviet Union are, from this point of view, similar reactions against and repressions of the non-ethnic ideals of both political constructions.

II

Any deconstructive reassessment of the political depends today, then, on a series of new assumptions about both society and subjectivity. Here deconstruction maintains its historical relation to psychoanalysis and Marxism alike, although by now these relations are so implicit that the crucial term in each case remains largely silent throughout the conference.

The unconscious is the conference's enabling notional secret, an Althusserian notion of the unconscious that understands subjects and ideology, texts and their reception, in reciprocal rather than exclusive terms. Avital Ronell's "testing" is a superb psychoanalytical representation of the subject. "Testing" suggests what the ego and any shape at all have in common—the doing and undoing of frames, edges, outlines, borders. "We exist in sway," says Ronnell, linking Kant with Feud and Lacan, and linking epistemology with psychoanalysis.

The conference's second chief notion, ideology, is well described by Barbara Johnson without being named. By asking "what speaks?" rather than "who speaks?," Johnson efficiently points out the dynamic and constitutive relation between ideology and the unconscious, and the way in which this relation fashions the ground of self and society alike. When Judith Butler asks, "Why do words wound?," the answer is that the unconscious is structured like a language.

III

In order to elaborate a deconstructive reassessment of the political, let us read a familiar and even topical text at some length. No twentieth-century text is more alluring for its presumable gender allegory than Virginia Woolf's *Orlando* (1928). And yet no twentieth-century text is also more strategically plain about its own deconstructive rather than irreducible notion of gender than *Orlando* is. Everyone knows the popular conception of *Orlando*—even the movies attest to it: an allegory about how perfect a human being would be could s/he combine the qualities of both genders. The emblem for *Orlando*'s apparently synthetic project is the book's *hommage* to androgyny, borrowed from Coleridge's picture of a harmonious imagination in the *Biographia Literaria* (1817). Woolf literalizes, or so it seems, Coleridge's idealizing descriptions of rich imaginative figures such as Shakespeare by switching Orlando's gender about halfway through the book. Woolf thus simultaneously preserves and changes Orlando's character as the rival demands of soul and history struggle beneath the full-throated ease of both the plot and Woolf's seamless use of language.

Culler's notion of performativity is dazzlingly evident as Woolf's text provides a virtual object lesson in how semiosis makes subjects from the ground up. What language brings into being in *Orlando* is gender as such. Even to call it "as such" is, of course, problematic, since gender's suchness or givenness is the function of a difference or a relation. Under the pressure of Woolf's language, *Orlando*'s presumably central notion of gender splits its husk.

The key to the novel, as the saying goes, lies in the sometimes odd structure of Woolf's prose, which as a rule is so well sutured that the means of its production slips by. In the novel's third chapter, the narrator announces, with an apparent straight face, that "everything, in fact, was something else" (143).[1] How can what is "in fact" be "something else"? By definition, a "fact" is what it is—just the fax, ma'am—but here, quite ironically, the self-evidence ordinarily associated with "fact" is also taken away from it by virtue of how its self-evidence is represented—as "something else."

This kind of rhetorical oddness occurs again and again in the texture of the book's language, often structuring sentences in uncannily similar—and equally disturbing—ways. "Everything was different," says the narrator early on (27), trying to give us a picture of the Elizabethan past by negation, even in a catalogue of vegetables, climates, and poets. How can a statement of nonidentity be a properly representational or descriptive one? "The arras" in "the hall" at Orlando's ancestral "home" "moved always" (45)— "moved always" is an oxymoron. Or, says the narrator, meditating on Orlando's future in the book's first chapter and thinking vaguely of official roles for him, he "was cut out for precisely some such career" (15). How can what is "precisely" also be "some such"? Similarly, if "openness . . . was the soul" of Orlando's "nature" (189), as the narrator says it is, then the outside—"openness"—and the inside—"soul"—are perilously and curiously identified.

The seeming imprecision in Woolf's language is, in fact, a rhetorical pattern—a principal one throughout the novel, and the way the novel itself goes about estimating as well as representing oppositions such as fact and fiction, text and world, and, of course, one gender and another.

The rhetorical pattern has as its counterpart the novel's larger structural pattern, which requires a similar transgression of the reader's assumptions once they have been put in place. Much as Woolf's sentences ask the reader to believe opposing or different kinds of propositions simultaneously, so, too, does the structure of the novel's fundamental illusionism. Orlando is at one and the same time the same person despite her change of sex midway through the book—her subjectivity is essential behind even gender. And yet Orlando is also a function of history, changing as she does in accord with the changes through which she lives. To define and represent gender, Orlando—and *Orlando*—both invoke history and deny it.

Rather than a problem, such structural irreconcilability is a strategy or device. Time must be invoked to describe something as timeless—Orlando's personality, for example—since the timeless can only be conceived of in its relation—its nonrelation—to time. And history can be thought of only in relation to a timelessness that is its foil or counterpart. In *Orlando*, everything, then—and remember, everything is something else—is as a rule put in place by its transgression. This strategy or device, both rhetorical and structural, I shall call Woolf's cross-writing—the transgression or crossing over of assumptions even as they are put in place.

Woolf theorizes cross-writing in *Orlando* by telling us that Orlando's own mind works in "violent see-saws" (46), not unlike Woolf's own clashing metaphors, "stopping at nothing," she says, "in between" (46). Sounding like Saussure (and Keats), Woolf gives cross-writing a differential model: "Nothing thicker than a knife's blade separates happiness from melancholy" (45). Of course not: to know one means to know its difference from the other. To accent this relativist or relational semiotics, Woolf uses the same metaphor that she uses in *Mrs. Dalloway* (1925) to show how difference works to constitute sameness: the clocks in London are off line, each ringing the same hour a bit differently from the others (60–61). Woolf's description of Shakespeare early in the novel also matches the structure of her cross-writing: "his mind was . . . a welter of opposites" (22). Queen Elizabeth, too, is drawn according to the same plan: qualities such as "innocence" and "simplicity" were "all the more dear to her for the dark background she set them against" (23).

Woolf tells us in the book's preface to be prepared for this double rhythm or movement. "The book," she says, "will inevitably wake expectations in the reader which the book itself can only disappoint" (viii). Expectation and disappointment, disappointment and expectation—this is a fair estimate of the semiotic rhythm the novel employs to have its way with us. The play of expectation and disappointment on the reader's part is necessary for any horizon or circumference—any edge or margin or frame that situates an object as such, whether animate or inanimate—to emerge at all, and as a function of compounding, of difference. Readers know, says Woolf, how to "make ... up from bare hints dropped here and there the whole boundary and circumference of a living person; can hear in what we only whisper a living voice; can see, often when we say nothing about it, exactly what he looked like, and know without a word to guide them precisely what he thought" (73).

Woolf reminds us of the kind of rhetorical sleight of hand at work here by calling attention to it and its mechanisms. "The most poetic" kind of "conversation," she says, "is precisely that which cannot be written down" (253). This creates not simply awe at the depth of the conversation in question (a conversation between Orlando and her nineteenth-century lover, Shelmerdine), but also awe at the fact that such "repletion" or fullness, as Woolf puts it (253), can be the effect of "a great blank here" (253). Even the opposition between life and literature is handled—is simultaneously established and undone—by crossover rhetoric. While life and literature are on the one hand distinct ("Green in nature is one thing, green in literature another" [17]), on the other hand, the Queen "read him"—Orlando—"like a page" (25).

When Orlando's change of gender comes, the way in which Woolf represents it, rhetorically at least, slides over us without a hitch. "He was a woman" (137). The fictional illusion succeeds despite—perhaps because of—the rhetorical impossibility. This is, as it turns out, simply a hyperbolic instance of the mixed metaphors that Woolf uses to describe practically everything. Even the novel's plot is made, ironically, out of transformation.

Far, then, from being a self-evident singularity, gender—like ethnicity, or like subjectivity itself—is always already the function of a relation in *Orlando*. A commonplace of structural feminism, it is interesting to see it rehearsed as early as 1928. Even androgyny is not fusion, but a structure of difference. One doesn't fuse the genders by crossing them—one puts them in place that way, and always has. To be fused, the genders must be different. Gender is a difference, not an essential characteristic, an elementary semiotic activity in all cultures that, in one way or another, is part of the basis upon which a given culture's world, and its subjects, are formed. Gender is a pure difference, a "pure performative," as Barbara Vinken puts it, whose role is merely paradigmatic, structuring a fundamental difference out of a formal necessity that is also necessarily political. As Orlando's confirmation of her new gender in the mirror suggests (138), form is itself always already political. The equivalence of politics and form is among the most provocative of the notions to which a deconstructive reassessment of the political leads. What is a politics of form?

Notes

1. All references are to Virginia Woolf, *Orlando*, rpt. (New York: Harcourt Brace & Co., 1973).

15

At the *Planchette* of Deconstruction is/in America

Gayatri Chakravorty Spivak

I missed the first flush of Deconstruction in America (1966). I bought *De la grammatologie* off a catalogue in the fastnesses of Iowa, my first place of work.[1] It was the mid-sixties. In those days postcoloniality was a dirty secret. It took one to know one. All by myself in Iowa, I was resonating with someone who, like me, was not quite not European. He was (un)peeling Western metaphysics as an insider/outsider. Although the theme of the conference which gave rise to this anthology is specifically Deconstruction is/in America, and the talk is of France and the United States, postcoloniality, in the name of the Other Heading and the Marrano, is surfacing in deconstruction more and more.[2] In these brief comments I will keep within the theme of the conference. The echo of that first resonance, before the name Jacques Derrida took on flesh for me, will no doubt sound as an undertone.

I cannot get a grip on deconstruction. I cannot grasp it in the grip of the *Begriff*. (I do not think of conceiving a concept when I think of my grip or grasp slipping on whatever would be a *Begriff* of deconstruction.) I cannot, then, get a grip on deconstruction.

This keeps me going farther and farther away from what seems to be its space. I have therefore not been able to contribute much to its in-house discussion. I keep trying that too, though. In the summer of 1993, travelling far away from the house of deconstruction, I wrote painstakingly for what I thought might be something of an in-house journal.[3] This is how I described what I was doing in that piece, "Responsibility," not knowing then that that was also the name of Derrida's current stream of teaching.

What is it then, I wrote as I was trying to set that question to work moving through North Africa and Asia by way of Strasbourg and Galway, what is it to be responsible to a changeful thought on the question of responsibility? To ask such a question is perhaps already to betray, in all its senses, the idea of academic responsibility in which one was trained—in an excellent University in a former colony—a serious, resistant colonial subject being constructed in the aftermath of the declaration of a negotiated independence. Discursive formations and presuppositions of education do not change miraculously because pieces of paper declaring independence have been signed. In fact, reasonableness seemed a protection against the kinds of violence unleashed by the seeming and sudden lifting of centuries of oppression. The idea of academic responsibility in which I was trained was therefore to give an objective account of an argument with textual demonstrations, and subsequently to evaluate it, on its own terms, as well as by the standards of an impartial judgement. By comparison with the imperatives of that austere responsibility, the first years of my teaching career, which began in the United States in 1965, seem to be haunted by demands of an extreme irresponsibility towards the alterity of history and augury: Do we like it? Is that relevant to us? And then to me?

To pose the question of responsibility to a thought precisely of responsibility from which a lesson of responsibility is learned goes against the grain of both those imperatives. For it is, first, to show that one is already partisan. And, secondly, it is to reveal that one's anxiety is for one's responsibility *to* the text, not the other way around. And yet, is there not something like a resemblance between those imperatives—requiring objectivity toward or relevance from the text—and my opening question? Have we not guessed that the early lesson of disinterested objectivity was in fact an unacknowledged partisanship for a sort of universalist humanism which dictated that one show, even if by the way, that the literary or philosophical text in general is good? And as for the other, does one not, given the current demand for thejustification of an interest in "deconstructive philosophical speculation" in a politically inclined female immigrant, demonstrate again and again, its relevance to such inclinations and such provenance?

How, then, to be responsible to the warning for "a community of well-meaning deconstructionists, reassured and reconciled with the world in ethical certainty, good conscience, satisfaction of services rendered, and the consciousness of duty accomplished (or more heroically still, yet to be accomplished")?[4]

Not being a philosopher by talent and training, I cannot philosophize the delicate ruptures involved in these double binds. That more profound speculation would look upon the night of non-knowledge in which all decisions are taken, even when it is the most detailed knowledge that has been set most responsibly to work. (This sentence already begs the question of responsibility, assumes its nature known.) During that summer as I moved about in the world of hegemonic and counter-hegemonic decision-making, I wrote that the space of my essay may be distinguished from those more perilous watches as the quicker tempo of the eve and the morning-after of that night, the night of non-knowledge when a decision tears time, the time of effect following just cause.[5] What the two spaces share is that "the limit of . . . [the] formalization . . . [of a problematic is] a sort of intemediary stage."[6]

I have paraphrased that essay at such length to show how, reading and learning from the texts of deconstruction, I seem to lose my grip more and more on how to do it on paper or in the classroom. I shift emphasis, from night, to evening, and morning after. I engage "the active and necessary marginalization of the strange guardians in the margin" in order to take the risk of reading.[7] (I was exhilarated recently to hear Derrida himself describe the matter of emphasis thus in an improvised discussion:

If you put the emphasis on the unicity of the existing one rather than Being as such at some point you will have the feeling that the other [Heideggerian] discourse is a moment of emptying—it speaks in an empty way about emptiness, not enough to disqualify it. You have to decide what you do with this emptiness, how you act historically out of this moment. It has to be the way you perform it and it makes a difference and that moment is decisive. If the absolutely indeterminate is universal, then you have to make decisions. Heidegger would agree with this. How do you act? You cannot avoid performativity. In order for this decision

you have to be free. Then we have to say what next? Whatever you do
next you sign with your own idiom.)[8]

By the implacable logic of performativity, I seem to fall back
these days on miming a progression of figures rather than following an argument. This is, I realize in amused despair, a sort of
thematization that annuls deconstruction yet once again. For example, having read *Of Spirit* (1989), I could do no better than to
offer, in that mimic in-house essay, a mere instantiation—and you
may recognize this as a cluster in *Of Spirit*—of the animal machine of fully programmed information, and a "European" combi-
natory whose power remains abyssal, so that the two sides seem
to engage in an interminable conversation, while a specter does
the rest.[9] I read a meeting of the European Parliament in Strasbourg on the World Bank's Flood Action Plan in Bangladesh by
the peculiar logic of these figures.

How rigorously can one maintain the distinction between the
messianic and messianism?[10] If we must "*know* still what the
messianic wants to say even if commitment [to it] is the destruction of the messianic by messianism . . . " and if "the question of
knowing which is the least grave of th[e] forms of complicity"
between the messianic and messianism "is always there," can we
insist on the distinction except as a repeated warning?[11]

I recall a two-part answer to my question (offered during the
conference at New York University in the fall, 1993) where Derrida situated himself as naming the discourse of a future that is
not a future present as messianic because he was himself written
in the interminable and indeterminate Book of the Peoples of the
Book. We read as we read and therefore I recognized in this gesture a vigilance that Derrida has ever practiced: a "regular erasure
of the archi-," remaining inside one's "text, . . . not sufficient to
operate the necessary transgression" (of generalization/universal-
ization?).[12]

Since then I have heard Derrida open up the understanding of
the Messiah not only by way of the *arrivant,* as in *Specters of Marx*
or *Aporias,* but as an attempt to figure the obscure structure of the
call to responsibility as tied to the originary and irreducible "auto-
affectaction" that is the is of the I.[13] I believe further that I have
heard Derrida expand the messianic, by way of the Resurrection,

into metempsychosis, thus stepping out of the strictly monotheistic enclosure. I believe he performs this by rewriting the teleological aspect of the resurrection and the cyclo-teleology of metempsychosis as a persistent *différance:* the condition that the other not only replace me but start replacing me now.[14]

I had understood messianic and messianism as examples, of the relationship between "the injunction or the order *[ordonnance]* of the *gift* ('give') . . . and the injunction or the order *[ordonnance]* of meaning."[15] Indeed, in the Derridian passage that I used to state my question, I had substituted "messianic" for "giving," and substituted "destruction of the gift by the gift," by "destruction of the messianic by messianism."

I have since then read the relevant pages of *Specters of Marx* more carefully, and the sharp contrast between the messianic and messianism that I had heard in Derrida's oratorical tone during the conference in 1993 seems surprisingly absent there. This is not the moment to discuss Derrid's election of that spirit of Marx which harkens to the messianic impulse. Yet a question lingers, and it may be necessary to put it more crudely. If I understand rightly, part of the project of the book is to transform Marx by historicizing him and thus open the space of a "new International." Asian Marxists have been attempting not only to historicize Marx but, and for some time, to read him against the predictive Eurocentric scenario. The Third World initiative, started in Asia, but reaching far beyond it, was an attempt at such a new International. I am aware that Derrida always speaks of a *Western* metaphysics because he does not wish to overstep the boundaries of what he knows and what writes him. The messianic and metempsychosis are thus not aberrant. But if one proposes a "new *International,*" should one not perhaps cast a glance at the fate of these other sustained efforts? Spectralizing the International Human Rights vision by asking it to include the economic sphere seems too European, too general, or to borrow Derrida's term, too "macrological." Otherwise, is one not perhaps retracing the steps, in spite of European applause, of the old *Second* international, which domesticated Socialism as European national projects of electorally dependent welfare statism, whose ruins Derrida correctly deplores? Who is the "we" here? Who prays for haunting, by what

ghost? For what it is worth, I point at "globe-girdling move-
ments," where the subject has shifted to the other side.[16]

At any rate, my question at the conference might have been no
more than an excuse for the kind of systemic interest with which
I seem obliged repeatedly to annul the spectrality of Derrida's
meditation on responsibility. During the roundtable discussion
that closed the conference, I offered a cryptic quotation from my
essay, mentioning that sixty pages had come in between:

Is it possible to imagine, since responsibility must bind the call of the
ethical to a response, that one must act here, in the context of the World
Bank's Flood Action Plan, as if responsibly to the specter called "com-
mune-ism," whose threat Development must desperately hold at bay?
That setting-to-work need not call on a European left monoculture.[17] The
Bangladeshi space of intimate learning, of human-animal-watery ground,
is after all an ongoing response to the weave of land and river *by* the
landless and on *common* waters. Nothing but an intermediary question
can be posed and left suspended in the space of an essay.

The echo of my first resonance with an unknown "postcolonial"
Derrida would remain, I had hoped, an undertone. It seems to be
the main sound now. Our theme is "Deconstruction is/in America."
I must tune myself back to it. (Just as "grip" calls up *Begriff* for
me, so does tuning call up *Bestimmung*. I must let myself be
determined by our common concern.)

If I had the time, I would point out how my old friend J. Hillis
Miller's take on "Cultural Studies" recalls that essay "Destroying
Literary Studies" by René Wellek, which introduced Derrida's
withdrawal of the title "Deconstruction in America" nearly ten
years ago.[18] But for the moment, I will content myself with notic-
ing that the translation of "l'Amérique, mais *c'est* la déconstruction," used repeatedly by Derrida, as "deconstruction *is* America"
loses the comma followed by the *mais*.

What Derrida withdraws or takes back—this gesture of withdrawal was part of his introductory speech in New York—is the
simplified English translation.

One of the most striking icons on the United States landscape
and its videographic simulacrum is the name America and the
U.S. flag (the "American" flag) attached to innumerable objects
and enterprises, with the accompanying sonic fallout. The United
States gives itself the right to the proper name "America,"—tac-

itly recognized in our title and our traffic with it—by way of a "but of course," close to the gallic *mais* with its stereotyped gesture, that is lost in the shuffle of translation to the way things are. And the hesitation, spaced by the comma in the sentence, serves to perform—in a blinding flash—a nameless performative where one makes excuses for breaking false promises by implying that promises can never, after all, be false because they can never be true. The "but of course" is lost in translating to the way things are, the harsh everyday normality of power. What I have described here is the way the U.S. treats not only its disenfranchised at home but also its "beneficiaries" abroad. This tacit everyday acceptance of the way things are is not the stuff of the broadstroke lists that Derrida painted black in his address.[19] They are but minor ruses: *post*modern *donor* countries borrowing a form from a *pre*-capitalist model to *give* aid that *coerces* the dazed recipient into a refined *debt-bondage;* just the normal business of giving aid; and at home, offers of *free* gifts everywhere—work that into the paradox of the gift![20] And if, in the bureaucratic theater of aid, one points this out with some moralistic embarrassment rather than in a thunderous denunciation, the varieties of patronizing to exasperated answers that come down, from all sides of a frontierless hybridity, can be generalized into versions of "L'Amerique, mais *c'est* la déconstruction!" What do you want, dummy? An unorganized Human Rights mindset ever-mindful of the economic cannot catch this micrology, perhaps precisely because, to use an archaic vocabulary, exploitation need not, strictly speaking, use extra-economic coercion, just mess with "common sense."

I want now to to speak briefly and crudely about the mindset of this frontierless hybrid. The main point of Professor Beaujour's essay is that deconstruction caught on here because the student body was untrained in philosophy. I was struck by his unwitting resemblance to some of those very United States students that he so patronized. Here comes the mindset: sitting in New York City, longing for a wilderness, all the while putting in a bit of national origin validation—in his case France. If the well-placed migrant is from a "developing nation," s/he will often speak in the name of the migrant underclass; celebrating Marx as a clandestine migrant (who typically flies *toward* capitalism) has something like a relationship to this habit (*Specters*, p. 174).

244 Gayatri Chakravorty Spivak

J. Hillis Miller's complaint about Cultural Studies does not take into account the critique of liberal multiculturalism within Cultural Studies. Among other things, that critique confronts the mindset described above. If I had the time, I would offer an example of how, learning from *Given Time* in my grip-slipping (dis)figuring way, I attempt, with students of that mindset, to confront the necessary impossibility of theorizing the name of woman, everywhere: a critique of multiculturalism in Cultural Studies. But that must wait. Today I can signal, not only teaching, but also new writing.[21] It will remain a signal, for, apart from the two brilliant allocated presentations, the Conference itself seemed not to be informed by the question of woman. Just as well for me, perhaps.

For if in the old days I liked best everything that led from those words in *Of Grammatology:* "the archè-writing is the origin of morality as of immorality. The non-ethical opening of ethics"; and if, later, passages like the one about setting-to-work in "The Principle of Reason" began to come alive for me, now I like best that statement about what Jacques Derrida likes even less.[22] I will quote again: "*I like even less* the community of well-meaning deconstructionists, reassured and reconciled with the world in ethical certainty, good conscience, satisfaction of services rendered, and the consciousness of duty accomplished (or more heroically still, yet to be accomplished)."

Cowering from the repeated exhortations to speak as an anthropological cliché, and a cliché of reversed gendering, with the postcolonial undertone loudspeaking on all sides, I take refuge in the indeterminacy of a less preferred space, even as I run from the orders to justify deconstruction in the areas that have resolutely defined themselves as its outside. At this writing's distance, it is perhaps not inappropriate to remind the reader that that Fall in New York, Derrida was weaving around Bartleby the Scrivener's "I prefer not to" the reverberations of a secret that will not be revealed.

Acknowledgments

My thanks to Mark Sanders for listening to the first version of this essay and to Forest Pyle for giving a fine first reading to the version for publication.

Notes

1. Jacques Derrida, *De la grammatalogie* (Paris: Seuil, 1967).
2. Derrida, *The Other Heading: Reflections on Today's Europe*, tr. Pascale-Anne Brault and Michael B. Naas (Bloomington: Indiana University Press, 1992); Derrida, "Awaiting (At) the Arrival," in *Aporias*, tr. Thomas Dutoit (Stanford: Stanford University Press, 1993), p. 81.
3. I felt such a lack of hospitality at the door that, hurt and baffled, I withdrew the piece in what one of the editors correctly diagnosed as "bad faith." Entitled "Responsibility," the piece will now appear in *boundary 2*, vol.21.no.3 (Fall 1994).
4. Derrida, "Passions: 'An Oblique Offering'," in David Wood, ed. *Derrida: A Critical Reader* (Cambridge: Blackwell, 1992), p. 15.
5. Derrida, "Force of Law: the 'Mystical Foundation of Authority'," in *Deconstruction and the Possibility of Justice, Cardozo Law Review* 11, 5–6 (July-Aug 1990), p.967.
6. Derrida, *Given Time: I.Counterfeit Money*, tr. Peggy Kamuf (Chicago: University of Chicago Press,1992), p.ix-x.
7. Spivak, "Theory in the Margin: Coetzee's *Foe* Reading Defoe's *Crusoe/Roxana*," in Jonathan Arac and Barbara Johnson eds., *Consequences of Theory* (Baltimore: Johns Hopkins University Press, 1991), p. 159.
8. Discussion, UCLA, April 28, 1994. This is not a printed piece but my own paraphrase. It should not be quoted directly as authored by Derrida. I realize that improvisation has its own rules, and take responsibility for the paraphrase.
9. Derrida, *Of Spirit: Heidegger and the Question*, tr. Geoffrey Bennington and Rachel Bowlby (Chicago: Univ. of Chicago Press, 1989).
10. Derrida, *Specters of Marx: the State of the Debt, the Work of Mourning and the New International*, tr. Peggy Kamuf (New York: Routledge, 1994) pp. 167–169.
11. *Given Time*, p. 30. Quotation modified, as explained below in the text.
12. Derrida, "Différance," in Alan Bass, tr. *Margins of Philosophy* (Chicago: University of Chicago Press, 1982), pp. 15, 12.
13. Derrida, *Specters*, p. 99f; Derrida, "Awaiting (At) the Arrival," in *Aporias*, p. 99; Again, this remark and what follows interwoven in the paragraph is a paraphrase of Derrida improvising (University of California, Irvine, May 3, 1994), and should not be quoted as authorized by him. I may be reading my own cruder speculations into him, since I have been groping towards a notion of "learning the lesson of the other in the house of the self by way of the irreducibility of auto-affection" ("Psychoanalysis and Feminism," end of Lecture 1, School of Criticism and Theory, Dartmouth College, August, 1993; forthcoming in Alan Schrift ed. *The Logic of the Gift*). Where does one's idiomatic signature or paraphrase begin?

14. Here, too, I may be contaminating the reading with the idiom and emphasis of my own interests: a) the relationship between the doctrine of *karma* (only minimally comparable, of course to the Hellenic metempsychosis) and the thinking of *ātman* (cognate with classical Greek *atmos*, invariably over the centuries transcendentalized as Self, but readable as "encircling air," obliging the recognition that the matrix of the ethical relation to the other is situated outside the ego, and the relation itself to be achieved, perhaps, through the study of the sense perceptions, —among them mentation—an othering of the self as object of concentration) is one between cyclo-teleology and living as *différance* (Spivak, " 'India', Echo, and Two Postscripts," in anthology being edited by David Wills, forthcoming; and at greater length in Bimal Krishna Matilal and Spivak, *Epic and Ethic*, New York: Routledge, forthcoming). b) the relationship between capitalism and socialism is a *différance*, articulated by Marx and mainstream Marxisms as a teleology (Spivak, "Supplementing Marxism," in Steven Cullenberg and Bernd Magnus eds., *Whither Marxism?*, New York: Routledge, forthcoming).

15. Derrida, *Given Time*, p. 30. "Ordonnance" is indeed untranslatable. But its implication, that there is a "givingness" *(donnance)* even in the order, was important for me, in the way I was thinking, because it seemed to suggest a certain entailment to messianism in the messianic as grasped by us.

16. Spivak, "Appendix," in Mahasweta Devi, *Imaginary Maps*, tr. Spivak (Calcutta: Thema, 1993), pp. 200–206; forthcoming from Routledge; and "Supplementing Marxism" *(op. cit.)*.

17. I borrow this term from Vandana Shiva, *Monocultures of the Mind: Perspectives on Biodiversity and Biotechnology* (London: Zed, 1993).

18. Reńe Wellek, "Destroying Literary Studies," *The New Criterion* (Dec. 1983), pp. 1–8. Derrida, *Mémoires for Paul de Man* (New York: Columbia Univ. Press, 1986), pp. 12–19. The next sentence quoted is from p. 18. The resemblance between Wellek's and Miller's positions comes clearer if we look at Miller, "The Work of Cultural Criticism in the Age of Digital Reproduction," in *Illustration* (Cambridge: Harvard Univ. Press, 1992), pp. 9–60. It is an uncanny resemblance, for Miller is among Wellek's named adversaries. Yet the same conserving concern that "[t]he hard work of reading the primary text [would] tend . . . to disappear" (Miller, p. 42, but see also the opening anecdote, p. 9, and the anecdote about the "children of the Sixties," p. 44) drives both essays. Miller is altogether more benign in tone ("Nothing could be further from the Nazi ideologues in political motivation, in subject-position, and in conceptual formulations than cultural critics like [David] Lloyd and [Abdul] JanMohamed" (p. 48). Although the implicit comparison with Nazis and communism always lurks in the background, for Miller it is more a question of sixties children play-

ing with fire. Miller would shame them into recognizing that cultural studies is too old fashioned a point of view to fit their hi-tech digital toys: "The danger is that the hardware and software developed for teaching and research with the new computer technologies will wittingly or unwittingly perpetuate outmoded ideological paradigms of historical or contextual explanation" (p. 40). But who are these children? It is still the children of the sixties—"the tenured radicals" (Roger Kimball, *The Tenured Radicals: How Politics Has Corrupted Our Higher Education* (New York: Harper's, 1990). For though some cultural studies texts are quoted, his real interlocutors are those who are "Making Sense of the Sixties" (p. 26). His critique of the idea that the university can be an arena of "revolutionary transformation," that teaching can lead to "universal justice," seems directed at 1968 and its aftermath. (The fear of 1968 is part of the deep structure of Columbia University, my place of employment.) Alas, pointing at the implications of the contradictions (which Miller calls aporias) in Benjamin's "The Work of Art in the Age of Mechanical Reproduction" (*Illuminations*, tr. Harry Zohn, New York: 1969, pp. 217–251) will lead unerringly to John Searle's *The Campus War: A Sympathetic Look At the University in Agony* (New York: World Pub., 1971), where the Berkeley radicals of the sixties are repeatedly accused of McCarthyism. Here again, J. Hillis Miller's innate good sense saves the day. But the uncanny resemblance to the self-declared chastisers of deconstruction troubles his friends.

It is clear that Wellek generalized from Yale. His real quarrel is with the Yale Derrida, de Man, Miller, Harold Bloom, Jonathan Culler (formerly at Yale). Miller's "Work of Cultural Criticism" is a generalization from two California campuses, Irvine and Berkeley, the latter represented by JanMohamed and Lloyd. But even a sense of his own adopted Southern California would have told Miller that the "identity"-controversy has hit the US multicultural field long since (so much so that attempting a bibliography in an incidental footnote is risible); it surfaces with diversified poignancy nearly every week in the Sunday magazine of *The Los Angeles Times*. In the event, the citation of Blanchot, Lyotard, Nancy, and David Carroll (p. 51)— exemplary thinkers, of course—as a group that could now solve the problem of identity for cultural studies is embarrassing.

Of course cultural studies is for Miller a problem attendant upon the immigration explosion in the US. You cannot argue globality from an "evening in Kathmandu." It is not surprising that he seems not to have heard of "hybridity" (a theme so pervasive and controversial in cultural studies that to give Homi Bhabha's work in general as a reference is a nod toward academic convention) or of "postnationality" (just as pervasive a debate which convention requires me to lay at the door of Arjun Appadurai, "Patriotism and Its Future," *Public*

Culture vol. 5, no. 3, Spring 93, p. 411–429, and the Public culture collective in general). As regards the canon debate, I may perhaps, and equally conventionally, cite my own two essays, "Marginality in the Teaching Machine," and "Scattered Speculation on the Question of Culture Studies" (Spivak, *Outside in the Teaching Machine*, New York: Routledge, 1993, pp. 53–76, 255–284; both pieces have been in print since 1990, *Outside*, copyright page). Any acquaintance with the complex text of global informatics would not have allowed Miller to exculpate technology from ideology (Miller, p. 39; the latter is admittedly confined by him to the precritical notion of motivation). What I wonder most, however, is how Miller comes to terms with certain profound tendencies in deconstruction today. (That he sees "reading . . . for Deconstruction . . . [as] the centre of a *humanistic* study that is oriented towards . . . understanding" [p. 17; emphasis mine] should perhaps tip us off about a serious in-coherence here.) How, with his view of reason in the university, can he make his peace with "Mochlos; or the Conflict of the Faculties" (in *Logomachia: The Conflict of the Faculties*, Richard Rand, ed., Lincoln: Univ. of Nebraska Press, 1992, pp.1–34) or the earlier "Principle of Reason: The University in the Eyes of its Pupils" (*Diacritics* vol. 13, no. 3, Fall 83, pp. 3–20)? How will his neat binary opposition between "rhetorical" and "thematic" reading take into account the interest in his differentation, ignoring their *différance* (*Margins of Philosophy*, p. 17); how come to terms with Derrida's caution that all formalization is an intermediary stage, judged elsewhere, responsible otherwise (see note 7). It is only because J. Hillis Miller is grounded in the best of the "humanist tradition," which will keep published critisism and personal friendship apart, that I will venture the following suggestion: In J. Hillis Miller's admonition to cultural studies we see de Manian deconstruction shackled to its lowest denominator: close reading. In spite of the deep sympathy between the two men, the actual critical practices of de Man and Derrida differ greatly. What was first broached in "The Rhetoric of Blindness: Jacques Derrida's Reading of Rousseau" (Paul de Man, *Blindness and Insight*, New Haven: Yale Univ. Press, 2d Edition, 1983, pp. 102–141) never disappeared. The difference shows in Derrida's emphasis on a performative that is not performed fully in the verbal text, or a recognition of the pathos of life and death in the text of philosophy. By contrast, the answer to Miller's question "What Are Cultural Studies?" (p.13) is, finally, "everything that is not literary studies," destroying literary studies. In conclusion, Miller sees "artwork and scholarship as inaugural performatives" (p.55). To appreciate how desperately cultural studies, a struggling and menaced discipline, is in that position, in terms of a textuality rather broader than "artwork and scholarship," he would have to enter the protocols of cultural studies with critical intimacy that produces deconstruction, whatever it may be. We forget at our peril that it was deconstructive thinking that allowed us to think "text" in so general a way (a secret to which Wellek and his followers remained obstinately blind). Here too I am, with all appropriate apologies, obliged to point at my own efforts: "Teaching for the Times," in Jan Nederveen Pieterse, ed. *The Decolonization of Imagination* (London: Zed Books, 1995) and "Narratives of Multiculturalism," in Thomas W. Keenan, ed. *Cultural Diversities* (forthcoming).

19. *Specters*, pp. 78–84.
20. The spectacular double bind of the paradox of the gift is laid out in *Given Time*, pp. 6–23.
21. "Diasporas Old and New: Women in the Transnational World," forthcoming in *Textual Practices*, March 2, 1994; and "Narratives of Multiculturalism" *(op. cit.)*.
22. Derrida, *Of Grammatology*, p. 140; "The Principle of Reason," pp. 18–19. For the reference to the following quoted passage, see note 5; emphasis mine.

16

Jaded in America

David Wills

The question of deconstruction in America devolves not upon the possibility of an affirmation or constative utterance—"it is a fashion," "its time has passed," "it is too powerful"—but rather upon the performance of an enunciative dehiscence such as that enacted by the title "Deconstruction is/in America." It would be easy to rehearse a history of deconstruction, indeed of deconstruction in America, that described the essential incoherence of any utterance, a history passing through texts like "Signature Event Context" (1977) and "Limited Inc." (1988), and recounting particulars of the introduction to the American academic scene of those ideas through the work of Jacques Derrida. The history of deconstruction in America is unavoidably tied up with Derrida's debate with Searle and with the idea of every utterance's selfdivision. One might even go on to recount the separate histories of philosophy's and literary studies' reactions and relations to deconstruction in terms of that same notion of originary self division.

The writing of such a history or such histories would give us more than a quarter of a century of deconstruction in relation to America. That might be reason enough to induce a sentiment of lassitude on the part of those who have lived or read those histories, a feeling that we know it well and can find little more to say about it. But if attention given to the appearance of *Spectres de Marx* (1993)[1] in France is any indication, and if, as I shall do here, we take deconstruction to be synonymous with the work of Jacques Derrida, then it is clear that its resources are far from being exhausted on either side of the Atlantic.

We have no need to repeat the history, a history not without its tragic and farcical side, in order to read the originary dehiscence of America's relation to deconstruction; we need go no further than the title that impels or inspires this discussion, and in particular the disarticulation of that title, the diacritical intervention that disturbs on the one hand the arrogance of the copula "deconstruction is America," and on the other hand the reductive and parochial circumscription of a "deconstruction in America." We need only do so, but we *must* also do so, for there is no doubt that deconstruction's relation to America, perhaps deconstruction in general, is being read more and more in terms as reductive and simplistic as those of the two utterances that the disarticulation of "Deconstruction is/in America" is eager to disturb. It is the very necessity of reading, of reading the disarticulations, that remains as the imperative of what we might now call a deconstructive legacy, as we rush, with it or without it, headlong, it sometimes seems, into a new paradigm of textual and informational processing and of the academic disciplines that take such matters to be their object, disciplines such as philosophy and literary studies.

If we start with 1966, the date of the Baltimore structuralism conference, as the point of introduction of deconstruction and of Jacques Derrida to the American academic scene, then it is clear more than a quarter of a century later that we are well into the second generation of that presence here. This is a simple fact of history as passage of time. It has its anecdotal side in the context of reference to deconstruction reaching such instances as the "Style" pages of the *New York Times* and the J-Crew catalog. But within the academic context we might read a not unrelated passing of a generation in the shift of attention or interest of scholars from deconstruction to, for example, what goes by the name of cultural studies. Both observations might lead us to think of deconstruction as a fashion: one that has come or gone, is here or there, one that is in or out, that *is* or *isn't*.

But if we continue to read, and we must—that is the pedagogical imperative of deconstruction that I seek, if only by the difference of a repetition, to reinforce here—we cannot, I repeat, allow such utterances to be installed with the constative force of simple statements. Deconstruction, by this reading, must remain a question. By the same token questions must remain about deconstruction and America some twenty-seven years into the history of their relation; questions about how it got here: whether it obtained accreditation through normal channels, or jumped ship, claimed asylum because of persecution at home, or married the first American it was able to seduce? And questions about where it is now: Is it just a familiar set of ideas that can be brought to bear on more pressing issues fueling current debates or theoretical approaches? Is it still relevant in an academic landscape transformed by cultural studies, queer theory, postcolonial analysis, and so on?

The gamble in what follows would be to preempt those questions by returning to the question that is posed by the originary self-division that deconstruction means, as that which haunts what Derrida, in a recalcitrant syntactic formulation that I do not have the space to discuss here, has recently called not the "idea" but the motif of deconstruction.[2] I call it a question simply because it is that which prevents or unsettles the constative singularity of the statement or answer, but also in order to refer to a text we recognize, *Of Spirit: Heidegger and the Question* (1989) by Jacques Derrida.[3] That text was produced in the context of a colloquium entitled "Heidegger: Open Questions." Once again we cannot pretend to effect a reading of that text here, but some of its resonances might be heard in what I have to say. In the first place there is something of an open question in the title "Deconstruction is/in America," an open question about the relation of deconstruction to America: what it is, what is "in" with respect to it; or what it is and, as the syntax says or a certain accent might say, what it *isin* (deconstruction is, after all, always spoken with a certain accent, being a state of exile with respect to one's own language). In the second place, haunting this discussion is the idea that deconstruction might have a darker side, that its questioning before the question(s) masks a form of mystagogy, a will-to-power that has not been sufficiently avowed, that would threaten to appear now that its supposed hegemony is challenged by competing discourses.

The "what *isin*" of deconstruction and America is the irreducibility of their relation. According to one reading of its syntax deconstruction isn't America, it is not America; for if deconstruction is *in* America, if it is the subset "d" of the set "a," then it cannot *be* America. On the other hand, the slash between "is" and "in" causes us to hear "deconstruction is America" as the alternative reading to the phrase "deconstruction in America," or indeed, "deconstruction is in America." We cannot therefore avoid hearing "deconstruction is America" in the title "Deconstruction is/in America." But by the same token we cannot hear just that, we cannot hear it inseparably from "deconstruction in America" and "deconstruction is in America." Deconstruction, I would suggest, thus becomes invaginated within America in the complex way Derrida has described in "The Law of Genre," "Living On: Border Lines,"[4] and other texts, whereby the enclosed subset can become as large as or larger than the set that encloses it. It is that syntactic difficulty, impossibility or monstrosity that takes on something of its spectral, if not virtual form, in the syntagm *isin*.

To come to the point, I want to say two things concerning what deconstruction is and *isin* with respect to America; or perhaps the same thing from two angles, in two versions. The first extends what I have already called the pedagogical imperative of reading in terms of the matter of haunting. To reinforce the very pedagogical importance of this, I might refer to such a haunting as a form of "apprehension," from the verb "to apprehend." As I have already suggested and as *Spectres de Marx* reminds us, reminding us also that it was never far away, there is more and more explicit reference to haunting *in* Derrida's work these days, a more and more constant evocation of something about to come upon us or apprehend us from the past, present, or future. Indeed Derrida's work *is* itself such a thing. It catches us, and at the same time haunts us, like an exciting anticipation that is also a terrifying anachronism. Derrida's work is so often characterized in terms of a threat, the threat of damage, the work of a wrecking crew; deconstruction is so often reduced to destruction. What is overlooked in such characterizations is what might be imperfectly described as the radically conservative side to his work. I say "imperfectly described" because the idea of radical conservatism has been and will be coopted by any number of reactionaries who would not hesitate to vilify everything in and around deconstruction. So I do not mean conservative in any way that would be of comfort to a conservative. But in shaking up our way of thinking, Derrida is, in a very real sense trying to save it; not to save it in any immutable form, but to keep it going, to keep us thinking. The anachronism that haunts us in Derrida is thus related to the profoundest sense of what the so-called humanities are about, and also to the point at which the humanities, today especially, face their profoundest crisis and their ultimate challenge. And even and especially beyond the humanities, into areas that couldn't be more relevant or imposing, the law, genetics, computing; everywhere that the questions of reading and of codes are raised. What can haunt in Derrida is the extent to which his volumes and volumes represent something of a last chance or last gasp—indistinguishable perhaps from a first chance or first gasp—the way in which, in a culture that, at the same time as it is being overwhelmed by what is called the information revolution, is rapidly forgetting or repressing its relation to language and to the word, forgetting how to read, no longer taking the time to read, perhaps preferring the passivity of looking (but that is a whole complicated question of its own). Against these trends Derrida forces us to stop, look, and read more closely. To slow down and reassess what we mean by fast and slow. To try something different, that is, to say no (but never a simplistic "just say no"), to say a kind of "no" to our addiction to speed, simplicity, transparency, and immediacy.

So I do say "conservative" by design, in order to refer to a special vigilance that deconstruction calls for, as well as in order to express something of the discomfort of the second-decade-but-perhaps-first-generation-deconstructionist that I am, or have become, with respect to the current reshaping of the theoretical landscape. To hold to the imperative of the kinds of reading that Derrida's work has rendered exemplary, modelled as they are on texts that as a general rule conform to canonical traditions, might sound defensive, conservative, even reactionary in the light of the critical interest in a wider variety of cultural forms and constructions that goes by the name of cultural studies. But the matter is more complex than that. In the first place one could argue that the shift from the "purely" literary or philosophical to manifestations of, for example, popular culture, would not have been possible without, among other things, the conceptions of textuality and re- or decontextualization that have been developed by Derrida. Furthermore, questions concerning the status and limits of the objects of critical theory are not solved by virtue of a loosening of disciplinary boundaries; on the contrary they become more acute. So the conservative voice speaks again, warning for heightened theoretical attention to the methods of analysis and against what sometimes amounts to uncritical description, to what Andrew Ross has called, in reference to one particular instance of it, the "euphoric, addictive thrill of the technological sublime"[5] for its own sake. It warns again against a slackening of our critical vigilance, against the presumption that the problematics of textuality and reading have disappeared from the critical enterprise once its objects do not belong to philosophy, or literature, or to the print medium. For those who have read Derrida, of whatever generation, it is clear that what he has to say only just begins where the so-called print medium leaves off, that it is not for nothing that deconstruction has proved so relevant to the visual arts and architecture, that from *Of Grammatology* (1974) on it recognized writing as an inscription generalizable across any number of disciplinary boundaries,[6] and finally that what I noted earlier concerning the specter and the virus mounts a challenge to reading that only the highest standards of competence and risk-taking in respect of it can rise to.

There is another form of conservatism that associates itself with a first-generation deconstruction and that explicitly concerns its relation to America. It locates that first generation or original deconstruction in a specific place—Paris, at a specific time—the late sixties, and in a specific intellectual climate—that of *mai 68*. That conservatism is surprised by the attention *still* given to Derrida's work in the United States, and more particularly by the facility with which it seems to have moved from its home within philosophy to the strange accommodation it has made with departments of English in the American academy. It is a conservatism that often finds expression in the positions held by both would-be supporters and detractors of deconstruction among French expatriates in Romance Language departments within that academy, but such a suspicion of the packaging or marketing of the exported product can as easily take place in France.[7]

The latter is not for me the radical conservatism that is deconstruction, although I think it needs to be said that it is neither a simple conservatism, nor is it entirely unrelated to a concern over the domestication of deconstruction that has been expressed from a number of quarters over the last decade and a half of its history. For although the important questions are not finally who owns deconstruction, whether American students have the same competence in philosophy as the French, and whether the French language (or, for that matter, cinema) should legislate to protect itself from hegemonic transatlantic advances, it is worthwhile to insist that deconstruction is not nationalizable, and that that goes for its Americanism as much as for its Frenchness. It is clear that a certain model of capitalism, a certain unexamined and triumphant faith in the natural good of the market, and a certain anti-intellectual mercantilism—some or all of which might be called American, although no doubt at bottom as little "American" as deconstruction is "French"—are at present coinciding with the fall of communism to presume a universality and a universal conformity that threaten to render criteria of difference, resistance and opposition highly problematic. With traditional discourses of both liberalism and liberation in retreat before the fact of American economic, scientific, and cultural domination, reactions ranging from nationalist reflex to intellectual inertia have sometimes found in deconstruction's complex configuration in this country something like the twin specters of American self-assurance and European decline. A reductive and uninformed analysis of the particulars of the American scene on the part of intellectuals in France, or else a refusal to deal with challenges to an intellectual tradition on the part of French professors working in America whose academic legitimacy partly derives from their embodiment of a nationality (and hence of an intellectual tradition and so on), can lead to a view of deconstruction in America, like political correctness in America, academic feminism or gay studies in America, as coterminous with the universal imposition of the American market. In both cases, economic and intellectual, challenges are being mounted to the status quo supposedly in the form of a "foreign" intervention.

I do not know to what extent I have accurately described this phenomenon which is, as I said, extremely complex. It would require a detailed analysis of particular cases, and I suspect that there would be some structural similarities between international cases and intranational cases of this form of conservatism vis-a-vis deconstruction. My point finally is, however, that in this context it is important to reinforce the revolutionary potential of deconstruction as a shifting set of strategies that should by definition disturb the status quo—witness reaction to it from the right in the United States—and that make it particularly important as an intervention, and as an international intervention, one that retains enormous potential for resisting the self-assurance of any hegemonic discourse or practice.

Let me now turn briefly to a second version of the unpronounceability of deconstruction's relation to America. Unpronounceable of course, because it isn't susceptible to pronouncements in a constative mode, and also because what *is in* the relation cannot properly be pronounced. This second version concerns that relation as an "event" in Derrida's work which is also more and more explicitly discussed in the texts of recent years, namely a particular configuration of the aporia, the gift and the secret, a configuration that finds one expression, and its *évènement* or *avènement*, in the *viens* ("come"). We might point to the "Of an Apocalyptic Tone" text of the 1980 Cerisy conference, as central in that regard, but there Derrida mentions also *Glas* (1986), *The Post Card* (1987), and "Pas"; and from there we can now look forward to *Aporias* (1993), and "Donner la mort."[8] In "Of an Apocalyptic Tone" Derrida refers to Blanchot, Levinas, and the Apocalypse of St. John, and calls the invitation and affirmation that is "come," that on the basis of which there is the event, "neither a desire nor an order, neither a prayer nor a request" (34). Saying that "I do not know what *it is,*" (ibid.) he develops the sense of *viens* as a function of difference of tone. If then we were to translate the tone of *viens* to the accent producing the unpronounceability or irreducibility of *isin* we might begin to talk about the relation between deconstruction and America as an event of coming.

"Coming to America" is of course a well-worn phrase and a whole history and mythology. America is that which one comes to: all "your tired, your poor, your huddled masses yearning to breathe free" have for two centuries defined America in that way; coming to it is quite simply what has made America. But deconstruction cannot arrive in that sense; it doesn't come to America. It can't be the title of a film with Eddie Murphy; it can't be that sort of circus however much some—some media, some institutions, some university departments—would want it to be or present it to be. On the other hand, we might say that deconstruction says "come" to America; that it can constitute that sort of affirmative and apocalyptic invitation. Let me develop a little further how that might be.

If, to the extent that it *isin* America, deconstruction comes close to coming to it, it might be first of all because there is something analogous between them. If they can both offer some sort of invitation it would be because they represent a sense of hospitality. This is a commonplace I am recounting here and without being able to determine what it is that makes American hospitality different from that of other countries, or deconstruction's different from that of other ideas or motifs, I shall simply take the risk of repeating or affirming it. In America there is a sense of hospitality that for me renders dismissive judgments of what deconstruction becomes here, such as those mentioned in the second type of conservatism above, importunate, even impolite or *badly brought up* (here I hide behind the alibi of translating from the French as in *questions mal relevées, propos mal posés*). Similarly, in deconstruction there is a generosity of ideas that works as a recognition of the principle of *parasitage*, that the host is always already altered by its invitees, so that whatever comes to it finds a place already prepared for it but at the same time a readiness to be transformed by it.

But however commonplace the affirmations I have just recounted, they should not amount to platitudes, to simple pronouncements. There is also in America much that is inhospitable in the extreme, especially to one who comes to it less tired, poor or huddled, from another Western industrialized democracy. There is the inhospitality of America's addiction to violence (a comparative analysis of the marketing, consumption and interdiction of firearms and drugs might finally explain the mechanism of psychological as opposed to physiological addiction). But I am not only referring to criminal violence for that addiction extends to state violence—that of unabashed militarism, that of the glaring intransigence of the death penalty. There is the inhospitality of homelessness, of endemic poverty, of overwork, and so on. Coming to America repeatedly involves the incomprehension, followed by some strangely complicitous acceptance, of that inhospitality. But there is one particular form of official inhospitality that should be mentioned in this regard, for it deals with the precise questions of immigration and viral epidemiology that have guided this whole discussion of how deconstruction *isin* America. I refer to the refusal of entry to HIV positive persons. To the extent that it is a virus, to the extent that it is HIV positive, deconstruction is forbidden entry, and can come to America only through various backdoors, by means of special exemptions and accompanied by restrictions of movement and association that belie the whole tradition of hospitality that Emma Lazarus waxed so eloquent about two hundred years ago. Not that such restrictions began with AIDS—one need only read the visa application form in force until very recently, I believe, regarding political association, sexual preference and so on that could be invoked to prevent entry to any perceived threat to American integrity.

Finally, to complete the uneven symmetry of this discussion of what, in coming, brings deconstruction into an analogous relation with America, it needs to be said that there is much that is resistant to assimilation in deconstruction (not to mention the farces and tragedies, the "affairs" of its own history that I evoked at the beginning). The complexities of the questions it poses, the challenges to received ideas and the stakes of thinking that it raises, mean that for being welcomed by it, one can never be comfortable with it. But more than that, there is the haunting I referred to earlier of a darker side to deconstruction, the notion

that it profits from its complexities to obfuscate and so exercises a
mystagogic power that can be invoked in the face of opposition
from differing points of view, new theoretical approaches, and so
on. There are still some, after all, who would argue that deconstruction represents a hegemonic discourse in the American academy even as others claim it is a fashion that has been relegated to
the pages of a J-Crew catalog. So it is doubtful that one can resolve
the question in those terms. The risk of mystagogy is, however, an
explicit consideration of the *viens*, and the central focus of discussion in "Of an Apocalyptic Tone":

> every discord or every tonal disorder, everything that detones and be-
> comes inadmissible *[irrecevable]* in general collocution, everything that is
> no longer identifiable on the basis of established codes . . . will necessarily
> pass for mystagogic, obscurantist, and apocalyptic. It will be made to
> pass for such. (30, translation modified)

This is the risk of deconstruction, the risk of its inhospitality, the
irreceivability of what, by means of a highly idiosyncratic form of
questioning, it sets loose within the context of intellectual debate
and has for the last twenty five years been setting loose within
America by saying "come" to it. It offers little succor to those who
are tired from the effort or tension of a suspended question, those
for whom the guest who is coming must quickly arrive in order to
just as quickly depart, those for whom the sense of apocalypse
resides entirely in a last judgment. On the other hand, if in saying,
or at least trying to pronounce "come" to America, deconstruction
isin it, then the aim of this short reflection is to have that heard as
something quite other than inarticulate, for it seems to me that a
deconstruction that *isin* America still sounds and resounds within
the space and upon the horizon of a certain eloquence.

Notes

1. Jacques Derrida, *Spectres de Marx* (Paris: Galilée, 1993). Translation
   forthcoming from Routledge.
2. "As for the logic of spectrality, inseparable from the idea of the idea (of
   the idealization of ideality as effect of iterability), inseparable from
   the very motif, let us not say any more the "idea" of deconstruction, it
   is at work, most often explicitly, in all the essays published over the

last twenty years . . . " (*Spectres de Marx*, p24n, my translation). The recalcitrance resides in the ambiguity between spectrality as a motif of deconstruction and spectrality as the motif that is deconstruction. A corollary of spectrality, or perhaps a further motif of it and of deconstruction, that is similarly explicit in Derrida yet absent from most discussion of deconstruction is the virus, referred to below. Discussion of that corollary, through the relations among spirit, mind and body, through the ontologies, biologies and pathologies, the ontopathogenetic, biotechnological and rhetoricoparasitological dehiscences that structure much of what we call life, death, and language, would be a "fashion" of deconstruction that has yet to be exposed at any length in either the academic or popular press. See "Rhétorique de la drogue," in *Points de suspension* (Paris: Galilée, 1992), especially p. 266n (translation forthcoming from Stanford University Press).

3. Jacques Derrida, *Of Spirit: Heidegger and the Question*. Trans. Geoffrey Bennington and Rachel Bowlby (Chicago: University of Chicago Press, 1989).

4. "The Law of Genre." *Glyph* 7 (1980); "Living On: Border Lines." In *Deconstruction and Criticism*. Ed. Harold Bloom et al. (New York: Seabury Press, 1979).

5. "Hacking Away At the Counterculture." In *Technoculture*. Ed. Constance Penley and Andrew Ross (Minneapolis: University of Minnesota Press, 1991), p. 131.

6. *Of Grammatology*. Trans. Gayatri Chakravorty Spivak (Baltimore: Johns Hopkins University Press, 1974), p.9.

7. In terms of French academics in America, although concerning more feminism and the role of English departments than deconstruction, see Naomi Schor; "The Righting of French Studies: Homosociality and the Killing of '*La pensée 68*'," *Profession* 92. A recent example of the French version might be found in allusions made by Michel Deguy at the 1992 Cerisy conference on Derrida's work ("*De la contemporanéité. Causerie pour Jacques Derrida*," in ed. Marie-Louise Mallet, *Passage des frontières*. Paris: Galilée, 1994). Deguy refers on the one hand to the "remarkable penetration" of Derrida's work in the United States as a sign of the American public's avidity "to taste (impossibly, by losing it *in* translation) this tone, this singularity, this work of the French language" (217) and on the other hand, recalling Freud's words, to this "new poison that the American (academic) body seeks . . . to evacuate by means of violent expectorations" (220, my translations). Although these remarks were far from the focus of Deguy's paper, discussion following it centered on them, especially in the context of the simultaneous appearance of Deguy's signature, along with many others, under an advertisement in *Le Monde* calling for measures to protect the French language from (mostly) American English ("*Appel. L'avenir de la langue française.*" *Le Monde*, 11 July 1992).

8. "Of an Apocalyptic Tone Recently Adopted in Philosophy." Trans. John P. Leavey. *Oxford Literary Review* 6:2 (1984) (cf. "D'un ton apocalyptique adopté naguère en philosophie," in ed. Philippe Lacoue-Labarthe and Jean-Luc Nancy, *Les Fins de l'homme. A partir du travail de Jacques Derrida.* Paris: Galilée, 1981); *Glas.* Trans. John P. Leavey and Richard Rand (Lincoln: University of Nebraska Press, 1986); *The Post Card: From Socrates to Freud and Beyond.* Trans. Alan Bass (Chicago: University of Chicago Press, 1987); "Pas," in *Parages* (Paris: Galilée, 1986); *Aporias.* Trans. Tom Dutoit (Stanford: Stanford University Press, 1993); "Donner la mort," in ed. Jean-Michel Rabaté and Michael Wetzel, *L'Ethique du don. Jacques Derrida et la pensée du don* (Paris: Transition, 1992), translation forthcoming from University of Chicago Press.

www.ingramcontent.com/pod-product-compliance
Lightning Source LLC
Chambersburg PA
CBHW032122020426
42334CB00016B/1040